APPLEWOOD'S
AMERICAN FRONTIER
SERIES

Commerce of the Prairies

Or, The Journal of a Santa Fe Trader during Eight Expeditions

Josiah Gregg

APPLEWOOD BOOKS
Carlisle, Massachusetts

Commerce of the Prairies
was originally published in
1851

ISBN: 978-1-4290-4528-5

APPLEWOOD'S AMERICAN FRONTIER SERIES

Thank you for purchasing an Applewood book. Applewood reprints America's lively classics—books from the past that are still of interest to modern readers. This facsimile was printed using many new technologies together to bring our tradition-bound mission to you. Applewood's facsimile edition of this work may include library stamps, scribbles, and margin notes as they exist in the original book. These interesting historical artifacts celebrate the place the book was read or the person who read the book. In addition to these artifacts, the work may have additional errors that were either in the original, in the digital scans, or introduced as we prepared the book for printing. If you believe the work has such errors, please let us know by writing to us at the address below.

For a free copy of our current print catalog featuring our bestselling books, write to:

APPLEWOOD BOOKS
P.O. Box 27
Carlisle, MA 01741

For more complete listings, visit us on the web at:
www.awb.com

Prepared for publishing by HP

ARRIVAL OF THE CARAVAN AT SANTA FÉ.

COMMERCE OF THE PRAIRIES

OR THE

Journal of a Santa Fé Trader,

DURING

EIGHT EXPEDITIONS ACROSS

THE GREAT WESTERN PRAIRIES,

AND

A RESIDENCE OF NEARLY NINE YEARS

IN

NORTHERN MEXICO.

Illustrated with Maps and Engravings.

BY JOSIAH GREGG.

IN TWO VOLUMES.

VOL. I.

FIFTH EDITION.

PHILADELPHIA:
J. W. MOORE, 193 CHESTNUT STREET.
- - - - - -
1851.

Entered according to the Act of Congress, in the year 1844, by
J. W. MOORE.
in the Clerk's office of the District Court for the Southern District of New York.

PREFACE.

IN adding another to the list of works which have already been published, appearing to bear more or less directly upon the subject matter of these volumes, I am aware that my labors make their appeal to the public under serious disadvantages. Topics which have occupied the pens of Irving and Murray and Hoffman, and more recently, of Kendall, the graphic historiographer of the "Texan Santa Fé Expedition," may fairly be supposed to have been so entirely exhausted, that the entrance of a new writer in the lists, whose name is wholly unknown to the republic of letters, and whose pretensions are so humble as mine, may be looked upon as an act of literary hardihood, for which there was neither occasion nor excuse. In view of this 'foregone conclusion,' I trust I may be pardoned for prefacing my literary offering with a few words in its justification,—which will afford me an occasion to explain the circumstances that first led to my acquaintance with life upon the Prairies and in Northern Mexico.

For some months preceding the year 1831, my health had been gradually declining under a complication of chronic diseases, which defied every plan of treatment that the sagacity and science of my medical friends could devise. This morbid condition of my system, which originated in the familiar miseries of dyspepsia and its kindred infirmities, had finally reduced me to such a state, that, for nearly a twelvemonth, I was not only disqualified for any systematic industry, but so debilitated as rarely to be able to extend my walks beyond the narrow precincts of my chamber. In this hopeless condition, my physicians advised me to take a trip across the Prairies, and, in the change of air and habits which such an adventure would involve, to seek that health which their science had failed to bestow. I accepted their suggestion, and, without hesitation, proceeded at once to make the necessary preparations for joining one of those spring Caravans which were annually starting from the United States, for Santa Fé.

The effects of this journey were in the first place to re-establish my health, and, in the second, to beget a passion for Prairie life which I never expect to survive. At the conclusion of the season which followed my first trip, I became interested as a proprietor in the Santa Fé Trade, and continued to be so, to a greater or less extent, for the eight succeeding years. During the whole of the above periods I crossed the Prairies eight different times; and, with the exception of the time thus spent in travelling to and fro, the greater part of the nine years of which I speak, were passed in Northern Mexico.

Having been actively engaged and largely interested in the commerce of that country and across the Prairies, for so long a period, I feel that I have at least had opportunities for observation, upon the subjects of which I have ventured to treat, superior to those enjoyed by any writers who have preceded me. But not even an attempt has before been made to present any full account of the origin of the Santa Fé Trade and modes of conducting it; nor of the early history and present condition of the people of New Mexico; nor of the Indian tribes by which the wild and unreclaimed regions of that department are inhabited. I think I may also assure my readers that most of the facts presented in my sketch of the natural history of the Prairies, and of the Indian tribes who inhabit them, are now published for the first time. As I have not sought to make a treatise upon these subjects, I have not felt compelled, for the purpose of giving my papers symmetry and completeness, to enter to any extent upon grounds which have already been occupied by other travellers; but have contented myself with presenting such matters and observations as I thought least likely to have come before under the notice of my readers.

I am perfectly sensible, however, that, in the selection of matter, and in the execution of my work, it is very far from being what it should be, and what, in more capable hands, it might have been. I only trust, that, with all its imperfections, it may be found to contain some new and not unimportant facts, which may be thought, in some measure, to justify my appearance for once in the capacity of a bookmaker; for which vocation, in all other respects, I am free to confess myself very poorly qualified.

This work has been prepared chiefly from a journal which I have been in the habit of keeping from my youth upward, and in which I was careful to preserve memoranda of my observations while engaged in the Santa Fé Trade,—though without the remotest intention of ever appropriating them to the present purpose. In addition, however, I have embraced every opportunity of procuring authentic information through others, upon such matters as were beyond my own sphere of observation. From materials thus collected I have received much assistance in the preparation of the chapters from the sixth to the fifteenth inclusive, of the first volume, which are chiefly devoted to the early history of New Mexico, and the manners, customs and institutions of its people. For favors thus conferred, I beg in particular to make my acknowledgments to ELISHA STANLEY, Esq., and Doctors SAMUEL B. HOBBS and DAVID WALDO, whose names have been long and favorably associated with the Santa Fé Trade.

Though myself cradled and educated upon the Indian border, and familiar with the Indian character from my infancy, I am yet greatly indebted, for information upon that subject, to many intelligent Indian traders, and others resident upon our border, with whose ample experience I have been frequently favored.

Yet, while I recognize my indebtedness to others, I feel bound, in self-defence, to reclaim in a single case, at least, the *waifs* of my own pen, which have been dignified with a place in the pages of a cotemporary writer. During the years 1841 and 1842, I contributed a number of letters upon the history and condition of the Santa Fé Trade, etc., to the Galveston "Daily Advertiser" and the "Arkansas Intelligencer," under the signatures of "J. G." and "G.," portions of which I have had occasion to insert in the present volumes. In Captain Marryat's recent work, entitled " Monsieur Violet," I was not a little annoyed (when I presume I ought to have been flattered) to find large portions of this correspondence copied, much of it *verbatim*, without the slightest intimation or acknowledgment whatever, of the source from whence they were procured. The public are already so familiar with the long series of literary larcenies of which that famous work was the product, that I should not have presumed to emphasize my own grievance at all here, but that the appearance of the same material, frequently in the same words, in these volumes, might, unless accompanied by some explanation, expose me to a charge of plagiarism myself, among those who may never have seen my original letters, or who are not yet aware that " Monsieur Violet" was an offering which had evidently been intended for the altar of Mercury rather than of Minerva.

In my historical sketches of New Mexico, it might have been naturally expected that some notice would be taken of the Texan Santa Fé Expedition of 1841, the events of which are so closely connected with the history of that country. I declined, however, to enter upon the topic; for I considered that none who had seen Mr. Kendall's account of that ill-fated enterprise, would have any inducement to consult these pages upon the subject; and for those who had not, I felt sure the best thing I could do, was to direct their attention at once to its attractive pages.

The maps which accompany the present work will be found, I believe, substantially correct; or more so, at least, than any others, of those regions, which have been published. They have been prepared, for the most part, from personal observations. Those portions of the country which I have not been able to observe myself, have chiefly been laid down from manuscript maps kindly furnished me by experienced and reliable traders and trappers, and also from the maps prepared under the supervision of United States surveyors.

The arrangement I have adopted seems to require a word of explanation. That the reader may the better understand the frequent notices, in the course of my personal narrative, of the Santa Fé Trade, the first chapter has been devoted to the development of its early history. And, though the results of my observations in Northern Mexico and upon the Prairies, as well as on the border, are sometimes interspersed through the narrative, I have, to a great degree, digested and arranged them into distinct chapters, occupying from the sixth to the fifteenth inclusive, of the first volume, and the seven last chapters, of the second. This plan was resorted to with a view of giving greater compactness to the work, and relieving the journal, as far as possible, from cumbrous details and needless repetitions.

J. G.

New York, June 12, 1844.

CONTENTS OF VOL. I.

CHAPTER I.

Page

Origin and progressive Development of the Santa Fé Trade—Captain Pike's Narrative—Pursley—La Lande—Expedition of McKnight and others—Glenn—Becknell—Cooper—Sufferings of Captain Becknell and his Companions—First Introduction of wheeled Vehicles—Colonel Marmaduke—Hostility of the Indians—Recriminations—Indian Ethics—Increase of Outrages—Major Riley's Escort—Annoyed by the Indians—Government Protection—Composition of a Caravan, . . . 17

CHAPTER II.

Head Quarters of the Santa Fé Trade—Independence and its *Locale*—A Prairie Trip an excellent Remedy for chronic Diseases—Supplies for the Journey—Wagons, Mules and Oxen—Art of Loading Wagons—Romancing Propensity of Travellers—The Departure—Storms and Wagon-covers—Quagmires—Tricks of marauding Indians—Council Grove—Fancy *versus* Reality—Electioneering on the Prairies—The Organization—Amateur Travellers and Loafers—Duties of the Watch—Costumes and Equipment of the Party—Timbers for the Journey, 32

CHAPTER III.

The 'Catch up'—Breaking up of the Encampment—Perversity of Mules—Under Way—The Diamond Spring—Eccentricities of Oxen—First Glance of the Antelope—Buffalo Herds and Prairie Novices—A John Gilpin Race—Culinary Preparations—A Buffalo Feast—Appetite of

Prairie Travellers—Troubles in Fording Streams—Fresh Alarms and their Causes—A Wolfish Frolic—Arkansas River—Pleasing Scenery—Character of the Country—Extraordinary Surgical Operation—The 'Pawnee Rock'—Salutary Effects of Alarms—New Order of March—Prairie Encampment and 'Upholstery'—Hoppling and Tethering of the 'Stock'—Crossing the Arkansas—Great Battle with Rattlesnakes—A Mustang Colt and a Mule Fracas—'The Caches'—Their Origin, and Signification of the Term, ... 50

CHAPTER IV.

A Desert Plain—Preparation for a 'Water-Scrape'—Accident to a French Doctor—Upsetting of a Wagon and its Consequences—A Party of Sioux Warriors—The first real Alarm—Confusion in the Camp—Friendly Demonstrations of the Indians—The Pipe of Peace—Squaws and Papooses—An Extemporary Village—Lose our Track—Search after the Lost River—Horrible Prospective—The Cimarron Found at last—A Night of Alarms—Indian Serenade and Thieving—Indian Diplomacy—Hailstones and Hurricanes—Position of the Captain of a Caravan—His Troubles, his Powers and Want of Powers—More Indians—Hostile Encounter—Results of the Skirmish—The 'Battle-Ground'—Col. Vizcarra and the Gros Ventres, ... 70

CHAPTER V.

A Beautiful Ravine—'Runners' Starting for Santa Fé—Fourth of July on the Prairies—The *Cibolero* or Buffalo-hunter—Mournful News of Captain Sublette's Company—Murder of Captain Smith and another of the Party by the Indians—Carelessness and Risks of Hunters—Captain Sublette's Peril—Character and Pursuits of the *Ciboleros*—The Art of Curing Meat—Purity of the Atmosphere—The 'Round Mound'—The Mirage or False Ponds—Philosophy thereof—Extensive and Interesting View—Exaggerated Accounts by Travellers of the Buffalo of the Prairies—Their Decrease—A 'Stampede'—Wagon Repairing—Rio Colorado or Canadian River—Meeting between old Friends—Mexican Escort—Disorganizing of the Caravan—Dreadful Thunder-storm—First Symptoms of Civilization—San Miguel—Arrival at Santa Fé—Entry of the Caravan—First Hours of Recreation—Interpreters and Custom-house Arrangements—A Glance at the Trade, etc., ... 87

CHAPTER VI.

Sketches of the Early History of Santa Fé—First Explorations—Why called New Mexico—Memorial of Oñate—His Colony—Captain Leyva's prior Settlement—Singular Stipulations of Oñate—Incentives presented by the Crown to Colonizers—Enormities of Spanish Conquerors—Progress of the new Colony—Cruel Labors of the Aborigines in the Mines—Revolt of the Indians in 1680—Massacre of the Spaniards—Santa Fé Besieged—Battles—Remaining Spanish Population finally evacuate the Province—Paso del Norte—Iuhuman Murder of a Spanish Priest—Final Recovery of the Country—Insurrection of 1837—A Prophecy—Shocking Massacre of the Governor and other distinguished Characters—American Merchants, and Neglect of our Government—Governor Armijo: his Intrigues and Success—Second Gathering of Insurgents and their final Defeat, ... 115

CHAPTER VII.

Geographical Position of New Mexico—Absence of navigable Streams—The Rio del Norte—Romantic Chasm—Story of a sunken River—Mr. Stanley's Excursion to a famous Lake—Santa Fé and its Localities—El Valle de Taos and its Fertility—Soil of New Mexico—The first Settler at Taos and his Contract with the Indians—Salubrity and Pleasantness of the Climate of New Mexico—Population—State of Agriculture—Staple Productions of the Country—Corn-fields and Fences—Irrigation and *Acequias*—*Tortillas* and *Tortilleras*—*Atole, Frijoles* and *Chile*—Singular Custom—Culinary and Table Affairs—Flax and Potato indigenous—Tobacco and *Punche*—Fruits—Peculiar Mode of cultivating the Grape—Forest Growths—*Piñon* and *Mezquite*—Mountain Cottonwood—*Palmilla* or Soap-plant—Pasturage, . . 137

CHAPTER VIII.

The Mines of New Mexico—Supposed Concealment of them by the Indians—Indian Superstition and Cozenage—Ruins of *La Gran Quivira*—Old Mines—*Placeres* or Mines of Gold Dust—Speculative Theories—Mode of Working the *Placeres*—Manners and Customs of the Miners—Arbitrary Restrictions of the Mexican Government upon Foreigners—Persecution of a Gachupin—Disastrous Effect of official Interference upon the Mining Interest—Disregard of American Rights and of the U. States Government—*Gambucinos* and their System—Gold found throughout New Mexico—Silver Mines—Copper, Zinc and Lead—*Salinas* or Salt Lakes—Sulphurous Springs—Gypsum, and Petrified Trees, . . . 162

CHAPTER IX.

Indifference on the Subject of Horse-breeding—*Caballos de Silla*—Popularity and Usefulness of the Mule—Mode of harnessing and lading Mules for a Journey—*Arrieros* and their System—The *Mulera* or Bell-mare—Surprising Feats of the Muleteers and *Vaqueros*—The *Lazo* and its Uses—Ridiculous Usages of the Country in regard to the Ownership of Animals—Anecdote of a Mexican Colonel—The *Burro* or domestic Ass and its Virtues—Shepherds and their Habits—The Itinerant Herds of the Plains—Sagacity of the Shepherd's Dog—The Sheep Trade—Destruction of Cattle by the Indians—Philosophical Notions of the Marauders—Excellent Mutton—Goats and their Utility—Wild Animals and their Character—A 'Bear Scrape'—Wolves, Panthers, Wild Birds and Reptiles—The Honey-bee, etc., ... 178

CHAPTER X.

Condition of the Arts and Sciences in New Mexico—Neglect of Education—Primary Schools—Geographical Ignorance—Female Accomplishments—Imported Refinements—Peculiarities of Language, etc.—Condition of the Public Press—State of Medical Science—The Mechanical Arts—Carpentry and Cabinet Work—State of Architecture—Dwelling Houses and their Peculiarities—Rustic Furniture—Curiously constructed Vehicles—Manufacture of Blankets—Other Fabrics—Want of Machinery, 197

CHAPTER XI.

Style of Dress in New Mexico—Riding-dress of the Caballero—Horse Trappings—The *Rebozo*—Passion for Jewelry—Apparel of the Female Peasantry—'Wheeled Tarantulas'—General Appearance of the People—Tawny Complexion—Singular Mode of Painting the Human Face—Striking Traits of Character—Alms-giving—Beggars and their Tricks—Wonderful Cure of Paralysis—Lack of Arms and Officers—Traits of Boldness among the Yeomanry—Politeness and Suavity of the Mexicans—Remarks of Mr. Poinsett—Peculiarities observed in Epistolary Intercourse—Salutations—*La Siesta*, . 211

CHAPTER XII.

Government of New Mexico—The Administration of Justice—Judicial Corruption—Prejudices against Americans—Partiality for the English—Anecdote of Governor Armijo and a Trapper—Outrage upon an American Physician—Violence suffered by the American Consul and others—Arbitrary Impositions upon Foreigners—*Contribucion de Guerra*—The Alcaldes and their System—The *Fueros*—Mode of punishing Delinquents and Criminals—Mexican System of Slavery—Thieves and Thieveries—Outrage upon an American Merchant—Gambling and Gambling-houses—Game of *Monte*—Anecdote of a Lady of Fashion—*Chuza*—Cockpits—*Correr el gallo*—*El Coleo*—Fandangoes—*Cigarritos*, . . . 225

CHAPTER XIII.

Military Hierarchy of Mexico—Religious Superstitions—Legend of *Neustra Señora de Guadalupe*—A profane Version of the Story—A curious Plan for manufacturing Water—Saints and Images—Processions—How to make it Rain—The Sacred Host—Fanaticism and Murder—Honors paid to a Bishop—Servility to Priests—Attendance at Public Worship—New Mexicans in Church—The Vesper Bells—Passion Week and the Ceremonies pertaining thereto—Ridiculous *Penitencia*—Whitewashing of Criminals—Matrimonial Connexions and Mode of Contracting them—Restrictions upon Lovers—Onerous Fees paid for Marriages and Burials—Anecdote of a *Ranchero*—Ditto of a Servant and of a Widow, illustrative of Priestly Extortion—Modes of Burial, and Burial Ground of the Heretics, ... 245

CHAPTER XIV.

The Pueblos—Their Character for Sobriety, Honesty, and Industry—Traditional descent from Montezuma—Their Languages—Former and present Population—The Pueblo of Pecos—Singular Habits of that ill-fated Tribe—Curious Tradition—Montezuma and the Sun—Legend of a Serpent—Religion and government—Secret Council—Laws and Customs—Excellent Provisions against Demoralization—Primitive Pastimes of the Pueblos—Their Architecture—Singular Structures of Taos, and other novel Fortifications—Primitive state of the Arts among the Pueblos—Style of Dress, Weapons, etc.—Their Diet—The *Guayave*. 267

CHAPTER XV.

The wild Tribes of New Mexico—Speculative Theories—Clavigero and the *Azteques*—Pueblo Bonito and other Ruins—Probable Relationship between the *Azteques* and Tribes of New Mexico—The several Nations of this Province—*Navajóes* and *Azteques*—Manufactures of the former—Their Agriculture, Religion, etc.—Mexican Cruelty to the Indians and its Consequences—Inroads of the Navajóes—Exploits of a Mexican Army—How to make a Hole in a powder-keg—The *Apaches* and their character—Their Food—Novel Mode of settling Disputes—Range of their marauding Excursions—Indian Traffic and imbecile Treaties—Devastation of the Country—Chihuahua Rodomontades—Juan José, a celebrated Apache Chief, and his tragical End, etc.—Massacre of Americans in Retaliation—A tragical Episode—*Proyecto de Guerra* and a 'gallant' Display—The *Yutas* and their Hostilities—A personal Adventure with them, but no Bloodshed—The Jicarillas. 282

CHAPTER XVI.

Incidents of a Return Trip from Santa Fé—Calibre of our Party—Return Caravans—Remittances—Death of Mr. Langham—Burial in the Desert—A sudden Attack—Confusion in the Camp—The Pawnees—A Wolfish Escort—Scarcity of Buffalo—Unprofitable Delusion—Arrival—Table of Camping Sites and Distances—Condition of the Town of Independence—The Mormons—Their Dishonesty and Immorality—Their high-handed Measures, and a Rising of the People—A fatal Skirmish—A chivalrous Parade of the Citizens—Expulsion of the Mormons—The Meteoric Shower, and Superstition, etc.—Wanderings and Improprieties of the 'Latter-day Saints'—Gov. Boggs' Recipe—The City of Nauvoo—Contemplated Retribution of the Mormons. . . 305

http://www.amazon.com

For detailed information about this and other orders, please visit Your Account. You can also print invoices, change your e-mail address and payment settings, alter your communication preferences, and much more – 24 hours a day – at http://www.amazon.com/your-account.

Returns Are Easy!

Visit http://www.amazon.com/returns to return any item – including gifts – in unopened or original condition within 30 days for a full refund (other restrictions apply). Please have your order ID ready.

Item Price	Total
$16.34	$16.34

Thanks for shopping at Amazon.com, and please come again!

$16.34
$3.99
$20.33
$20.33
$0.00

Your order of August 10, 2011 (Order ID 105-8797853-6302654)

Qty.	Item
1	**IN THIS SHIPMENT** **Commerce of the Prairies** Paperback (** P-3-B57F121 **) 1429045280 1429045280

Subtotal
Shipping & Handling
Order Total
Paid via credit/debit
Balance due

This shipment completes your order.

Have feedback on how we packaged your order? Tell us at www.amazon.com/packaging.

COMMERCE OF THE PRAIRIES.

CHAPTER I.

Origin and progressive Development of the Santa Fé Trade—Captain Pike's Narrative — Pursley— La Lande — Expedition of McKnight and others—Glenn—Becknell—Cooper — Sufferings of Captain Becknell and his Companions — First Introduction of wheeled Vehicles—Colonel Marmaduke — Hostility of the Indians — Recriminations—Indian Ethics—Increase of Outrages—Major Riley's Escort—Annoyed by the Indians—Government Protection—Composition of a Caravan.

THE overland trade between the United States and the northern provinces of Mexico, seems to have had no very definite origin; having been rather the result of accident than of any organized plan of commercial establishment. For a number of years its importance attracted no attention whatever. From Captain Pike's narrative we learn, that one James Pursley, after much wandering over the wild and then unexplored regions west of the Mississippi, finally fell in with some Indians on the Platte river, near its source in the Rocky Mountains; and obtaining information from them respecting the settlements of New Mexico, he set out in company with a party of these savages, and descended, in 1805, to Santa Fé, where he remained for several years—perhaps till his death. It does not appear, however, that he took with him any considerable amount of merchandise.

Although Captain Pike speaks of Pursley as the first *American* that ever crossed the desert plains into the Spanish provinces, it is nevertheless related by the same writer, that, in consequence of information obtained by the trappers, through the Indians, relative to this isolated province, a merchant of Kaskaskia, named Morrison, had already dispatched, as early as 1804, a *French Creole*, by the name of La Lande, up Platte river, with directions to push his way into Santa Fé, if the passage was at all practicable. The ingenious emissary was perfectly successful in his enterprise; but the kind and generous treatment of the natives overcame at once his patriotism and his probity. He neither returned to his employer nor accounted for the proceeds of his adventure. His expansive intellect readily conceived the advantages of setting up in business for himself upon this 'borrowed' capital; which he accordingly did, and remained there, not only unmolested, but honored and esteemed till his death, which occurred some fifteen or twenty years afterward—leaving a large family, and sufficient property to entitle him to the fame of *rico* among his neighbors.

The Santa Fé trade attracted very little notice, however, until the return of Captain Pike,* whose exciting descriptions of the new El Dorado spread like wildfire throughout the western country. In 1812, an expedition was fitted out under the auspices of Messrs. McKnight, Beard, Chambers, and several others (in all about a dozen), who, following the directions of Captain Pike across the dreary western wilds, finally succeeded in reaching

* This celebrated officer, who was afterwards promoted to the rank of General, and died in the achievement of the glorious victory at York, Upper Canada, in 1813, was sent, in 1806, on an exploring expedition up the Arkansas, with instructions to pass to the sources of Red River, for which those of the Canadian were then mistaken. Captain Pike, however, even passed around the head of the latter; and, crossing the mountain with an almost incredible degree of peril and suffering, he descended upon the Rio del Norte with his little party, then but fifteen in number. Believing himself now upon Red River, within the then assumed bounds of the United States, he erected a small fortification for his company, till the opening of the spring of 1807 should enable him to continue his descent to Natchitoches. As he was within the Mexican territory, however, and but sixty to eighty miles from the northern settlements, his position was soon discovered, and a force sent out to take him into Santa Fé, which, by a treacherous manœuvre, was effected without opposition. The Spanish officer assured him that the Governor, learning he had missed his way, had sent animals and an escort to convey his men and baggage to a navigable point on *Red River* (Rio Colorado), and that his Excellency desired very much to see him at Santa Fé, which might be taken on their way. As soon, however, as the Governor had Captain Pike in his power, he sent him with his men to the Commandant General at Chihuahua, where most of his papers were seized, and he and his party were sent under an escort, via San Antonio de Bexar, to the United States.

The narrative of Captain Pike gives a full account of this expedition, both previous and subsequent to its interruption by the Spaniards; but as this work is now rarely met with, the foregoing note may not be deemed altogether supererogatory. Many will believe and assert to the present day, however, that this expedition had some connection with the famous project of Aaron Burr; yet the noble and patriotic character of the officer who conducted it, will not permit us to countenance such an aspersion.

Santa Fé in safety. But these new adventurers were destined to experience trials and disappointments of which they had formed no conception. Believing that the declaration of Independence by Hidalgo, in 1810, had completely removed those injurious restrictions which had hitherto rendered all foreign intercourse, except by special permission from the Spanish Government, illegal, they were wholly unprepared to encounter the embarrassments with which despotism and tyranny invariably obstruct the path of the stranger. They were doubtless ignorant that the patriotic chief Hidalgo had already been arrested and executed, that the royalists had once more regained the ascendency, and that all foreigners, but particularly Americans, were now viewed with unusual suspicion. The result was that the luckless traders, immediately upon their arrival, were seized as spies, their goods and chattels confiscated, and themselves thrown into the *calabozos* of Chihuahua, where most of them were kept in rigorous confinement for the space of nine years; when the republican forces under Iturbide getting again in the ascendant, McKnight and his comrades were finally set at liberty. It is said that two of the party contrived, early in 1821, to return to the United States in a canoe, which they succeeded in forcing down the Canadian fork of the Arkansas. The stories promulgated by these men soon induced others to launch into the same field of enterprise, among whom was a merchant of Ohio, named Glenn, who, at the time, had an Indian trading-house near the mouth of the Verdigris river. Having taken the circuitous route up the Arkansas towards the mountains, this pioneer trader encountered a great deal of trouble and privation, but eventually reached Santa Fé with his little caravan, before the close of 1821, in perfect safety.

During the same year, Captain Becknell, of Missouri, with four trusty companions, went out to Santa Fé by the far western prairie route. This intrepid little band started from the vicinity of Franklin, with the original purpose of trading with the Iatan or Comanche Indians; but having fallen in accidentally with a party of Mexican rangers, when near the Mountains, they were easily prevailed upon to accompany them to the new emporium, where, notwithstanding the trifling amount of merchandise they were possessed of, they realized a very handsome profit. The fact is, that up to this date New Mexico had derived all her supplies from the Internal Provinces by the way of Vera Cruz; but at such exorbitant rates, that common calicoes, and even bleached and brown domestic goods, sold as high as two and three dollars per *vara* (or Spanish yard of thirty-three inches). Becknell returned to the United States alone the succeeding winter, leaving the rest of his company at Santa Fé.

The favorable reports brought by the enterprising Captain, stimulated others to embark in the trade; and early in the following May, Colonel Cooper and sons, from the same neighborhood, accompanied by several others (their whole number about fifteen), set out with four or five thousand dollars' worth of goods, which they transported upon packhorses. They steered directly for Taos, where they arrived without any remarkable occurrence.

The next effort of Captain Becknell was attended with very different success. With a company amounting to near thirty men, and perhaps five thousand dollars' worth of goods of various descriptions, he started from Missouri, about a month after Colonel Cooper. Being an excellent woodsman, and anxious to avoid the circuitous route of the Upper Arkansas country, he resolved this time, after having reached that point on the Arkansas river since known as the 'Caches,' to steer more directly for Santa Fé, entertaining little or no suspicion of the terrible trials which awaited him across the pathless desert. With no other guide but the starry heavens, and, it may be, a pocket-compass, the party embarked upon the arid plains which extended far and wide before them to the Cimarron river.

The adventurous band pursued their forward course without being able to procure any water, except from the scanty supply they carried in their canteens. As this source of relief was completely exhausted after two days' march, the sufferings of both men and beasts had driven them almost to distraction.

The forlorn band were at last reduced to the cruel necessity of killing their dogs, and cutting off the ears of their mules, in the vain hope of assuaging their burning thirst with the hot blood. This only served to irritate the parched palates, and madden the senses of the sufferers. Frantic with despair, in prospect of the horrible death which now stared them in the face, they scattered in every direction in search of that element which they had left behind them in such abundance, but without success.

Frequently led astray by the deceptive glimmer of the mirage, or false ponds, as those treacherous oases of the desert are called, and not suspecting (as was really the case) that they had already arrived near the banks of the Cimarron, they resolved to retrace their steps to the Arkansas. But they now were no longer equal to the task, and would undoubtedly have perished in those arid regions, had not a buffalo, fresh from the river's side, and with a stomach distended with water, been discovered by some of the party, just as the last rays of hope were receding from their vision. The hapless intruder was immediately dispatched, and an invigorating draught procured from its stomach. I have since heard one of the parties to that expedition declare, that nothing ever passed his lips which gave him such exquisite delight as his first draught of that filthy beverage.

This providential relief enabled some of the strongest men of the party to reach the river, where they filled their canteens, and then hurried back to the assistance of their comrades, many of whom they found prostrate on the ground, and incapable of further exertion. By degrees, however, they were all enabled to resume their journey; and following the course of the Arkansas for several days, thereby avoiding the arid regions which had occasioned them so much suffering, they succeeded in reaching Taos (sixty or seventy miles north of Santa Fé) without further difficulty. Although travellers have since suffered excessively with thirst upon the same desert, yet, having become better acquainted with the topography of the country, no other equally thrilling incidents have subsequently transpired.

It is from this period—the year 1822—that the virtual commencement of the SANTA FÉ TRADE may be dated. The next remarkable era in its history is the first attempt to introduce wagons in these expeditions. This was made in 1824 by a company of traders, about eighty in number, among whom were several gentlemen of intelligence from Missouri, who contributed, by their superior skill and undaunted energy, to render the enterprise completely successful. A portion of this company employed pack-mules: among the rest were owned twenty-five wheeled vehicles, of which one or two were stout road-wagons, two were carts, and the rest dearborn carriages—the whole conveying some $25,000 or $30,000 worth of merchandise. Colonel Marmaduke, the present Governor of the State of Missouri, having formed one of the party, has been pleased to place his diary of that eventful journey at my disposal; but want of space necessarily compels me to pass over the many interesting and exciting incidents which it contains. Suffice it to say that the caravan reached Santa Fé with much less difficulty than must have been anticipated from a first experiment with wheeled vehicles. The route, indeed, appears to have presented fewer obstacles than any ordinary road of equal length in the United States.

It was not until several years after this experiment, however, that adventurers with large capital began seriously to embark in the Santa Fé trade. The early traders having but seldom experienced any molestations from the Indians, generally crossed the plains in detached bands, each individual rarely carrying more than two or three hundred dollars' worth of stock. This peaceful season, however, did not last very long; and it is greatly to be feared that the traders were not always innocent of having instigated the savage hostilities that ensued in after years. Many seemed to forget the wholesome precept, that they should not be savages themselves because they dealt with savages. Instead of cultivating friendly feelings with those few who remained peaceful and honest, there was an occasional one always disposed to kill, even in cold blood, every Indian that fell into their power, merely because some of the tribe had committed some outrage either against themselves or their friends.

Since the commencement of this trade, returning parties have performed the homeward journey across the plains with the proceeds of their enterprise, partly in specie, and partly in furs, buffalo rugs and animals. Occasionally, these straggling bands would be set upon by marauding Indians, but if well armed and of resolute spirit, they found very little difficulty in persuading the savages to let them pass unmolested; for, as Mr. Storrs very justly remarks, in his representation presented by Colonel Benton, in 1825, to the United States Senate, the Indians are always willing to compromise when they find that they cannot rob "without losing the lives of their warriors, which they hardly ever risk, unless for revenge or in open warfare."

The case was very different with those who through carelessness or recklessness ventured upon the wild prairies without a sufficient supply of arms. A story is told of a small band of twelve men, who, while encamped on the Cimarron river, in 1826, with but four serviceable guns between them, were visited by a party of Indians (believed to be Arrapahoes), who made at first strong demonstrations of friendship and good will. Observing the defenceless condition of the traders, they went away, but soon returned about thirty strong, each provided with a *lazo*, and all on foot. The chief then began by informing the Americans that his men were tired of walking, and must have horses. Thinking it folly to offer any resistance, the terrified traders told them if one animal apiece would satisfy them, to go and catch them. This they soon did; but finding their requests so easily complied with, the Indians held a little parley together, which resulted in a new demand for more— they must now have two apiece. "Well, catch them!" was the acquiescent reply of the unfortunate band—upon which the savages mounted those they had already secured, and, swinging their lazos over their heads, plunged among the stock with a furious yell, and drove off the entire *caballada* of near five hundred head of horses, mules and asses.

The fall of 1828 proved still more fatal to the traders on their homeward trip; for by this time the Indians had learned to form a correct estimate of the stock with which the return companies were generally provided. Two young men named McNees and Monroe, having carelessly lain down to sleep on the banks of a stream, since known as McNees's creek, were barbarously shot, with their own guns, as it was supposed, in very sight of the caravan. When their comrades came up, they found McNees lifeless, and the other almost expiring. In this state the latter was carried nearly forty miles to the Cimarron river, where he died, and was buried according to the custom of the Prairies.*

---

* These funerals are usually performed in a very summary manner. A grave is dug in a convenient spot, and the corpse, with no other shroud than its own clothes, and only a blanket for a coffin, is consigned to the earth. The grave is then usually filled up with stones or poles, as a safe-guard against the voracious wolves of the prairies.

Just as the funeral ceremonies were about to be concluded, six or seven Indians appeared on the opposite side of the Cimarron. Some of the party proposed inviting them to a parley, while the rest, burning for revenge, evinced a desire to fire upon them at once. It is more than probable, however, that the Indians were not only innocent but ignorant of the outrage that had been committed, or they would hardly have ventured to approach the caravan. Being quick of perception, they very soon saw the belligerent attitude assumed by some of the company, and therefore wheeled round and attempted to escape. One shot was fired, which wounded a horse and brought the Indian to the ground, when he was instantly riddled with balls! Almost simultaneously another discharge of several guns followed, by which all the rest were either killed or mortally wounded, except one, who escaped to bear to his tribe the news of their dreadful catastrophe!

These wanton cruelties had a most disastrous effect upon the prospects of the trade; for the exasperated children of the desert became more and more hostile to the 'pale faces,' against whom they continued to wage a cruel war for many successive years. In fact, this same party suffered very severely a few days afterwards. They were pursued by the enraged comrades of the slain savages to the Arkansas river, where they were robbed of nearly a thousand head of mules and horses. But the Indians were not yet satisfied. Having beset a company of about twenty men, who followed shortly after, they killed one of their number, and subsequently took from them all the animals they had in their possession. The unfortunate band were now not only compelled to advance on foot, but were even constrained to carry nearly a thousand dollars each upon their backs to the Arkansas river, where it was *cached* (concealed in the ground) till a conveyance was procured to transfer it to the United States.

Such repeated and daring outrages induced the traders to petition the Federal Government for an escort of United States troops. The request having been granted, Major Riley, with three companies of infantry and one of riflemen, was ordered to accompany the caravan which left in the spring of 1829. The escort stopped at Chouteau's Island, on the Arkansas river, and the traders thence pursued their journey through the sand-hills beyond. They had hardly advanced six or seven miles, when a startling incident occurred which made them wish once more for the company of the gallant Major and his well-disciplined troops. A vanguard of three men, riding a few hundred yards ahead, had just dismounted for the purpose of satisfying their thirst, when a band of Kiawas, one of the most savage tribes that infest the western prairies, rushed upon them from the immense hillocks of sand which lay scattered in all directions. The three men sprang upon their animals, but two only who had horses were enabled to make their escape to the wagons; the third, a Mr. Lamme, who was unfortunately mounted upon a mule, was overtaken, slain and scalped before any one could come to his assistance. Somewhat alarmed at the boldness of the Indians, the traders dispatched an express to Major Riley, who immediately ordered his tents to be struck; and such was the rapidity of his movements, that when he appeared before the anxious caravan every one was lost in astonishment. The reinforcement having arrived in the night, the enemy could have obtained no knowledge of the fact, and would no doubt have renewed the attack in the morning, when they would have received a wholesome lesson from the troops, had not the *reveille* been sounded through mistake, at which they precipitately retreated. The escort now continued with the company as far as Sand creek, when, perceiving no further signs of danger, they returned to the Arkansas, to await the return of the caravan in the ensuing fall.

The position of Major Riley on the Arkansas was one of serious and continual danger. Scarce a day passed without his being subjected to some new annoyance from predatory Indians. The latter appeared, indeed, resolved to check all further concourse of the whites upon the Prairies; and fearful of the terrible extremes to which their excesses might be carried, the traders continued to unite in single caravans during many years afterwards, for the sake of mutual protection.

This escort under Major Riley, and one composed of about sixty dragoons, commanded by Captain Wharton, in 1834, constituted the only government protection ever afforded to the Santa Fé trade, until 1843, when large escorts under Captain Cook accompanied two different caravans as far as the Arkansas river.

Of the composition and organization of these trading caravans, I shall take occasion to speak, from my own experience, in the following chapters.

CHAPTER II

Head Quarters of the Santa Fé Trade—Independence and its *Locale*—A Prairie Trip an excellent Remedy for Chronic Diseases—Supplies for the Journey—Wagons, Mules and Oxen—Art of Loading Wagons—Romancing Propensity of Travellers—The Departure—Storms and Wagon-covers—Quagmires—Tricks of marauding Indians—Council Grove—Fancy *versus* Reality—Electioneering on the Prairies—The Organization—Amateur Travellers and Loafers—Duties of the Watch—Costumes and Equipment of the Party—Timbers for the Journey.

PEOPLE who reside at a distance, and especially at the North, have generally considered St. Louis as the emporium of the Santa Fé Trade; but that city, in truth, has never been a place of rendezvous, nor even of outfit, except for a small portion of the traders who have started from its immediate vicinity. The town of Franklin on the Missouri river, over a hundred and fifty miles further to the westward, seems truly to have been the cradle of our trade; and, in conjunction with several neighboring towns, continued for many years to furnish the greater number of these adventurous traders. Even subsequently to 1831, many wagons have been fitted out and started from this interior section. But as the navigation of the Missouri river had considerably advanced towards the year 1831, and the advantages of some point of debarkation nearer the western frontier were very evident, whereby upwards of a hundred miles of troublesome land-carriage, over unimproved and often miry roads, might be avoided, the new town of INDEPENDENCE, but twelve miles from the Indian border and two or three south of the Missouri river, being the most eligible point, soon began to take the lead as a place of debarkation, outfit and departure, which, in spite of all opposition, it has ever since maintained. It is to this beautiful spot, already grown up to be a thriving town, that the prairie adventurer, whether in search of wealth, health or amusement, is latterly in the habit of repairing, about the first of May, as the caravans usually set out some time during that month. Here they purchase their provisions for the road, and many of their mules, oxen, and even some of their wagons—in short, load all their vehicles, and make their final preparations for a long journey across the prairie wilderness.

As Independence is a point of convenient access (the Missouri river being navigable at all times from March till November), it has become the general 'port of embarkation' for every part of the great western and northern 'prairie ocean.' Besides the Santa Fé caravans, most of the Rocky Mountain traders and trappers, as well as emigrants to Oregon, take this town in their route. During the season of departure, therefore, it is a place of much bustle and active business.

Among the concourse of travellers at this 'starting point,' besides traders and tourists, a number of pale-faced invalids are generally to be met with. The Prairies have, in fact, become very celebrated for their sanative effects—more justly so, no doubt, than the most fashionable watering-places of the North. Most chronic diseases, particularly liver complaints, dyspepsias, and similar affections, are often radically cured; owing, no doubt, to the peculiarities of diet, and the regular exercise incident to prairie life, as well as to the purity of the atmosphere of those elevated unembarrassed regions. An invalid myself, I can answer for the efficacy of the remedy, at least in my own case. Though, like other valetudinarians, I was disposed to provide an ample supply of such commodities as I deemed necessary for my comfort and health, I was not long upon the prairies before I discovered that most of such extra preparations were unnecessary, or at least quite dispensable. A few knick-knacks, as a little tea, rice, fruits, crackers, etc., suffice very well for the first fortnight, after which the invalid is generally able to take the fare of the hunter and teamster. Though I set out myself in a carriage, before the close of the first week I saddled my pony; and when we reached the buffalo range, I was not only as eager for the chase as the sturdiest of my companions, but I enjoyed far more exquisitely my share of the buffalo, than all the delicacies which were ever devised to provoke the most fastidious appetite.

The ordinary supplies for each man's consumption during the journey, are about fifty pounds of flour, as many more of bacon, ten of coffee and twenty of sugar, and a little salt. Beans, crackers, and trifles of that description, are comfortable appendages, but being looked upon as *dispensable* luxuries, are seldom to be found in any of the stores on the road. The buffalo is chiefly depended upon for fresh meat, and great is the joy of the traveller when that noble animal first appears in sight.

The wagons now most in use upon the Prairies are manufactured in Pittsburg; and are usually drawn by eight mules or the same number of oxen. Of late years, however, I have seen much larger vehicles employed, with ten or twelve mules harnessed to each, and a cargo of goods of about five thousand pounds in weight. At an early period the horse was more frequently in use, as mules were not found in great abundance; but as soon as the means for procuring these animals increased, the horse was gradually and finally discarded, except occasionally for riding and the chase.

Oxen having been employed by Major Riley for the baggage wagons of the escort which was furnished the caravan of 1829, they were found, to the surprise of the traders, to perform almost equal to mules. Since that time, upon an average about half of the wagons in these expeditions have been drawn by oxen. They possess many advantages, such as pulling heavier loads than the same number of mules, particularly through muddy or sandy places; but they generally fall off in strength as the prairie grass becomes drier and shorter, and often arrive at their destination in a most shocking plight. In this condition I have seen them sacrificed at Santa Fé for ten dollars the pair; though in more favorable seasons, they sometimes remain strong enough to be driven back to the United States the same fall. Therefore, although the original cost of a team of mules is much greater, the loss ultimately sustained by them is usually less,—to say nothing of the comfort of being able to travel faster and more at ease. The inferiority of oxen as regards endurance is partially owing to the tenderness of their feet; for there are very few among the thousands who have travelled on the Prairies that ever knew how to shoe them properly. Many have resorted to the curious expedient of shoeing their animals with 'moccasins' made of raw buffalo-skin, which does remarkably well as long as the weather remains dry; but when wet, they are soon worn through. Even mules, for the most part, perform the entire trip wiihout being shod at all; though the hoofs often become very smooth, which frequently renders all their movements on the dry grassy surface nearly as laborious as if they were treading on ice.

The supplies being at length procured, and

all necessary preliminaries systematically gone through, the trader begins the difficult task of loading his wagons. Those who understand their business, take every precaution so to stow away their packages that no jolting on the road can afterwards disturb the order in which they had been disposed. The ingenuity displayed on these occasions has frequently been such, that after a tedious journey of eight hundred miles, the goods have been found to have sustained much less injury, than they would have experienced on a turnpike-road, or from the ordinary handling of property upon our western steam-boats.

The next great difficulty the traders have to encounter is in training those animals that have never before been worked, which is frequently attended by an immensity of trouble. There is nothing, however, in the mode of harnessing and conducting teams in prairie travelling, which differs materially from that practised on the public highways throughout the States,—the representations of certain travellers to the contrary, notwithstanding. From the amusing descriptions which are sometimes given by this class of writers, one would be apt to suppose that they had never seen a wagon or a team of mules before, or that they had just emerged for the first time from the purlieus of a large city. The propensity evinced by these writers for giving an air of romance to everything they have either seen or heard, would seem to imply a conviction on their part, that no statement of unvarnished facts can ever be stamped with the seal of the world's approbation—that a work, in order to prove permanently attractive, should teem with absurdities and abound in exaggerated details. How far such an assumption would be correct, I shall not pause to inquire.

At last all are fairly launched upon the broad prairie—the miseries of preparation are over—the thousand anxieties occasioned by wearisome consultations and delays are felt no more. The charioteer, as he smacks his whip, feels a bounding elasticity of soul within him, which he finds it impossible to restrain; —even the mules prick up their ears with a peculiarly conceited air, as if in anticipation of that change of scene which will presently follow. Harmony and good feeling prevail everywhere. The hilarious song, the *bon mot* and the witty repartee, go round in quick succession; and before people have had leisure to take cognizance of the fact, the lively village of Independence, with its multitude of associations, is already lost to the eye.

It was on the 15th of May, 1831, and one of the brightest and most lovely of all the days in the calendar, that our little party set out from Independence. The general rendezvous at Council Grove was our immediate destination. It is usual for the traders to travel thus far in detached parties, and to assemble there for the purpose of entering into some kind of organization, for mutual security and defence during the remainder of the journey. It was from thence that the formation of the *Caravan* was to be dated, and the chief interest of our journey to commence: therefore, to this point we all looked forward with great anxiety. The intermediate travel was marked by very few events of any interest. As the wagons had gone before us, and we were riding in a light carriage, we were able to reach the Round Grove, about thirty-five miles distant, on the first day, where we joined the rear division of the caravan, comprising about thirty wagons.

On the following day we had a foretaste of those protracted, drizzling spells of rain, which, at this season of the year, so much infest the frontier prairies. It began sprinkling about dark, and continued pouring without let or hinderance for forty-eight hours in succession; and as the rain was accompanied by a heavy north-wester, and our camp was pitched in the open prairie, without a stick of available timber within a mile of us, it must be allowed that the whole formed a prelude anything but flattering to valetudinarians. For my own part, finding the dearborn carriage in which I had a berth not exactly water-proof, I rolled myself in a blanket and lay snugly coiled upon a tier of boxes and bales, under cover of a wagon, and thus managed to escape a very severe drenching.

It may be proper to observe here, for the benefit of future travellers, that in order to make a secure shelter for the cargo, against the inclemencies of the weather, there should be spread upon each wagon a pair of stout Osnaburg sheets, with one of sufficient width to reach the bottom of the body on each side, so as to protect the goods from driving rains. By omitting this important precaution many packages of merchandise have been seriously injured. Some have preferred lining the exterior of the wagon-body by tacking a simple strip of sheeting all around it. On the outward trips especially, a pair of Mackinaw blankets can be advantageously spread betwixt the two sheets, which effectually secures the roof against the worst of storms. This contrivance has also the merit of turning the blankets into a profitable item of trade, by enabling the owners to evade the custom-house officers, who would otherwise seize them as contraband articles.

The mischief of the storm did not exhaust itself, however, upon our persons. The loose animals sought shelter in the groves at a considerable distance from the encampment, and the wagoners being loth to turn out in search of them during the rain, not a few of course, when applied for, were missing. This, however, is no uncommon occurrence. Travellers generally experience far more annoyance from the straying of cattle during the first hundred miles, than at any time afterwards; because, apprehending no danger from the wild Indians (who rarely approach within two hundred miles of the border), they seldom keep any watch, although that is the v time when a cattle-guard is most needed. It is only after some weeks' travel that the animals begin to feel attached to the caravan, which they then consider about as much their home as the stock-yard of a dairy farm.

After leaving this spot the troubles and vicissitudes of our journey began in good earnest; for on reaching the narrow ridge which separates the Osage and Kansas waters (known as 'the Narrows'), we encountered a region of very troublesome quagmires. On such occasions it is quite common for a wagon to sink to the hubs in mud, while the surface of the soil all around would appear perfectly dry and smooth. To extricate each other's wagons we had frequently to employ double and triple teams, with 'all hands to the wheels' in addition—often led by the proprietors themselves up to the waist in mud and water.

Three or four days after this, and while crossing the head branches of the Osage river, we experienced a momentary alarm. Conspicuously elevated upon a rod by the roadside, we found a paper purporting to have been written by the Kansas agent, stating that a band of Pawnees were said to be lurking in the vicinity! The first excitement over, however, the majority of our party came to the conclusion that it was either a hoax of some of the company in advance, or else a stratagem of the Kaws (or Kansas Indians), who, as well as the Osages, prowl about those prairies, and steal from the caravans, during the passage, when they entertain the slightest hope that their maraudings will be laid to others. They seldom venture further, however, than to seize upon an occasional stray animal, which they frequently do with the view alone of obtaining a reward for returning it to its owner. As to the Pawnees, the most experienced traders were well aware that they had not been known to frequent those latitudes since the commencement of the Santa Fé trade. But what contributed as much as anything else to lull the fears of the timid, was an accession to our forces of seventeen wagons which we overtook the same evening.

Early on the 26th of May we reached the long looked-for rendèzvous of Council Grove, where we joined the main body of the caravan. Lest this imposing title suggest to the reader a snug and thriving village, it should be observed, that, on the day of our departure from Independence, we passed the last human abode upon our route; therefore, from the borders of Missouri to those of New Mexico not even an Indian settlement greeted our eyes.

This point is nearly a hundred and fifty miles from Independence, and consists of a continuous stripe of timber nearly half a mile in width, comprising the richest varieties of trees; such as oak, walnut, ash, elm, hickory, etc., and extending all along the valleys of a small stream known as 'Council Grove creek,' the principal branch of the Neosho river. This stream is bordered by the most fertile bottoms and beautiful upland prairies, well adapted to cultivation: such indeed is the general character of the country from thence to Independence. All who have traversed these delightful regions, look forward with anxiety to the day when the Indian title to the land shall be extinguished, and flourishing 'white' settlements dispel the gloom which at present prevails over this uninhabited region. Much of this prolific country now belongs to the Shawnees and other Indians of the border, though some portion of it has never been allotted to any tribe.

Frequent attempts have been made by travellers to invest the Council Grove with a romantic sort of interest, of which the following fabulous vagary, which I find in a letter that went the rounds of our journals, is an amusing sample: " Here the Pawnee, Arapaho, Comanche, Loup and Eutaw Indians, all of whom were at war with each other, meet and smoke the pipe once a year." Now it is more than probable that not a soul of most of the tribes mentioned above ever saw the Council Grove. Whatever may be the interest attached to this place, however, on account of its historical or fanciful associations, one thing is very certain,—that the novice, even here, is sure to imagine himself in the midst of lurking savages. These visionary fears are always a source of no little merriment to the veteran of the field, who does not hesitate to travel, with a single wagon and a comrade or two, or even alone, from the Arkansas river to Independence.

The facts connected with the designation of this spot are simply these. Messrs. Reeves, Sibley and Mathers, having been commissioned by the United States, in the year 1825, to mark a road from the confines of Missouri to Sante Fé, met on this spot with some bands of Osages, with whom they concluded a treaty, whereby the Indians agreed to allow all citizens of the United States and Mexico to pass unmolested, and even to lend their aid to those engaged in the Santa Fé trade; for which they were to receive a gratification of eight hundred dollars in merchandise. The commissioners, on this occasion, gave to the place the name of 'Council Grove.'

But, although the route examined by the Commissioners named above, was partially marked out as far as the Arkansas, by raised mounds, it seems to have been of but little service to travellers, who continued to follow the trail previously made by the wagons, which is now the settled road to the region of the short 'buffalo grass.'

The designation of 'Council Grove,' after all, is perhaps the most appropriate that could be given to this place; for *we* there held a 'grand council,' at which the respective claims of the different 'aspirants to office' were considered, leaders selected, and a system of government agreed upon,—as is the standing custom of these promiscuous caravans. One would have supposed that electioneering and 'party spirit' would hardly have penetrated so far into the wilderness: but so it was. Even in our little community we had our 'office-seekers' and their 'political adherents,' as earnest and as devoted as any of the modern school of politicians in the midst of civilization. After a great deal of bickering and wordy warfare, however, all the 'candidates' found it expedient to decline, and a gentleman by the name of Stanley, without seeking, or even desiring the 'office,' was unanimously proclaimed 'Captain of the Caravan.' The powers of this officer were undefined by any 'constitutional provision,' and consequently vague and uncertain: orders being only viewed as mere requests, they are often obeyed or neglected at the caprice of the subordinates. It is necessary to observe, however, that the captain is expected to direct the order of travel during the day, and to designate the camping-ground at night; with many other functions of a general character, in the exercise of which the company find it convenient to acquiesce. But the little attention that is paid to his commands in cases of emergency, I will leave the reader to become acquainted with, as I did, by observing their manifestations during the progress of the expedition.

But after this comes the principal task of organizing. The proprietors are first notified by 'proclamation' to furnish a list of their men and wagons. The latter are generally apportioned into four 'divisions,' particularly when the company is large—and ours consisted of nearly a hundred wagons,* besides a dozen of dearborns and other small vehicles, and two small cannons (a four and six pounder), each mounted upon a carriage. To each of these divisions, a 'lieutenant' was appointed, whose duty it was to inspect every ravine and creek on the route, select the best crossings, and superintend what is called in prairie parlance, the 'forming' of each encampment.

Upon the calling of the roll, we were found to muster an efficient force of nearly two hundred men without counting invalids or other disabled bodies, who, as a matter of course, are exempt from duty. There is nothing so much dreaded by inexperienced travellers as the ordeal of guard duty. But no matter what the condition or employment of the individual may be, no one has the smallest chance of evading the 'common law of the prairies.' The amateur tourist and the listless loafer are precisely in the same wholesome predicament—they must all take their regular turn at the watch. There is usually a set of genteel idlers attached to every caravan, whose wits are forever at work in devising schemes for whiling away their irksome hours at the expense of others. By embarking in these 'trips of pleasure,' they are enabled to live without expense; for the hospitable traders seldom refuse to accommodate even a loafing compa-

---

* About half of these wagons were drawn by ox-teams, the rest by mules.—The capital in merchandise of the whole caravan was about $200,000.

nion with a berth at their mess without charge. But then these lounging *attachés* are expected at least to do good service by way of guard duty. None are even permitted to furnish a substitute, as is frequently done in military expeditions, for he that would undertake to stand the tour of another besides his own, would scarcely be watchful enough for the dangers of the Prairies. Even the invalid must be able to produce unequivocal proofs of his inability, or it is a chance if the plea is admitted. For my own part, although I started on the 'sick list,' and though the prairie sentinel must stand fast and brook the severest storm (for then it is that the strictest watch is necessary), I do not remember ever having missed my post but once during the whole journey.

The usual number of watches is eight, each standing a fourth of every alternate night. When the party is small the number is generally reduced; while in the case of very small bands, they are sometimes compelled for safety's sake to keep one watch on duty half the night. With large caravans the captain usually appoints eight 'sergeants of the guard,' each of whom takes an equal portion of men under his command.

The heterogeneous appearance of our company, consisting of men from every class and grade of society, with a little sprinkling of the softer sex, would have formed an excellent subject for an artist's pencil. It may appear, perhaps, a little extraordinary that females should have ventured across the Prairies under such forlorn auspices. Those who accompanied us, however, were members of a Spanish family who had been banished in 1829, in pursuance of a decree of the Mexican congress, and were now returning to their homes in consequence of a suspension of the decree. Other females, however, have crossed the prairies to Santa Fé at different times, among whom I have known two respectable French ladies, who now reside in Chihuahua.

The wild and motley aspect of the caravan can be but imperfectly conceived without an idea of the costumes of its various members. The most 'fashionable' prairie dress is the fustian frock of the city-bred merchant furnished with a multitude of pockets capable of accommodating a variety of 'extra tackling.' Then there is the backwoodsman with his linsey or leather hunting-shirt—the farmer with his blue jean coat—the wagoner with his flannel-sleeve vest—besides an assortment of other costumes which go to fill up the picture.

In the article of fire-arms there is also an equally interesting medley. The frontier hunter sticks to his rifle, as nothing could induce him to carry what he terms in derision 'the scatter-gun.' The sportsman from the interior flourishes his double-barrelled fowling-piece with equal confidence in its superiority. The latter is certainly the most convenient description of gun that can be carried on this journey; as a charge of buck-shot in night attacks (which are the most common), will of course be more likely to do execution than a single rifle-ball fired at random. The 'repeating' arms have lately been brought into use upon the Prairies, and they are certainly very formidable weapons, particularly when used against an ignorant savage foe. A great many were furnished beside with a bountiful supply of pistols and knives of every description, so that the party made altogether a very brigand-like appearance.

During our delay at the Council Grove, the laborers were employed in procuring timber for axle-trees and other wagon repairs, of which a supply is always laid in before leaving this region of substantial growths; for henceforward there is no wood on the route fit for these purposes; not even in the mountains of Santa Fé do we meet with any serviceable timber. The supply procured here is generally lashed under the wagons, in which way a log is not unfrequently carried to Santa Fé, and even sometimes back again.

CHAPTER III.

The 'Catch up'—Breaking up of the Encampment—Perversity of Mules—Under way—The Diamond Spring—Eccentricities of Oxen—First Glance of the Antelope—Buffalo Herds and Prairie Novices—A John Gilpin Race—Culinary Preparations—A Buffalo Feast—Appetite of Prairie Travellers—Troubles in Fording Streams—Fresh Alarms and their Causes—A Wolfish Frolic—Arkansas River—Pleasing Scenery—Character of the Country—Extraordinary Surgical Operation—The 'Pawnee Rock'—Salutary Effects of Alarms—New Order of March—Prairie Encampment and 'Upholstery'—Hoppling and Tethering of the 'Stock'—Crossing the Arkansas—Great Battle with Rattlesnakes—A Mustang Colt and a Mule Fracas—'The Caches'—Origin and Signification of the Term.

OWING to the delays of organizing and other preparations, we did not leave the Council Grove camp till May 27th. Although the usual hour of starting with the prairie caravans is after an early breakfast, yet, on this occasion, we were hindered till in the afternoon. The familiar note of preparation, "Catch up! catch up!" was now sounded from the captain's camp, and re-echoed from every division and scattered group along the valley. On such occasions, a scene of confusion ensues, which must be seen to be appreciated. The woods and dales resound with the gleeful yells of the light-hearted wagon ers, who, weary of inaction, and filled with joy at the prospect of getting under way, become clamorous in the extreme. Scarcely does the jockey on the race-course ply his whip more promptly at that magic word 'Go,' than do these emulous wagoners fly to harnessing their mules at the spirit-stirring sound of 'Catch up.' Each teamster vies with his fellows who shall be soonest ready; and it is a matter of boastful pride to be the first to cry out—"All's set!"

The uproarious bustle which follows—the hallooing of those in pursuit of animals—the exclamations which the unruly brutes call forth from their wrathful drivers; together with the clatter of bells—the rattle of yokes and harness—the jingle of chains—all conspire to produce a clamorous confusion, which would be altogether incomprehensible without the assistance of the eyes; while these alone would hardly suffice to unravel the labyrinthian manœuvres and hurly-burly of this precipitate breaking up. It is sometimes amusing to observe the athletic wagoner hurrying an animal to its post—to see him 'heave upon' the halter of a stubborn mule, while the brute as obstinately 'sets back,' determined not to 'move a peg' till his own good pleasure thinks it proper to do so—his whole manner seeming to say, "Wait till your hurry's over!" I have more than once seen a driver hitch a harnessed animal to the halter, and by that process haul 'his mulishness' forward, while each of his four projected feet would leave a furrow behind; until at last the perplexed master would wrathfully exclaim, "A mule will be a mule any way you can fix it!"

"All's set!" is finally heard from some teamster—"All's set," is directly responded from every quarter. "Stretch out!" immediately vociferates the captain. Then, the 'heps!' of drivers—the cracking of whips—the trampling of feet—the occasional creak of wheels—the rumbling of wagons—form a new scene of exquisite confusion, which I shall not attempt further to describe. "Fall in!" is heard from head-quarters, and the wagons are forthwith strung out upon the long inclined plain, which stretches to the heights beyond Council Grove.

After fifteen miles' progress, we arrived at the 'Diamond Spring' (a crystal fountain discharging itself into a small brook), to which, in later years, caravans have sometimes advanced, before 'organizing.' Near twenty-five miles beyond we crossed the Cottonwood fork of the Neosho, a creek still smaller than that of Council Grove, and our camp was pitched immediately in its further valley.

When caravans are able to cross in the evening, they seldom stop on the near side of a stream—first, because if it happen to rain during the night, it may become flooded, and cause both detention and trouble: again, though the stream be not impassable after rain, the banks become slippery and difficult to ascend. A third and still more important reason is, that, even supposing the contingency of rain does not occur, teams will rarely pull as well in 'cold collars,' as wagoners term it—that is, when fresh geared—as in the progress of a day's travel. When a heavy pull is just at hand in the morning, wagoners sometimes resort to the expedient of driving a circuit upon the prairie, before venturing to 'take the bank.'

We experienced a temporary alarm during the evening, while we lay encamped at Cottonwood, which was rather more boisterous than serious in its consequences. The wagons had been 'formed' across the neck of a bend in the creek, into which the cattle were turned, mostly in their yokes; for though, when thoroughly trained, teamsters usually unyoke their oxen every night, yet at first they often leave them coupled, to save the trouble of re-yoking them in their unruly state. A little after dark, these animals started simultaneously, with a thundering noise and rattle of the yokes, towards the outlet protected by the wagons, but for which obstacle they might have escaped far into the prairie, and have been irrecoverably lost, or, at least, have occasioned much trouble and delay to recover them. The cause of the fright was not discovered; but oxen are exceedingly whimsical creatures when surrounded by unfamiliar objects. One will sometimes take a fright at the jingle of his own yoke-irons, or the cough of his mate, and, by a sudden flounce, set the whole herd in a flurry. This was probably the case in the present instance;

although some of our easily excited companions immediately surmised that the oxen had scented a lurking Pawnee.

Our route lay through uninterrupted prairie for about forty miles—in fact I may say, for five hundred miles, excepting the very narrow fringes of timber along the borders of the streams. The antelope of the high prairies which we now occasionally saw, is sometimes found as far east as Council Grove; and as a few old buffaloes have sometimes been met with about Cottonwood, we now began to look out for this desirable game. Some scattering bulls are generally to be seen first, forming as it would appear the 'van' or 'piquet guards' of the main droves with their cows and calves. The buffalo are usually found much further east early in the spring, than during the rest of the year, on account of the long grass, which shoots up earlier in the season than the short pasturage of the plains.

Our hopes of game were destined soon to be realized; for early on the second day after leaving Cottonwood (a few miles beyond the principal Turkey creek), our eyes were greeted with the sight of a herd amounting to nearly a hundred head of buffalo, quietly grazing in the distance before us. Half of our company had probably never seen a buffalo before (at least in its wild state); and the excitement that the first sight of these 'prairie beeves' occasions among a party of novices, beggars all description. Every horseman was off in a scamper; and some of the wagoners, leaving their teams to take care of themselves, seized their guns and joined the race afoot. Here went one with his rifle or yager—there another with his double-barrelled shot-gun—a third with his holster-pistols—a Mexican perhaps with his lance—another with his bow and arrows—and numbers joined without any arms whatever, merely for the 'pleasures of the chase'—all helter-skelter—a regular John Gilpin race, truly 'neck or naught.' The fleetest of the pursuers were soon in the midst of the game, which scattered in all directions, like a flock of birds upon the descent of a hawk.

A few 'beeves' were killed during the chase; and as soon as our camp was pitched, the bustle of kindling fires and preparing for supper commenced. The new adventurers were curious to taste this prairie luxury; while we all had been so long upon salt provisions—now nearly a month—that our appetites were in exquisite condition to relish fresh meat. The fires had scarcely been kindled when the fumes of broiling meat pervaded the surrounding atmosphere; while all huddled about, anxiously watching their cookeries, and regaling their senses in anticipation upon the savory odors which issued from them.

For the edification of the reader, who has no doubt some curiosity on the subject, I will briefly mention, that the 'kitchen and table ware' of the traders usually consists of a skillet, a frying-pan, a sheet-iron camp-kettle, a coffee-pot, and each man with his tin cup and a butcher's knife. The culinary operations being finished, the pan and kettle are set upon the grassy turf, around which all take a 'lowly seat,' and crack their gleesome jokes, while from their greasy hands they swallow their savory viands—all with a relish rarely experienced at the well-spread tables of the most fashionable and wealthy.

The insatiable appetite acquired by travellers upon the Prairies is almost incredible, and the quantity of coffee drank is still more so. It is an unfailing and apparently indispensable beverage, served at every meal—even under the broiling noon-day sun, the wagoner will rarely fail to replenish a second time, his huge tin cup.

Early the next day we reached the 'Little Arkansas,' which, although endowed with an imposing name, is only a small creek with a current but five or six yards wide. But, though small, its steep banks and miry bed annoyed us exceedingly in crossing. It is the practice upon the prairies on all such occasions, for several men to go in advance with axes, spades and mattocks, and, by digging the banks and erecting temporary bridges, to have all in readiness by the time the wagons arrive. A bridge over a quagmire is made in a few minutes, by cross-laying it with brush (willows are best, but even long grass is often employed as a substitute), and covering it with earth,—across which a hundred wagons will often pass in safety.

We had now arrived at the point nearest

to the border, I believe, where any outrages have been perpetrated upon the traders to Santa Fé. One of the early packing companies lost their animals on this spot, and had to send back for a new supply.

Next day we reached Cow creek, where all the difficulties encountered at Little Arkansas had to be reconquered: but after digging, bridging, shouldering the wheels, with the usual accompaniment of whooping, swearing and cracking of whips, we soon got safely across and encamped in the valley beyond. Alarms now began to accumulate more rapidly upon us. A couple of persons had a few days before been chased to the wagons by a band of——buffalo; and this evening the encampment was barely formed when two hunters came bolting in with information that a hundred, perhaps of the same 'enemy,' were at hand—at least this was the current opinion afterwards. The hubbub occasioned by this fearful news had scarcely subsided, when another arrived on a panting horse, crying out "Indians! Indians! I've just escaped from a couple, who pursued me to the very camp!" "To arms! to arms!" resounded from every quarter—and just then a wolf, attracted by the fumes of broiling buffalo bones, sent up a most hideous howl across the creek. "Some one in distress!" was instantly shouted: "To his relief!" vociferated the crowd—and off they bolted, one and all, arms in hand, hurly-burly—leaving the camp entirely unprotected; so that had an enemy been at hand indeed, and approached us from the opposite direction, they might easily have taken possession of the wagons. Before they had all returned, however, a couple of hunters came in and laughed very heartily at the expense of the first alarmist, whom they had just chased into the camp.

Half a day's drive after leaving this camp of 'false alarms' brought us to the valley of Arkansas river. This point is about 270 miles from Independence. From the adjacent heights the landscape presents an imposing and picturesque appearance. Beneath a ledge of wave-like yellow sandy ridges and hillocks spreading far beyond, descends the majestic river (averaging at least a quarter of a mile in width), bespeckled with verdant islets, thickly set with cottonwood timber. The banks are very low and barren, with the exception of an occasional grove of stunted trees, hiding behind a swamp or sand-hill, placed there as it were to protect it from the fire of the prairies, which in most parts keeps down every perennial growth. In many places, indeed, where there are no islands, the river is so entirely bare of trees, that the unthinking traveller might approach almost to its very brink, without suspecting its presence.

Thus far, many of the prairies have a fine and productive appearance, though the Neosho river (or Council Grove) seems to form the western boundary of the truly rich and beautiful country of the border. Up to that point the prairies are similar to those of Missouri—the soil equally exuberant and fertile; while all the country that lies beyond, is of a far more barren character—vegetation of every kind is more stinted—the gay flowers more scarce, and the scanty timber of a very inferior quality: indeed, the streams, from Council Grove westward, are lined with very little else than cottonwood, barely interspersed here and there with an occasional elm or hackberry.

Following up the course of this stream for some twenty miles, now along the valley, and again traversing the points of projecting eminences, we reached Walnut creek. I have heard of a surgical operation performed at this point, in the summer of 1826, which, though not done exactly *secundum artem*, might suggest some novel reflections to the man of science. A few days before the caravan had reached this place, a Mr. Broadus, in attempting to draw his rifle from a wagon muzzle foremost, discharged its contents into his arm. The bone being dreadfully shattered, the unfortunate man was advised to submit to an amputation at once; otherwise, it being in the month of August, and excessively warm, mortification would soon ensue. But Broadus obstinately refused to consent to this course, till death began to stare him in the face. By this time, however, the whole arm had become gangrened, some spots having already appeared above the place where the operation should have been performed. The invalid's case was therefore considered perfectly hopeless, and he was given up by all his comrades, who thought of little else than to consign him to the grave.

But being unwilling to resign himself to the fate which appeared frowning over him, without a last effort, he obtained the consent of two or three of the party, who undertook to amputate his arm merely to gratify the wishes of the dying man; for in such a light they viewed him. Their only 'case of instruments' consisted of a handsaw, a butcher's knife and a large iron bolt. The teeth of the saw being considered too coarse, they went to work, and soon had a set of fine teeth filed on the back. The knife having been whetted keen, and the iron bolt laid upon the fire, they commenced the operation: and in less time than it takes to tell it, the arm was opened round to the bone, which was almost in an instant sawed off; and with the whizzing hot iron the whole stump was so effectually seared as to close the arteries completely. Bandages were now applied, and the company proceeded on their journey as though nothing had occurred. The arm commenced healing rapidly, and in a few weeks the patient was sound and well, and is perhaps still living, to bear witness to the superiority of the 'hot iron' over ligatures, in 'taking up' arteries.

On the following day our route lay mostly over a level plain, which usually teems with buffalo, and is beautifully adapted to the chase. At the distance of about fifteen miles, the attention of the traveller is directed to the

Pawnee Rock,' so called, it is said, on account of a battle's having once been fought hard by, between the Pawnees and some other tribe. It is situated at the projecting point of a ridge, and upon its surface are furrowed, in uncouth but legible characters, numerous dates, and the names of various travellers who have chanced to pass that way.

We encamped at Ash creek, where we again experienced sundry alarms in consequence of 'Indian sign,' that was discovered in the creek valley, such as unextinguished fires, about which were found some old moccasins,—a sure indication of the recent retreat of savages from the vicinity. These constant alarms, however, although too frequently the result of groundless and unmanly fears, are not without their salutary effects upon the party. They serve to keep one constantly on the alert, and to sharpen those faculties of observation which would otherwise become blunted or inactive. Thus far also we had marched in two lines only; but, after crossing the Pawnee Fork, each of the four divisions drove on in a separate file, which became henceforth the order of march till we reached the border of the mountains. By moving in long lines as we did before, the march is continually interrupted; for every accident which delays a wagon ahead stops all those behind. By marching four abreast, this difficulty is partially obviated, and the wagons can also be thrown more readily into a condition of defence in case of attack.

Upon encamping the wagons are formed into a 'hollow square' (each division to a side), constituting at once an enclosure (or *corral*) for the animals when needed, and a fortification against the Indians. Not to embarrass this cattle-pen, the camp fires are all lighted outside of the wagons. Outside of the wagons, also, the travellers spread their beds, which consist, for the most part, of buffalo-rugs and blankets. Many content themselves with a single Mackinaw; but a pair constitutes the most regular pallet; and he that is provided with a buffalo-rug into the bargain, is deemed luxuriously supplied. It is most usual to sleep out in the open air, as well to be at hand in case of attack, as indeed for comfort; for the serene sky of the Prairies affords the most agreeable and wholesome canopy. That deleterious attribute of night air and dews, so dangerous in other climates, is but little experienced upon the high plains: on the contrary, the serene evening air seems to affect the health rather favorably than otherwise. Tents are so rare on these expeditions that, in a caravan of two hundred men, I have not seen a dozen. In time of rain the traveller resorts to his wagon, which affords a far more secure shelter than a tent; for if the latter is not beaten down by the storms which so often accompany rain upon the prairies, the ground underneath is at least apt to be flooded. During dry weather, however, even the invalid prefers the open air.

Prior to the date of our trip it had been customary to secure the horses by hoppling them. The 'fore-hopple' (a leathern strap or rope manacle upon the fore-legs) being most convenient, was more frequently used; though the 'side-line' (a hopple connecting a fore and a hind leg) is the most secure; for with this an animal can hardly increase his pace beyond a hobbling walk; whereas, with the fore-hopple, a frighted horse will scamper off with nearly as much velocity as though he were unshackled. But, better than either of these is the practice which the caravans have since adopted of tethering the mules at night around the wagons, at proper intervals, with ropes twenty-five or thirty feet in length, tied to stakes fifteen to twenty inches long, driven into the ground; a supply of which, as well as mallets, the wagoners always carry with them.

It is amusing to witness the disputes which often arise among wagoners about their 'staking ground.' Each teamster is allowed, by our 'common law,' a space of about a hundred yards immediately fronting his wagon, which he is ever ready to defend, if a neighbor shows a disposition to encroach upon his soil. If any animals are found 'staked' beyond the 'chartered limits,' it is the duty of the guard to 'knock them up,' and turn them into the *corral.* Of later years the tethering of oxen has also been resorted to with advantage. It was thought at first that animals thus confined by ropes could not procure a sufficient supply of food; but experience has allayed all apprehension on the subject. In fact, as the camp is always pitched in the most luxuriantly clothed patches of prairie that can be selected, a mule is seldom able to dispatch in the course of one night, all the grass within his reach. Again, when animals are permitted to range at liberty, they are apt to mince and nibble at the tenderest blades and spend their time in roaming from point to point, in search of what is most agreeable to their 'epicurean palates;' whereas if they are restricted by a rope, they will at once fall to with earnestness and clip the pasturage as it comes.

Although the buffalo had been scarce for a few days,—frightened off, no doubt, by the Indians whose 'sign' we saw about Ash creek, they soon became exceedingly abundant. The larger droves of these animals are sometimes a source of great annoyance to the caravans, as, by running near our loose stock, there is frequent danger of their causing *stampedes* (or general scamper), in which case mules, horses and oxen have been known to run away among the buffalo, as though they had been a gang of their own species. A company of traders, in 1824, lost twenty or thirty of their animals in this way. Hunters have also been deprived of their horses in the same way. Leaping from them in haste, in order to take a more determinate aim at a buffalo, the horse has been known to take fright, and following the fleeing game, has disappeared with saddle, bridle, pistols and all—most probably never to be heard of again. In fact, to look for stock upon these prairies, would be emphatically to 'search for a needle in a haystack;' not only because they are virtually boundless, but that being everywhere alive with herds of buffalo, from which horses cannot be distinguished at a distance, one knows not whither to turn in search after the stray animals.

We had lately been visited by frequent showers of rain, and upon observing the Arkansas river, it was found to be rising, which seemed portentous of the troubles which the 'June freshet' might occasion us in crossing it; and, as it was already the 11th of this month, this annual occurrence was now hourly expected. On some occasions caravans have been obliged to construct what is called a 'buffalo-boat,' which is done by stretching the hides of these animals over a frame of poles, or, what is still more common, over an empty wagon-body. The 'June freshets,' however, are seldom of long duration; and, during the greatest portion of the year, the channel is very shallow. Still the bed of the river being in many places filled with quicksand, it is requisite to examine and mark out the best ford with stakes, before one undertakes to cross. The wagons are then driven over usually by double teams, which should never be permitted to stop, else animals and wagons are apt to founder, and the loading is liable to be damaged. I have witnessed a whole team down at once, rendering it necessary to unharness and drag each mule out separately: in fact, more than common exertion is sometimes required to prevent these dumpish animals from drowning in their fright and struggles through the water, though the current be but shallow at the place. Hence it is that oxen are much safer for fording streams than mules. As for ourselves, we forded the river without serious difficulty.

Rattlesnakes are proverbially abundant upon all these prairies, and as there is seldom to be found either stick or stone with which to kill them, one hears almost a constant popping of rifles or pistols among the vanguard, to clear the route of these disagreeable occupants, lest they should bite our animals. As we were toiling up through the sandy hillocks which border the southern banks of the Arkansas, the day being exceedingly warm, we came upon a perfect den of these reptiles. I will not say 'thousands,' though this perhaps were nearer the truth—but hundreds at least were coiled or crawling in every direction. They were no sooner discovered than we were upon them with guns and pistols, determined to let none of them escape.

In the midst of this amusing scramble among the snakes, a wild mustang colt, which had, somehow or other, become separated from its dam, came bolting among our relay of loose stock to add to the confusion. One of our mules, evidently impressed with the impertinence of the intruder, sprang forward and attacked it, with the apparent intention of executing summary chastisement; while another mule, with more benignity of temper than its irascible compeer, engaged most lustily in defence of the unfortunate little mustang. As the contest was carried on among the wagons, the teamsters soon became very uproarious; so that the whole, with the snake fracas, made up a capital scene of confusion. When the mule skirmish would have ended, if no one had interfered, is a question which remained undetermined; for some of our company, in view of the consequences that might result from the contest, rather inhumanly took sides with the assailing mule; and soon after they entered the lists, a rifle ball relieved the poor colt from its earthly embarrassments, and the company from further domestic disturbance. Peace once more restored, we soon got under way, and that evening pitched our camp opposite the celebrated 'Caches,' a place where some of the earliest adventurers had been compelled to conceal their merchandise.

The history of the origin of these 'Caches' may be of sufficient interest to merit a brief recital. Beard, of the unfortunate party of 1812, alluded to in the first chapter, having returned to the United States in 1822, together with Chambers, who had descended the Canadian river the year before, induced some small capitalists of St. Louis to join in an enterprise, and then undertook to return to Santa Fé the same fall, with a small party and an assortment of merchandise. Reaching the Arkansas late in the season, they were overtaken by a heavy snow storm, and driven to take shelter on a large island. A rigorous winter ensued, which forced them to remain pent up in that place for three long months. During this time the greater portion of their animals perished; so that, when the spring began to open, they were unable to continue their journey with their goods. In this emergency they made a *cache* some distance above, on the north side of the river, where they stowed away the most of their merchandise. From thence they proceeded to Taos, where they procured mules, and returned to get their hidden property.

Few travellers pass this way without visiting these mossy pits, some of which remain partly unfilled to the present day. In the vicinity, or a few miles to the eastward perhaps, passes the hundredth degree of longitude west from Greenwich, which, from the Arkansas to Red River, forms the boundary between the United States and the Mexican, or rather the Texan territory.

The term *cache*, meaning a *place of concealment*, was originally used by the Canadian French trappers and traders. It is made by digging a hole in the ground, somewhat in the shape of a jug, which is lined with dry sticks, grass, or anything else that will protect its contents from the dampness of the earth. In this place the goods to be concealed are carefully stowed away; and the aperture is then so effectually closed as to protect them from the rains. In *caching*, a great deal of skill is often required, to leave no signs whereby the cunning savage might discover the place of deposit. To this end, the excavated earth is carried to some distance and carefully concealed, or thrown into a stream, if one be at hand. The place selected for a cache is usually some rolling point, sufficiently elevated to be secure from inundations. If it be well set with grass, a solid piece of turf is cut out large enough for the entrance. The turf is afterward laid back, and taking root, in a short time no signs remain of its ever having been molested. However, as every locality does not afford a turfy site, the camp fire is sometimes built upon the place, or the animals are penned over it, which effectually destroys all traces of the cache.

This mode of concealing goods seems to have been in use from the time of the earliest French voyagers in America. Father Hennepin, during his passage down the Mississippi river, in 1680, describes an operation of this kind in the following terms: " We took up the green Sodd, and laid it by, and digg'd a hole in the Earth where we put our Goods, and cover'd them with pieces of Timber and Earth, and then put in again the green Turf; so that 'twas impossible to suspect that any Hole had been digg'd under it, for we flung the Earth into the River." Returning a few weeks after, they found the cache all safe and sound.

CHAPTER IV.

A Desert Plain—Preparation for a 'Water-Scrape'—Accident to a French Doctor—Upsetting of a Wagon and its Consequences—A Party of Sioux Warriors—The first real Alarm—Confusion in the Camp—Friendly Demonstrations of the Indians—The Pipe of Peace—Squaws and Papooses—An Extemporary Village—Lose our Track—Search after the Lost River—Horrible Prospective—The Cimarron Found at last—A Night of Alarms—Indian Serenade and Thieving—Indian Diplomacy—Hail-stones and Hurricanes—Position of the Captain of a Caravan—His Troubles, his Powers and Want of Powers—More Indians—Hostile Encounter—Results of the Skirmish—The 'Battle-Ground'—Col. Vizcarra and the Gros Ventres.

Our route had already led us up the course of the Arkansas river for over a hundred miles, yet the earlier caravans often passed from fifty to a hundred further up before crossing the river; therefore nothing like a regular ford had ever been established. Nor was there a road, not even a trail, anywhere across the famous plain, extending between the Arkansas and Cimarron rivers, a distance of over fifty miles, which now lay before us—the scene of such frequent sufferings in former times for want of water. It having been determined upon, however, to strike across this dreaded desert the following morning, the whole party was busy in preparing for the ' water scrape,' as these droughty drives are very appropriately called by prairie travellers. This tract of country may truly be styled the grand 'prairie ocean;' for not a single landmark is to be seen for more than forty miles—scarcely a visible eminence by which to direct one's course. All is as level as the sea, and the compass was our surest, as well as principal guide.

In view of this passage, as well as that of many other dry stretches upon the route, the traveller should be apprised of the necessity of providing a water-cask holding at least five gallons to each wagon, in which a supply for drinking and cooking may be carried along to serve in cases of emergency.

The evening before the embarking of a caravan upon this plain, the captain's voice is usually heard above the din and clatter of the camp, ordering to "fill up the water kegs,"—a precaution which cannot be repeated too often, as new adventurers are usually ignorant of the necessity of providing a supply sufficient to meet every contingency that may befal during two or more days' journey over this arid region. The cooks are equally engrossed by their respective vocations: some are making bread, others preparing viands, and all tasking their ingenuity to lay by such stores as may be deemed expedient for at least two days' consumption. On the following morning (June 14th), the words 'catch up' again resounded through the camp, and the caravan was once more in motion.

For the first five miles we had a heavy pull

among the sandy hillocks; but soon the broad and level plain opened before us. We had hardly left the river's side, however, when we experienced a delay of some hours, in consequence of an accident which came very nigh proving fatal to a French doctor of our company. Fearful lest his stout top-heavy dearborn should upset whilst skirting the slope of a hill, he placed himself below in order to sustain it with his hands. But, in spite of all his exertions, the carriage tumbled over, crushing and mashing him most frightfully. He was taken out senseless, and but little hopes were at first entertained of his recovery. Having revived, however, soon after, we were enabled to resume our march; and, in the course of time, the wounded patient entirely recovered.

The next day we fortunately had a heavy shower, which afforded us abundance of water. Having also swerved considerably toward the south, we fell into a more uneven section of country, where we had to cross a brook swelled by the recent rain, into which one of the wagons was unfortunately overset. This, however, was not a very uncommon occurrence; for unruly oxen, when thirsty, will often rush into a pool in despite of the driver, dragging the wagon over every object in their way, at the imminent risk of turning it topsy-turvy into the water. We were now compelled to make a halt, and all hands flocked to the assistance of the owner of the damaged cargo. In a few minutes about an acre of ground was completely covered with calicoes, and other domestic goods, presenting altogether an interesting spectacle.

All were busily occupied at this work when some objects were seen moving in the distance, which at first were mistaken for buffalo; but were speedily identified as horsemen. Anxiety was depicted in every countenance. Could it be possible that the party of Capt. Sublette, which was nearly a month ahead of us, had been lost in these dreary solitudes? or was it the band of Capt. Bent, who was expected to follow some time after us? This anxious suspense, however, lasted only for a few minutes; and the cry of " Indians!" soon made the welkin ring. Still they appeared to approach too slowly for the western prairie tribes. A little nearer, and we soon perceived that they carried a flag, which turned out to be that of the United States. This welcome sight allayed at once all uneasiness; as it is well known that most savages, when friendly, approach the whites with a hoisted flag, provided they have one. It turned out to be a party of about eighty Sioux, who were on a tour upon the Prairies for the purpose of trading with, stealing from or marauding upon the south-western nations. Our communications were carried on entirely by signs; yet we understood them perfectly to say, that there were immense numbers of Indians ahead, upon the Cimarron river, whom they described by symbolic language to be Blackfeet and Co manches; a most agreeable prospect for the imagination to dwell upon!

We now moved on slowly and leisurely, for all anxiety on the subject of water had been happily set at rest by frequent falls of rain. But imagine our consternation and dismay, when, upon descending into the valley of the Cimarron, on the morning of the 19th of June, a band of Indian warriors on horseback suddenly appeared before us from behind the ravines—an imposing array of death-dealing savages! There was no merriment in this! It was a genuine alarm—a tangible reality! These warriors, however, as we soon discovered, were only the van-guard of a 'countless host,' who were by this time pouring over the opposite ridge, and galloping directly towards us.

The wagons were soon irregularly 'formed' upon the hill-side: but in accordance with the habitual carelessness of caravan traders, a great portion of the men were unprepared for the emergency. Scores of guns were 'empty,' and as many more had been wetted by the recent showers, and would not 'go off.' Here was one calling for balls—another for powder—a third for flints. Exclamations, such as, "I've broke my ramrod"—"I've spilt my caps"—"I've rammed down a ball without powder"—"My gun is 'choked;' give me yours"—were heard from different quarters; while a timorous 'greenhorn' would perhaps cry out, "Here, take my gun, you can out-shoot me!" The more daring bolted off to encounter the enemy at once, while the timid and cautious took a stand with presented rifle behind the wagons. The Indians who were in advance made a bold attempt to press upon us, which came near costing them dearly ; for some of our fiery backwoodsmen more than once had their rusty but unerring rifles directed upon the intruders, some of whom would inevitably have fallen before their deadly aim, had not a few of the more prudent traders interposed. The savages made demonstrations no less hostile, rushing, with ready sprung bows, upon a portion of our men who had gone in search of water; and mischief would, perhaps, have ensued, had not the impetuosity of the warriors been checked by the wise men of the nation.

The Indians were collecting around us, however, in such great numbers, that it was deemed expedient to force them away, so as to resume our march, or at least to take a more advantageous position. Our company was therefore mustered and drawn up in 'line of battle ;' and, accompanied by the sound of a drum and fife, we marched towards the main group of the Indians. The latter seemed far more delighted than frightened with this strange parade and music, a spectacle they had, no doubt, never witnessed before, and perhaps looked upon the whole movement rather as a complimentary salute than a hostile array ; for there was no interpreter through whom any communication could be conveyed to them. But, whatever may have been their impressions, one thing is certain,—that the principal chief (who was dressed in a long red coat of strouding, or coarse cloth) appeared to have full confidence in the virtues of his calumet; which he lighted, and came boldly forward to meet our warlike corps, serenely smoking the 'pipe of peace.' Our captain, now taking a whiff with the savage chief, directed him by signs to cause his warriors to retire. This most of them did, to rejoin the long train of squaws and papooses with the baggage, who followed in the rear, and were just then seen emerging from beyond the hills. Having slowly descended to the banks of the stream, they pitched their wigwams or lodges; over five hundred of which soon bespeckled the ample valley before us, and at once gave to its recently meagre surface the aspect of an immense Indian village. The entire number of the Indians, when collected together, could not have been less than from two to three thousand—although some of our company insisted that there were at least four thousand souls. In such a case they must have mustered nearly a thousand warriors, while we were but little over two hundred strong. Still, our superior arms and the protection afforded by the wagons, gave us considerably the advantage, even supposing an equality in point of valor. However, the appearance of the squaws and children soon convinced us, that, for the present, at least, they had no hostile intentions; so we also descended into the valley and formed our camp a few hundred yards below them. The 'capitanes,' or head men of the whites and Indians, shortly after met, and, again smoking the calumet, agreed to be friends.

Although we were now on the very banks of the Cimarron, even the most experienced traders of our party, whether through fright or ignorance, seemed utterly unconscious of the fact. Having made our descent, far below the usual point of approach, and there being not a drop of water found in the sandy bed of the river, it was mistaken for Sand creek, and we accordingly proceeded without noticing it. Therefore, after our 'big talk' was concluded, and dinner dispatched, we again set out southward, in search of the Cimarron. As we were starting, warriors, squaws and papooses now commenced flocking about us, gazing at our wagons with amazement; for many of them had never, perhaps, seen such vehicles before. A few chiefs and others followed us to our next encampment; but these were sent away at night.

Our guards were now doubled, as a night attack was apprehended; for although we were well aware that Indians never commit outrages with their families at hand, yet it was feared that they might either send them away or conceal them during the night. A little after dark, these fears seemed about to be realized; as a party of thirty or forty Indians were seen coming up towards the encampment. Immediate preparations were made to attack them, when they turned out to be a band of squaws, with merely a few men as gallants—all of whom were summarily turned adrift, without waiting to speculate upon the objects of their visit. The next morning a few others made their appearance, which we treated in precisely the same manner, as a horse was missing, which it was presumed the Indians had stolen.

We continued our march southward in search of the 'lost river.' After a few miles' travel we encountered a ledge of sand-hills, which obstructed our course, and forced us to turn westward and follow their border for the rest of the day. Finding but little water that night, and none at all the next day, we began by noon to be sadly frightened; for nothing is more alarming to the prairie traveller than a 'water-scrape.' The impression soon became general that we were *lost*—lost on that inhospitable desert, which had been the theatre of so many former scenes of suffering! and our course impeded by sand-hills! A council of the veteran travellers was called to take our emergency into consideration. It was at once resolved to strike in a northwesterly direction in search of the 'dry ravine' we had left behind us, which was now supposed to have been the Cimarron.

We had just set out, when a couple of Indians approached us, bringing the horse we had lost the night before; an apparent demonstration of good faith which could hardly have been anticipated. It was evidently an effort to ingratiate themselves in our favor, and establish an intercourse—perhaps a traffic. But the outrages upon Major Riley, as well as upon a caravan, not two years before, perpetrated probably by the same Indians, were fresh in the memory of all; so that none of us were willing to confide in their friendly professions. On inquiring by means of signs for the nearest water, they pointed to the direction we were travelling: and finally taking the lead, they led us, by the shortest way, to the valley of the long-sought Cimarron, which, with its delightful green-grass glades and flowing torrent (very different in appearance from where we had crossed it below), had all the aspect of an 'elysian vale,' compared with what we had seen for some time past. We pitched our camp in the valley, much rejoiced at having again 'made a port.'

We were not destined to rest long in peace, however. About midnight we were all aroused by a cry of alarm, the like of which had not been heard since the day Don Quixote had his famous adventure with the fulling-mills; and I am not quite sure but some of our party suffered as much from fright as poor Sancho Panza did on that memorable occasion. But Don Quixote and Sancho only heard the thumping of the mills and the roaring of the waters; while we heard the thumping of the Indian drums, accompanied by occasional yells, which our excited fancies immediately construed into notes of the fearful war-song.

After the whole company had been under arms for an hour or two, finding the cause of alarm approached no nearer, we again retired to rest. But a little before daylight we were again startled by the announcement—" The Indians are coming!—they are upon the very camp!" In a moment every man was up in arms; and several guns were presented to 'salute' the visitors, when, to our extreme mortification, they were found to be but eight or ten in number. They were immediately dispatched, by signs, and directed to remain away till morning—which they did.

On the following day, we had been in motion but a few minutes, when the Indians began flocking around us in large numbers, and by the time we encamped in the evening, we had perhaps a thousand of these pertinacious creatures, males and females, of all ages and descriptions, about us. At night, every means, without resorting to absolute violence, was employed to drive them away, but without entire success. At this time a small band of warriors took the round of our camp, and 'serenaded' us with a monotonous song of *hee-o-hehs*, with the view, I suppose, of gaining permission to remain; hoping, no doubt, to be able to 'drive a fair business' at pilfering during the night. In fact, a few small articles were already missing, and it was now discovered that they had purloined a pig of lead (between fifty and a hundred pounds weight) from one of the cannon-carriages, where it had been carelessly left. This increased the uneasiness which already prevailed to a considerable extent; and many of us would imagine it already moulded into bullets, which we were perhaps destined to receive before morning from the muzzles of their fusils. Some were even so liberal as to express a willingness to pardon the theft, rather than give the Indians the trouble of sending it back in so hasty a manner. After a tedious night of suspense and conjecture, it was no small relief to those whose feelings had been so highly wrought upon, to find, on waking up in the morning, that every man still retained his scalp.

We started at a much earlier hour, this morning, in hopes to leave our Indian tormentors behind; but they were too wide-awake for us. By the time the wagoners had completed the task of gearing their teams, the squaws had 'geared' their dogs, and loaded them with their lodge poles and covers, and other light 'plunder,' and were travelling fast in our wake. Much to our comfort, however, the greatest portion abandoned us before night; but the next day several of the chiefs overtook us again at noon, seeming anxious to renew the 'treaty of peace.' The truth is, the former treaty had never been 'sealed'— they had received no presents, which form an indispensable ratification of all their 'treaties' with the whites. Some fifty or sixty dollars' worth of goods having been made up for them, they now left us apparently satisfied; and although they continued to return and annoy us for a couple of days longer; they at last entirely disappeared.

It was generally supposed at the time that there was a great number of Comanches and Arrapahoes among this troop of savages; but they were principally if not altogether Blackfeet and Gros Ventres. We afterward learned that on their return to the northern mountains, they met with a terrible defeat from the Sioux and other neighboring tribes, in which they were said to have lost more than half their number.

We now encountered a great deal of wet weather; in fact this region is famous for cold protracted rains of two or three days' duration. Storms of hail-stones larger than hen's eggs are not uncommon, frequently accompanied by the most tremendous hurricanes. The violence of the wind is sometimes so great that, as I have heard, two road-wagons were once capsized by one of these terrible thunder-gusts; the rain, at the same time, floating the plain to the depth of several inches. In short, I doubt if there is any known region out of the tropics, that can 'head' the great prairies in 'getting up' thunder-storms, combining so many of the elements of the awful and sublime.

During these storms the guards were often very careless. This was emphatically the case with us, notwithstanding our knowledge of the proximity of a horde of savages. In fact, the caravan was subject to so little control that the patience of Capt. Stanley underwent some very severe trials; so much so that he threatened more than once to resign. Truly, there is not a better school for testing a man's temper, than the command of a promiscuous caravan of independent traders. The rank of captain is, of course, but little more than nominal. Every proprietor of a two-horse wagon is apt to assume as much authority as the commander himself, and to issue his orders without the least consultation at head-quarters. It is easy then to conceive that the captain has anything but an enviable berth. He is expected to keep order while few are disposed to obey—loaded with execrations for every mishap, whether accidental or otherwise; and when he attempts to remonstrate he only renders himself ridiculous, being entirely without power to enforce his commands. It is to be regretted that some system of 'maritime law' has not been introduced among these traders to secure subordination, which can never be attained while the commander is invested with no legal authority. For my own part, I can see no reason why the captain of a prairie caravan should not have as much power to call his men to account for disobedience or mutiny, as the captain of a ship upon the high seas.

After following the course of the Cimarron for two days longer, we at length reached a place called the 'Willow Bar,' where we took the usual mid-day respite of two or three hours, to afford the animals time to feed, and our cooks to prepare dinner. Our wagons were regularly 'formed,' and the animals turned loose to graze at leisure, with only a 'day-guard' to watch them. Those who had finished their dinners lay stretched upon their blankets, and were just beginning to enjoy the luxury of a siesta—when all of a sudden, the fearful and oft-reiterated cry of "Indians!" turned this scene of repose into one of bustle and confusion.

From the opposite ridge at the distance of a mile, a swarm of savages were seen coming upon us, at full charge, and their hideous whoop and yell soon resounded through the valley. Such a jumbling of promiscuous voices I never expect to hear again. Every one fancied himself a commander, and vociferated his orders accordingly. The air was absolutely rent with the cries of " Let's charge 'em, boys!"—" Fire upon 'em, boys!"—" Reserve! don't fire till they come nearer!"— while the voice of our captain was scarcely distinguishable in his attempts to prevent such rash proceedings. As the prairie Indians often approach their friends as well as enemies in this way, Captain Stanley was unwilling to proceed to extremities, lest they might be peacefully inclined. But a 'popping salute,' and the whizzing of fusil balls over our heads, soon explained their intentions. We returned them several rifle shots by way of compliment, but without effect, as they were at too great a distance.

A dozen cannoniers now surrounded our 'artillery,' which was charged with canister Each of them had, of course, something to say. "Elevate her; she'll ground," one would suggest. "She'll overshoot, now," rejoined another. At last, after raising and lowering the six-pounder several times, during which process the Indians had time to retreat beyond reach of shot, the match was finally applied, and—bang! went the gun, but the charge grounded mid-way. This was followed by two or three shots with single ball, but apparently without effect; although there were some with sharp eyes, who fancied they saw Indians or horses wounded at every fire. We came off equally unscathed from the conflict, barring a horse of but little value, which ran away, and was taken by the enemy. The Indians were about a hundred in number, and supposed to be Comanches, though they might have been a band of warriors belonging to the party we had just left behind.

The novices were not a little discouraged at these frequent inroads of the enemy, although it is very seldom that any lives are lost in encounters with them. In the course of twenty years since the commencement of this trade, I do not believe there have been a dozen deaths upon the Santa Fé route, even including those who have been killed off by disease, as well as by the Indians.

On the following day we encamped near the 'Battle Ground,' famous for a skirmish which a caravan of traders, in company with a detachment of Mexican troops, under the command of Col. Vizcarra, had in 1829 with a band of Gros Ventres. The united companies had just encamped on the Cimarron, near the site of the burial catastrophe which occurred the preceding year. A party of about a hundred and twenty Indians soon after approached them on foot; but as the Americans were but little disposed to admit friendly intercourse between them, they passed into the camp of the Mexican commander, who received them amicably—a circumstance not altogether agreeable to the traders. As the Indians seemed disposed to remain till morning, Col. Vizcarra promised that they should be disarmed for the night; but the cunning wretches made some excuse to delay the surrender of their weapons, until the opportunity being favorable for a *coup de main*, they sprang to their feet, raised a fearful yell, and fired upon the unsuspecting party. Their aim seems chiefly to have been to take the life of the Mexican colonel; and it is said that a Taos Indian who formed one of the Mexican escort, seeing a gun levelled at his commander, sprang forward and received the ball in his own body, from the effects of which he instantly expired! The Indians were pursued for several miles into the hills, and a considerable number killed and wounded. Of the Americans not one received the slightest injury; but of the Mexican dragoons, a captain and two or three privates were killed.

CHAPTER V.

A Beautiful Ravine—'Runners' Starting for Santa Fé—Fourth of July on the Prairies—The *Cibolero* or Buffalo-hunter—Mournful News of Captain Sublette's Company—Murder of Captain Smith and another of the party by the Indians—Carelessness and Risks of Hunters—Captain Sublette's Peril—Character and Pursuits of the *Ciboleros*—The Art of Curing Meat—Purity of the Atmosphere—The 'Round Mound'—The Mirage or False Ponds—Philosophy thereof—Extensive and Interesting View—Exaggerated Accounts by Travellers of the Buffalo of the Prairies—Their Decrease—A 'Stampede'—Wagon Repairing—Rio Colorado or Canadian River—Meeting between old Friends—Mexican Escort—Disorganizing of the Caravan—Dreadful Thunder-storm—First Symptoms of Civilization—San Miguel—Arrival at Santa Fé—Entry of the Caravan—First Hours of Recreation—Interpreters and Custom-house Arrangements—A Glance at the Trade, etc.

It was on the last day of June that we arrived at the 'Upper Spring,' which is a small fountain breaking into a ravine that declines towards the Cimarron some three or four miles to the north. The scarcity of water in these desert regions, gives to every little spring an importance which, of course, in more favored countries it would not enjoy. We halted at noon on the brook below, and then branched off towards the waters of the Canadian, in an average direction of about thirty degrees south of west. As the wagon-road passes upon the adjacent ridge a quarter of a mile to the south of this spring, some of us, to procure a draught of its refreshing water, pursued a path along the ravine, winding through dense thickets of underbrush, matted with green-briers and grape-vines, which, with the wild-currant and plum-bushes, were all bent under their unripe fruit. The wildness of this place, with its towering cliffs, craggy spurs, and deep-cut crevices, became doubly impressive to us, as we reflected that we were in the very midst of the most savage haunts. Often will the lonely traveller, as he plods his weary way in silence, imagine in each click of a pebble, the snap of a firelock, and in every rebound of a twig, the whisk of an arrow. After regaling ourselves with a draught of the delicious beverage which gushed from the pure fountain, we ascended the rugged heights and rejoined the caravan half a mile beyond.

We had now a plain and perfectly distinguishable track before us, and a party of *avant-couriers*, known in the technical parlance of the Prairies as 'runners,' soon began to make preparations for pushing forward in advance of the caravan into Santa Fé, though we were yet more than two hundred miles from that city. It is customary for these runners to take their departure from the caravans in the night, in order to evade the vigilance of any enemy that might be lurking around the encampment. They are generally proprietors or agents; and their principal purpose is to procure and send back a supply of provisions, to secure good store-houses, and what is no less important, to obtain an agreeable understanding with the officers of the custom-house.

The second day after the departure of the runners, as we lay encamped at McNees's creek, the Fourth of July dawned upon us. Scarce had gray twilight brushed his dusky brow, when our patriotic camp gave lively demonstrations of that joy which plays around the heart of every American on the anniversary of this triumphant day. The roar of our artillery and rifle platoons resounded from every hill, while the rumbling of the drum and the shrill whistle of the fife, imparted a degree of martial interest to the scene which was well calculated to stir the souls of men. There was no limit to the huzzas and enthusiastic ejaculations of our people; and at every new shout the dales around sent forth a gladsome response. This anniversary is always hailed with heart-felt joy by the wayfarer in the remote desert; for here the strifes and intrigues of party-spirit are unknown: nothing intrudes, in these wild solitudes, to mar that harmony of feeling, and almost pious exultation, which every true-hearted American experiences on this great day.

The next day's march brought us in front of the Rabbit-Ear Mounds, which might now be seen at a distance of eight or ten miles south of us, and which before the present track was established, served as a guide to travellers.

The first caravan of wagons that crossed these plains, passed on the south side of these mounds, having abandoned our present route at the 'Cold Spring,' where we encamped on the night of the 1st of July. Although the route we were travelling swerves somewhat too much to the north, that pursued by the early caravans as stated above, made still a greater circuit to the south, and was by far the most inconvenient.

As we were proceeding on our march, we observed a horseman approaching, who excited at first considerable curiosity. His picturesque costume, and peculiarity of deportment, however, soon showed him to be a Mexican *Cibolero* or buffalo-hunter. These hardy devotees of the chase usually wear leathern trousers and jackets, and flat straw hats; while, swung upon the shoulder of each hangs his *carcage* or quiver of bow and arrows. The long handle of their lance being set in a case, and suspended by the side with a strap from the pommel of the saddle, leaves the point waving high over the head, with a tassel of gay parti-colored stuffs dangling at the tip of the scabbard. Their fusil, if they happen to have one, is suspended in like manner at the other side, with a stopper in the muzzle fantastically tasselled.

The *Cibolero* saluted us with demonstrations of joy; nor were we less delighted at meeting with him; for we were now able to obtain information from Santa Fé, whence no news had been received since the return of the caravan the preceding fall. Traders and idlers, with equal curiosity, clustered around the new visitor; every one who could speak a word of Spanish having some question to ask :—" What prospects?"— " How are goods?"—" What news from the South?"—while the more experienced traders interested themselves chiefly to ascertain the condition of the custom-house, and who were the present revenue officers; for unpropitious changes sometimes occur during the absence of the caravans.

But whatever joy we at first experienced was soon converted into mourning, by a piece of most melancholy news—the tragical death of a celebrated veteran mountain adventurer. It has already been mentioned that Capt. Sublette and others had started near a month in advance of our company. We had frequently seen their trail, and once or twice had received some vague information of their whereabouts through the Indians, but nothing satisfactory. Our visitor now informed us that a captain of this band had been assassinated by the Indians; and from his description we presumed it to be Capt. Smith, one of the partners,—which was afterwards confirmed, with many particulars of the adventures of this company.

Capt. Smith and his companions were new beginners in the Santa Fé trade, but being veteran pioneers of the Rocky Mountains, they concluded they could go anywhere; and imprudently set out without a single person in their company at all competent to guide them on the route. They had some twenty-odd wagons, and about eighty men. There being a plain track to the Arkansas river, they did very well thus far; but from thence to the Cimarron, not a single trail was to be found, save the innumerable buffalo paths, with which these plains are furrowed, and which are exceedingly perplexing to the bewildered prairie traveller. In a great many places which I have observed, they have all the appearance of immense highways, over which entire armies would seem to have frequently passed. They generally lead from one watering place to another; but as these reservoirs very often turn out to be dry, the thirsty traveller who follows them in search of water, is liable to constant disappointment.

When Capt. Sublette's party entered this arid plain, it was parched with drought; and they were doomed to wander about for several days, with all the horrors of a death from thirst staring them continually in the face. In this perilous situation, Capt. Smith resolved at last to pursue one of these seductive buffalo paths, in hopes it might lead to the margin of some stream or pond. He set out alone; for besides the temerity which desperation always inspires, he had ever been a stranger to fear; indeed, he was one of the most undaunted spirits that had ever traversed the Rocky Mountains; and if but one-half of what has been told of him be true,—of his bold enterprises—his perilous wanderings—

his skirmishings with the savages—his hairbreadth escapes, etc.—he would surely be entitled to one of the most exalted seats in the Olympus of Prairie mythology. But, alas! unfortunate Captain Smith! after having so often dodged the arrow and eluded the snare of the wily Mountain Indian, little could he have thought, while jogging along under a scorching sun, that his bones were destined to bleach upon those arid sands! He had already wandered many miles away from his comrades, when, on turning over an eminence, his eyes were joyfully greeted with the appearance of a small stream meandering through the valley that spread before him. It was the Cimarron. He hurried forward to slake the fire of his parched lips—but, imagine his disappointment, at finding in the channel only a bed of dry sand! With his hands, however, he soon scratched out a basin a foot or two deep, into which the water slowly oozed from the saturated sand. While with his head bent down, in the effort to quench his burning thirst in the fountain, he was pierced by the arrows of a gang of Comanches, who were lying in wait for him! Yet he struggled bravely to the last; and, as the Indians themselves have since related, killed two or three of their party before he was overpowered.

Every kind of fatality seems to have attended this little caravan. Among other calamities, we also learned that a clerk in their company, named Minter, had been killed by a band of Pawnees, before they crossed the Arkansas. This, I believe, is the only instance of loss of life among the traders while engaged in hunting: although the scarcity of accidents can hardly be said to be the result of prudence. There is not a day, from the time a caravan reaches the 'buffalo range,' that hunters do not commit some indiscretion, such as straying at a distance of five and even ten miles from the caravan, frequently alone, and seldom in bands of more than two or three together. In this state, they must frequently be spied by prowling savages; so that the frequency of escape, under such circumstances, must be partly attributed to the cowardice of the Indians: indeed, generally speaking, the latter are very loth to charge upon even a single armed man, unless they can take him at a decided disadvantage. Therefore, it is at all times imprudent to fire at the first approach of Indians; for, seeing their guns empty, the savages would charge upon them; while very small bands of hunters have been known to keep large numbers of the enemy at bay, by presenting their rifles, but reserving their fire, till assistance was at hand.

The companions of Capt. Smith, having descended upon the Cimarron at another point, appear to have remained ignorant of the terrible fate that had befallen him, until they were informed of the circumstances by some Mexican traders, who had ascertained the facts from the murderous savages themselves. Not long after, this band of Capt. Sublette very narrowly escaped a total destruction. They had fallen in with that immense horde of Blackfeet and Gros Ventres, with whom we afterwards met, and, as the traders were literally but a handful among their thousands, they fancied themselves for awhile in imminent peril of being virtually 'eaten up.' But as Capt. Sublette possessed considerable experience, he was at no loss how to deal with these treacherous savages; so that although the latter assumed a menacing attitude, he passed them without any serious molestation, and finally arrived at Santa Fé in safety.

But to return to our *Cibolero*. He was desirous to sell us some provisions, which, by the by, were welcome enough; for most of the company were out of bread, and meat was becoming very scarce, having seen but few buffalo since our first encounter with the Indians on the Cimarron. Our visitor soon retired to his camp hard by, and, with several of his comrades, afterwards brought us an abundance of dry buffalo beef, and some bags of coarse oven-toasted loaves, a kind of hard bread, much used by Mexican travellers. It is prepared by opening the ordinary leavened rolls, and toasting them brown in an oven. Though exceedingly hard and insipid while dry, it becomes not only soft but palatable when soaked in water—or better still in 'hot coffee.' But what we procured on this occasion was unusually stale and coarse, prepared expressly for barter with the Comanches, in case they should meet any : yet bread was bread, emphatically, with us just then.

A word concerning the *Ciboleros* may not be altogether uninteresting. Every year, large parties of New-Mexicans, some provided with mules and asses, others with *carretas* or truckle-carts and oxen, drive out into these prairies to procure a supply of buffalo beef for their families. They hunt, like the wild Indians, chiefly on horseback, and with bow and arrow, or lance, with which they soon load their carts and mules. They find no difficulty in curing their meat even in midsummer, by slicing it thin and spreading or suspending it in the sun; or, if in haste, it is slightly barbecued. During the curing operation they often follow the Indian practice of beating or kneading the slices with their feet, which they contend contributes to its preservation.

Here the extraordinary purity of the atmosphere is remarkably exemplified. The caravans cure meat in the same simple manner, except the process of kneading. A line is stretched from corner to corner on each side of a wagon-body, and strung with slices of beef, which remains from day to day till it is sufficiently cured to be stacked away. This is done without salt, and yet it very rarely putrifies. Besides, as blow-flies are unknown here, there is nothing to favor putrefaction. While speaking of flies, I might as well remark, that, after passing beyond the region of the tall grass, between the Missouri frontier and Arkansas river, the horse-fly also is unknown. Judging from the prairies on our border, we had naturally anticipated a great deal of mischief from these brute-tormentors; in which we were very agreeably disappointed.

But I have not yet done with the meat-curing operations. While in the midst of the buffalo range, travellers usually take the precaution of laying up a supply of beef for exigencies in the absence of the 'prairie cattle.' We had somewhat neglected this provision in time of abundance, by which we had come near being reduced to extremities. Caravans sometimes lie by a day or two to provide a supply of meat; when numbers of buffalo are slaughtered, and the flesh 'jerked,' or slightly barbecued, by placing it upon a scaffold over a fire. The same method is resorted to by Mexicans when the weather is too damp or cloudy for the meat to dry in the open air.

We were now approaching the 'Round Mound,' a beautiful round-topped cone, rising nearly a thousand feet above the level of the plain by which it is for the most part surrounded. We were yet at least three miles from this mound, when a party set out on foot to ascend it, in order to get a view of the surrounding country. They felt confident it was but half a mile off—at most, three-quarters; but finding the distance so much greater than they had anticipated, many began to lag behind, and soon rejoined the wagons. The optical illusions occasioned by the rarified and transparent atmosphere of these elevated plains, are often truly remarkable, affording another exemplification of its purity. One would almost fancy himself looking through a spy-glass, for objects frequently appear at scarce one-fourth of their real distance—frequently much magnified, and more especially elevated. I have often seen flocks of antelopes mistaken for droves of elks or wild horses, and when at a great distance, even for horsemen; whereby frequent alarms are occasioned. I have also known tufts of grass or weeds, or mere buffalo bones scattered on the prairies, to stretch upward to the height of several feet, so as to present the appearance of so many human beings. Ravens in the same way are not unfrequently taken for Indians, as well as for buffalo; and a herd of the latter upon a distant plain often appear so increased in bulk that they would be mistaken by the inexperienced for a grove of trees. This is usually attended with a continual waving and looming, which often so writhe and distort distant objects as to render them too indistinct to be discriminated. The illusion seems to be occasioned by gaseous vapors rising from the ground while the beaming rays of the sun are darting upon it.

But the most curious, and at the same time the most perplexing phenomenon, occasioned by optical deception, is the *mirage*, or, as familiarly called upon the Prairies, the 'false ponds.' Even the experienced traveller is often deceived by these upon the arid plains, where a disappointment is most severely felt. The thirsty wayfarer, after jogging for hours under a burning sky, at length espies a pond—yes, it must be water—it looks too natural for him to be mistaken. He quickens his pace, enjoying in anticipation the pleasure of a refreshing draught: but lo! as he approaches, it recedes or entirely disappears; and when upon its apparent site, he is ready to doubt his own vision—he finds but a parched plain under his feet. It is not until he has been thus a dozen times deceived, that he is willing to relinquish the pursuit: and then, perhaps, when he really does see a pond, he will pass it unexamined, for fear of another disappointment.

The philosophy of these 'false ponds' seems generally not well understood. They have usually been attributed to *refraction*, by which a section of the bordering sky would appear below the horizon: but there can be no doubt that they are the effect of *reflection*, upon a gas emanating perhaps from the sun-scorched earth and vegetable matter. Or it may be that a surcharge of carbonic acid, precipitated upon the flats and sinks of those plains, by the action of the sun, produces the effect. At least, it appears of sufficient density, when viewed very obliquely, to reflect the objects beyond: and thus the opposite sky being reflected in the *pond of gas*, gives the appearance of water. As a proof that it is the effect of reflection, I have often observed the distant trees and hilly protuberances which project above the horizon beyond, distinctly inverted in the 'pond;' whereas, were it the result of refraction, these would appear erect, only cast below the surface. Indeed, many are the singular atmospheric phenomena observable upon the plains, which would afford a field of interesting research for the curious natural philosopher.

At last, some of the most persevering of our adventurers succeeded in ascending the summit of the Round Mound, which commands a full and advantageous view of the surrounding country, in some directions to the distance of a hundred miles or more. Looking southward a varied country is seen, of hills, plains, mounds, and sandy undulations; but on the whole northern side, extensive plains spread out, studded occasionally with variegated peaks and ridges. Far beyond these, to the north-westward, and low in the horizon a silvery stripe appears upon an azure base, resembling a list of chalk-white clouds. This is the perennially snow-capped summit of the eastern spur of the Rocky Mountains.

These immense bordering plains, and even the hills with which they are interspersed, are wholly destitute of timber, except a chance scattering tree upon the margins of the bluffs and ravines, which but scantily serves to variegate the landscape. Not even a buffalo was now to be seen to relieve the dull monotony of the scene; although at some seasons (and particularly in the fall) these prairies are literally strewed with herds of this animal. Then, 'thousands and tens of thousands' might at times be seen from this eminence. But the buffalo is a migratory animal, and even in the midst of the Prairies where they are generally so very abundant, we sometimes travel for days without seeing a single one; though no signs of hunter or Indian can be discovered. To say the truth, however, I have never seen them anywhere upon the Prairies so abundant as some travellers have represented—in dense masses, darkening the whole country. I have only found them in scattered herds, of a few scores, hundreds, or sometimes thousands in each, and where in the greatest numbers, dispersed far and wide; but with large intervals between. Yet they are very sensibly and rapidly decreasing. There is a current notion that the whites frighten them away; but, I would ask, where do they go to? To be sure, to use a hunter's phrase, they 'frighten a few out of their skins;' yet for every one killed by the whites, more than a hundred, perhaps a thousand, fall by the hands of the savages. From these, however, there is truly 'nowhere to flee;' for they follow them wheresoever they go: while the poor brutes instinctively learn to avoid the fixed establishments, and, to some degree, the regular travelling routes of the whites.

As the caravan was passing under the northern base of the Round Mound, it presented a very fine and imposing spectacle to those who were upon its summit. The wagons marched slowly in four parallel columns, but in broken lines, often at intervals of many rods between. The unceasing 'crack, crack,' of the wagoners' whips, resembling the frequent reports of distant guns, almost made one believe that a skirmish was actually taking place between two hostile parties: and a hostile engagement it virtually was to the poor brutes, at least; for the merciless application of the whip would sometimes make the blood spirt from their sides—and that often without any apparent motive of the wanton *carrettieri*, other than to amuse themselves with the flourishing and loud popping of their lashes!

The rear wagons are usually left without a guard; for all the loose horsemen incline to be ahead, where they are to be seen moving in scattered groups, sometimes a mile or more in advance. As our camp was pitched but a mile west of the Round Mound, those who lingered upon its summit could have an interesting view of the evolutions of 'forming' the wagons, in which the drivers by this time had become very expert. When marching four abreast, the two exterior lines spread out and then meet at the front angle; while the two inner lines keep close together until they reach the point of the rear angle, when they wheel suddenly out and close with the hinder ends of the other two; thus systematically concluding a right-lined quadrangle, with a gap left at the rear corner for the introduction of the animals.

MARCH OF THE CARAVAN.

Our encampment was in a beautiful plain, but without water, of which, however, we had had a good supply at noon. Our cattle, as was the usual custom, after having grazed without for a few hours, were now shut up in the pen of the wagons. Our men were all wrapt in peaceful slumber, except the guard, who kept their silent watch around the encampment; when all of a sudden, about the ominous hour of midnight, a tremendous uproar was heard, which caused every man to start in terror from his blanket couch, with arms in hand. Some animal, it appeared, had taken fright at a dog, and by a sudden start, set all around him in violent motion: the panic spread simultaneously throughout the pen; and a scene of rattle, clash, and 'lumbering,' ensued, which far surpassed everything we had yet witnessed. A general 'stampede' (*estampida*, as the Mexicans say) was the result. Notwithstanding the wagons were tightly bound together, wheel to wheel, with ropes or chains, and several stretched across the gaps at the corners of the *corral*, the oxen soon burst their way out; and though mostly yoked in pairs, they went scampering over the plains, as though Tam O'Shanter's 'cutty-sark' Nannie had been at their tails. All attempts to stop them were vain; for it would require 'Auld Clootie' himself to check the headway of a drove of oxen, when once thoroughly frightened. Early the following morning we made active exertions to get up a sufficient quantity of teams to start the caravan. At Rock Creek, a distance of six or seven miles, we were joined by those who had gone in pursuit of the stock. All the oxen were found, except some half a dozen, which were never recovered. No mules were lost: a few that had broken loose were speedily retaken. The fact is, that though mules are generally easiest scared, oxen are decidedly the worst when once started. The principal advantage of the latter in this respect, is, that Indians have but little inducement to steal them, and therefore few attempts would be made upon a caravan of oxen.

We were now entering a region of rough, and in some places, rocky road, as the streams which intervene from this to the mountains are all bordered with fine sandstone. These rugged passes acted very severely upon our wagons, as the wheels were by this time becoming loose and 'shackling,' from the shrink of the wood, occasioned by the extreme dryness and rarity of this elevated atmosphere. The spokes of some were beginning to reel in the hubs, so that it became necessary to brace them with 'false spokes,' firmly bound with 'buffalo tug.' On some occasions, the wagon tires have become so loose upon the felloes as to tumble off while travelling. The most effective mode of tightening slackened tires (at least that most practised on the plains, as there is rarely a portable forge in company), is by driving strips of hoop-iron around between the tire and felloe—simple wedges of wood are sometimes made to supply the place of iron. During halts I have seen a dozen wheels being repaired at the same time, occasioning such a clitter-clatter of hammers, that one would almost fancy himself in a ship-yard.

Emerging from this region of asperities, we soon passed the 'Point of Rocks,' as a diminutive 'spur' projecting from the north is called, at the foot of which springs a charming little fount of water. This is but thirty or forty miles from the principal mountains, along whose border, similar detached ridges and hills are frequently to be seen. The next day, having descended from the table plain, we reached the principal branch of the Canadian river, which is here but a rippling brook, hardly a dozen paces in width, though eighty miles from its source in the mountains to the north. The bottom being of solid rock, this ford is appropriately called by the ciboleros, *el Vado de Piedras.* The banks are very low and easy to ascend. The stream is called *Rio Colorado* by the Mexicans, and is known among Americans by its literal translation of *Red River.* This circumstance perhaps gave rise to the belief that it was the head branch of our main stream of this name :* but the

---

* Previous to the year 1820, this ' *Rio Colorado*' seems universally to have been considered as the principal source of *Red River ;* but in the expedition of Maj. Long, during that year, he discovered this to be the head branch of the Canadian. The discovery cost him somewhat dearly too ; for striking a branch of the Colorado near the Mountains, he followed down its course, believing it to be of the main Red River. He was not fully undeceived till he arrived at its junction with the Arkansas ; whereby he failed in a principal object of the expedition—the exploration of the true sources of ' Red River of Natchitoches '

nearest waters of the legitimate 'Red River of Natchitoches,' are still a hundred miles to the south of this road.

In descending to the Rio Colorado, we met a dozen or more of our countrymen from Taos, to which town (sixty or seventy miles distant) there is a direct but rugged route across the mountains. It was a joyous encounter, for among them we found some of our old acquaintances whom we had not seen for many years. During our boyhood we had 'spelt' together in the same country school, and roamed the wild woods with many a childish glee. They turned about with us, and the remainder of our march was passed in answering their inquiries after their relatives and friends in the United States.

Before reaching the stream, we encountered another party of visitors, being chiefly custom-house agents or clerks, who, accompanied by a military escort, had come out to guard the caravan to the Capital. The ostensible purpose of this escort was to prevent smuggling,—a company of troops being thus dispatched every year, with strict injunctions to watch the caravans. This custom appears since to have nearly grown out of use: and well might it be discontinued altogether, for any one disposed to smuggle would find no difficulty in securing the services of these preventive guards, who, for a trifling *douceur*, would prove very efficient auxiliaries, rather than obstacles to the success of any such designs. As we were forming in the valley opposite where the escort was encamped, Col. Vizcarra, the commandant, honored us with a salute from his artillery, which was promptly responded to by our little cannon.

Considering ourselves at last out of danger of Indian hostilities (although still nearly a hundred and forty miles from Santa Fé); and not unwilling to give our 'guard' as much trouble as possible, we abandoned the organization of our caravan a few miles beyond the Colorado; its members wending their way to the Capital in almost as many detached parties as there were proprietors. The road from this to San Miguel (a town nearly a hundred miles distant), leads in a southwestern direction along the base of, and almost parallel with, that spur of snow-clad mountains, which has already been mentioned, bearing down east of the Rio del Norte.

This region is particularly celebrated for violent showers, hail-storms, and frightful thunder-gusts. The sudden cooling and contraction of the atmosphere which follows these falls of rain, very often reverses the current of the lower stratum of air; so that a cloud which has just ceased pouring its contents and been wafted away, is in a few minutes brought back, and drenches the traveller with another torrent. I was deeply impressed with a scene I witnessed in the summer of 1832, about two days' journey beyond the Colorado, which I may be excused for alluding to in this connection. We were encamped at noon, when a murky cloud issued from behind the mountains, and, after hovering over us for a few minutes, gave vent to one of those tremendous peals of thunder which seem peculiar to those regions, making the elements tremble, and leaving us so stunned and confounded that some seconds elapsed before each man was able to convince himself that he had not been struck by lightning. A sulphureous stench filled the atmosphere; but the thunderbolt had skipped over the wagons and lighted upon the *caballada*, which was grazing hard by; some of which were afterward seen stretched upon the plain. It was not a little singular to find an ox lying lifeless from the stroke, while his mate stood uninjured by his side, and under the same yoke.

Some distance beyond the Colorado, a party of about a dozen (which I joined) left the wagons to go ahead to Santa Fé. Fifty miles beyond the main branch of this stream we passed the last of the Canadian waters, known to foreigners as the *Mora*.* From thence to the *Gallinas*,† the first of the Rio del Norte waters, the road stretches over an elevated plain, unobstructed by any mountainous ridge. At Gallinas creek, we found

---

* As *mora* means *mulberry*, and this fruit is to be found at the mouth of this stream, one would suppose that it had acquired its name from that fact, did not the Mexicans always call it *Rio de lo de Mora*, thus leaving it to be inferred that the name had originated from some individual called Mora, who had settled upon it.

† Called *Rio de las Gallinas* by Mexicans. Though *gallina* is literally *hen*, it is here also applied to the *turkey* (usually with a 'surname,' as *gallina de la tierra*). It is therefore *Turkey* river

a large flock of sheep grazing upon the adjacent plain; while a little hovel at the foot of a cliff showed it to be a *rancho*. A swarthy *ranchero* soon made his appearance, from whom we procured a treat of goat's milk, with some dirty ewe's milk 'curdle cheese' to supply the place of bread.

Some twenty miles from this place we entered San Miguel, the first settlement of any note upon our route. This consists of irregular clusters of mud-wall huts, and is situated in the fertile valley of Rio Pecos, a silvery little river which ripples from the snowy mountains of Santa Fé—from which city this frontier village is nearly fifty miles to the southeast. The road makes this great southern bend, to find a passway through the broken extremity of the spur of mountains before alluded to, which from this point south is cut up into detached ridges and table plains. This mountain section of the road, even in its present unimproved condition, presents but few difficult passes, and might, with little labor, be put in good order.

A few miles before reaching the city, the road again emerges into an open plain. Ascending a table ridge, we spied in an extended valley to the northwest, occasional groups of trees, skirted with verdant corn and wheat fields, with here and there a square block-like protuberance reared in the midst. A little further, and just ahead of us to the north, irregular clusters of the same opened to our view. " Oh, we are approaching the suburbs!" thought I, on perceiving the cornfields, and what I supposed to be brick-kilns scattered in every direction. These and other observations of the same nature becoming audible, a friend at my elbow said, " It is true those are heaps of unburnt bricks, nevertheless they are *houses*—this is the city of Santa Fé."

Five or six days after our arrival, the caravan at last hove in sight, and wagon after wagon was seen pouring down the last declivity at about a miles distance from the city. To judge from the clamorous rejoicings of the men, and the state of agreeable excitement which the muleteers seemed to be laboring under, the spectacle must have been as new to them as it had been to me. It was truly a scene for the artist's pencil to revel in. Even the animals seemed to participate in the humor of their riders, who grew more and more merry and obstreperous as they descended towards the city. I doubt, in short, whether the first sight of the walls of Jerusalem were beheld by the crusaders with much more tumultuous and soul-enrapturing joy.

The arrival produced a great deal of bustle and excitement among the natives. "*Los Americanos!*"—"*Los carros!*"—"*La entrada de la caravana!*" were to be heard in every direction; and crowds of women and boys flocked around to see the new-comers; while crowds of *léperos* hung about as usual to see what they could pilfer. The wagoners were by no means free from excitement on this occasion. Informed of the 'ordeal' they had to pass, they had spent the previous morning in 'rubbing up;' and now they were prepared, with clean faces, sleek combed hair, and their choicest Sunday suit, to meet the 'fair eyes' of glistening black that were sure to stare at them as they passed. There was yet another preparation to be made in order to 'show off' to advantage. Each wagoner must tie a bran new 'cracker' to the lash of his whip; for, on driving through the streets and the *plaza pública*, every one strives to outvie his comrades in the dexterity with which he flourishes this favorite badge of his authority.

Our wagons were soon discharged in the ware-rooms of the Custom-house; and a few days' leisure being now at our disposal, we had time to take that recreation which a fatiguing journey of ten weeks had rendered so necessary. The wagoners, and many of the traders, particularly the novices, flocked to the numerous fandangoes, which are regularly kept up after the arrival of a caravan. But the merchants generally were anxiously and actively engaged in their affairs—striving who should first get his goods out of the custom-house, and obtain a chance at the 'hard chink' of the numerous country dealers, who annually resort to the capital on these occasions.

Now comes the harvest for those idle interpreters, who make a business of 'passing goods,' as they term it; for as but a small portion of the traders are able to write the Spanish language, they are obliged to employ these legal go-betweens, who pledge themselves, for a stipulated fee, to make the 'arrangements,' and translate the *manifiestos* (that is, bills of merchandise to be *manifested* at the custom-house), and to act the part of interpreters throughout.

The inspection ensues, but this is rarely carried on with rigid adherence to rules; for an 'actuated sympathy' for the merchants, and a 'specific desire' to promote the trade, cause the inspector to open a few of such packages only, as will exhibit the least discrepancy with the manifest.

The *derechos de arancel* (tariff imposts) of Mexico are extremely oppressive, averaging about a hundred per cent. upon the United States' cost of an ordinary 'Santa Fé assortment.' Those on cotton textures are particularly so. According to the Arancel of 1837 (and it was still heavier before), all plain-wove cottons, whether white or printed, pay twelve and a half cents duty per *vara*, besides the *derecho de consumo* (consumption duty), which brings it up to at least fifteen. But it is scarcely necessary to add that there are believed to be very few ports in the Republic at which these rigid exactions are strictly executed. An 'arrangement'—a compromise is expected, in which the officers are sure at least to provide for themselves. At some ports, a custom has been said to prevail, of dividing the legal duties into three equal parts: one for the officers—a second for the merchants—the other for the government.

For a few years, Gov. Armijo of Santa Fé, established a tariff of *his own*, entirely arbitrary,—exacting five hundred dollars for each wagon-load, whether large or small—of fine or coarse goods! Of course this was very advantageous to such traders as had large wagons and costly assortments, while it was no less onerous to those with smaller vehicles or coarse heavy goods. As might have been anticipated, the traders soon took to conveying their merchandise only in the largest wagons, drawn by ten or twelve mules, and omitting the coarser and more weighty articles of trade. This caused the governor to return to an *ad valorem* system, though still without regard to the *Arancel general* of the nation. How much of these duties found their way into the public treasury, I will not venture to assert.

The arrival of a caravan at Santa Fé changes the aspect of the place at once. Instead of the idleness and stagnation which its streets exhibited before, one now sees everywhere the bustle, noise and activity of a lively market town. As the Mexicans very rarely speak English, the negotiations are mostly conducted in Spanish.

Taking the circuit of the stores, I found they usually contained general assortments, much like those to be met with in the retail variety stores of the west. The stocks of the inexperienced merchants are apt to abound in unsalable goods—*mulas*, as the Mexicans figuratively term them.

Although a fair variety of dry goods, silks, hardware, &c., is to be found in this market, domestic cottons, both bleached and brown, constitute the great staple, of which nearly equal quantities ought to enter into a 'Santa Fé assortment.' The demand for these goods is such that at least one half of our stocks of merchandise is made up of them. However, although they afford a greater nominal per centum than many other articles, the profits are reduced by their freight and heavy duty. In all the Southern markets, where they enter into competition, there is a decided preference given to the American manufactures over the British, as the former are more heavy and durable. The demand for calicoes is also considerable, but this kind of goods affords much less profit. The quantity in an assortment should be about equal to half that of domestics. Cotton velvets, and drillings (whether bleached, brown or blue, and especially the latter), have also been in much request. But all the coarser cotton goods, whether shirtings, calicoes or drillings, &c., were prohibited by the *Arancel* of 1837; and still continue to be, with some modifications.

CHAPTER VI.

Sketches of the Early History of Santa Fé—First Explorations—Why called New Mexico—Memorial of Oñate—His Colony—Captain Leyva's prior Settlement—Singular Stipulations of Oñate—Incentives presented by the Crown to Colonizers—Enormities of Spanish Conquerors — Progress of the new Colony—Cruel Labors of the Aborigines in the mines—Revolt of the Indians in 1680—Massacre of the Spaniards—Santa Fé Besieged—Battles—Remaining Spanish Population finally evacuate the Province—Paso del Norte—Inhuman Murder of a Spanish Priest—Final Recovery of the Country—Insurrection of 1837—A Prophecy—Shocking Massacre of the Governor and other distinguished Characters — American Merchants, and Neglect of our Government—Governor Armijo: his Intrigues and Success—Second Gathering of Insurgents and their final Defeat.

HAVING resided for nearly nine years in Northern Mexico, and enjoyed opportunities for observation which do not always fall to the lot of a trader, it has occurred to me that a few sketches of the country—the first settlements—the early, as well as more recent struggles with the aboriginal inhabitants—their traditions and antiquities—together with some account of the manners and customs of the people, etc., would not be altogether unacceptable to the reader. The dearth of information which has hitherto prevailed on this subject, is my best apology for travelling out of my immediate track, and trespassing as it were upon the department of the regular historian.

The province of NEW MEXICO, of which SANTA FÉ, the capital, was one of the first establishments, dates among the earliest settlements made in America. By some traditions it is related that a small band of adventurers proceeded thus far north shortly after the capture of the city of Mexico by Hernan Cortés. The historian Mariana speaks of some attempts having been made, during the career of this renowned chieftain in America, to conquer and take possession of these regions. This, however, is somewhat doubtful; for it is hardly probable that the Spaniards, with all their mania for gold, would have pushed their conquests two thousand miles into the interior at so early a day, traversing the settlements of hostile savages, and leaving unexplored intermediate regions, not only more beautiful, but far more productive of the precious metals.

Herrera, writing of the events of 1550, mentions New Mexico as a known province lying north of New Galicia, though as yet only inhabited by the aborigines. It was probably called New Mexico from the resemblance of its inhabitants to those of the city of Mexico and its environs. They appear to have assimilated in their habits, their agriculture, their manufactures and their houses; while those of the intermediate country (the Chichimecos, &c.) were in a much ruder state, leading a more wandering life, and possessing much less knowledge of agriculture, arts, etc.

The only paper found in the archives at Santa Fé which gives any clue to the first settlement of New Mexico, is the memorial of one Don Juan de Oñate, a citizen of Zacatecas, dated September 21, 1595, of which I have been furnished with a copy through the politeness of Don Guadalupe Miranda, Secretary of State at Santa Fé. This petition prayed for the permission and assistance of the vice-regal government at Mexico, to establish a colony on the Rio del Norte in the region already known as New Mexico; which having been granted, it was carried into effect, as I infer from the documents, during the following spring.

This appears to have been the first *legal* colony established in the province; yet we gather from different clauses in Oñate's memorial, that an adventurer known as Captain Francisco de Leyva Bonillo had previously entered the province with some followers, without the king's permission, whom Oñate was authorized to arrest and punish. Some historians insist that New Mexico was first visited by a few missionaries in 1581; and there is a tradition in the country which fixes the first settlement in 1583—both having reference no doubt to the party of Leyva.

Oñate bound himself to take into New Mexico two hundred soldiers, and a sufficiency of provisions for the first year's support of the colony; with abundance of horses, black cattle, sheep, etc., as also merchandise, agricultural utensils, tools and materials for mechanics' purposes; and all at his own cost, or rather at the ultimate expense of the colonists.

This adventurer, in the course of his memorial, also stipulates for some extraordinary provisions on the part of the King: such as, artillery and other arms, ammunitions, etc.—six priests, with a full complement of books, ornaments and church accoutrements—a loan of $20,000 from the royal treasury—a grant of thirty leagues square of land wheresoever he might choose to select it, with all the vassals (Indians) residing upon it—his family to be ennobled, with the hereditary title of Marquis—the office of Governor, with the titles of *Adelantado* and the rank of Captain-general for four generations—a salary of 8,000 ducats of Castile per annum—the privilege of working mines exempt from the usual crown-tax—permission to parcel out the aborigines among his officers and men; and, besides other favors to his brothers and relatives, to have "Indians recommended to their charge," which, in other words, was the privilege of making slaves of them to work in the mines—with many other distinctions, immunities and powers to himself, sufficient to establish him in an authority far more despotic than any modern monarch of Europe would venture to assume. And although these exorbitant demands were not all conceded, they go to demonstrate by what incentives of pecuniary interest, as well as of honors, the Spanish monarchs sought the "*descubrimiento, pacificacion y conversion,*" as they modestly termed it, of the poor aborigines of America.

The memorial referred to is extremely lengthy, being encumbered with numerous marginal notes, each containing the decree of assent or dissent of the Viceroy. All this, however, serves rather to illustrate the ancient manners and customs of the Spaniards in those feudal days—the formalities observed in undertaking an exploring and christianizing enterprise—than to afford any historical data of the expedition.

In every part of this singular document there may be traced evidences of that sordid lust for gold and power, which so disgraced all the Spanish conquests in America; and that religious fanaticism—that crusading spirit, which martyrized so many thousands of the aborigines of the New World under Spanish authority.

But to return to Oñate: In one article, this adventurer, or contractor, or whatever else we may choose to call him, inquires, "In case the natives are unwilling to come quietly to the acknowledgment of the true Christian faith, and listen to the evangelical word, and give obedience to the king our sovereign, what shall be done with them? that we may proceed according to the laws of the Catholic Church, and the ordinances of his Majesty. And what tributes, that they may be christianly borne, shall be imposed upon them, as well for the crown as for the adventurers?"—showing that these 'missionaries' (as they were wont to call themselves) not only robbed the Indians of their country and treasure, and made menial slaves of them, but exacted tribute beside—promulgated the gospel at the point of the bayonet, and administered baptism by force of arms—compelling them to acknowledge the 'apostolic Roman Catholic faith,' of which they had not the slightest idea. Cervantes, who wrote his Don Quixote about this time, no doubt intended to make a hit at this cruel spirit of religious bigotry, by making his hero command his captives to acknowledge the superiority of his Dulcinea's beauty over that of all others; and when they protest that they have never seen her, he declares, that "the importance consists in this—that without seeing her, you have it to believe, confess, affirm, swear and defend."

It is much to be regretted that there are no records to be found of the wars and massacres, the numberless incidents and wild adventures which one would presume to have occurred during the first three-quarters of a century of the colonization of New Mexico. It is probable, however, that, as the aborigines seem to have been at first of a remarkably pacific and docile character, the conqueror met with but little difficulty in carrying out his original plans of settlement. Quietly acquiescing in both the civil and religious authority of the invaders, the yoke was easily riveted upon them, as they had neither intelligence nor spirit to resist, until goaded to desperation.

The colony had progressed very rapidly, the settlements extending into every quarter of the territory—villages, and even towns of considerable importance were reared in remote sections; of which there now remain but the ruins, with scarce a tradition to tell the fate of the once flourishing population. Many valuable mines were discovered and worked, as tradition relates, the locations of which have been lost, or (as the Mexicans say) concealed by the Indians, in order to prevent a repetition of the brutal outrages they had suffered in them. Whether this was the case or not, they surely had cause enough for wishing to conceal those with which they were acquainted; for in these very mines they had been forced to perform, under the lash, the most laborious tasks, till human strength could endure no more. Even then, perhaps, they would not have ventured upon resistance, but for the instigations of an eloquent warrior from a distant tribe, who pretended to have inherited the power of Montezuma, of whose subjects all these Indians, even to the present day, consider themselves the descendants. Tecumseh-like, our hero united the different tribes, and laid the plan of a conspiracy and general massacre of their oppressors; declaring that all who did not enter into the plot, should share the fate of the Spaniards. I have been furnished, through the kindness of the Secretary of

State before mentioned, with an account of this insurrection and consequent massacre of the Spanish population, taken from the journal of Don Antonio de Otermin, governor and commandant at the time, which was preserved in the public archives at Santa Fé.

It appears that the night of the 13th of August, 1680, was the time fixed for a general insurrection of all the tribes and *Pueblos*.* At a stated hour the massacre of the Spanish population was to commence. Every soul was to be butchered without distinction of sex or age—with the exception of such young and handsome females as they might wish to preserve for wives! Although this conspiracy had evidently been in agitation for a great while, such strict secrecy had been maintained, that nothing was known or even suspected, till a few days before the appointed time. It is said that not a single woman was let into the secret, for fear of endangering the success of the cause; but it was finally disclosed by two Indian chiefs themselves to the governor; and about the same time information of the conspiracy was received from some curates and officers of Taos.

Gov. Otermin, seeing the perilous situation of the country, lost no time in dispatching general orders for gathering the people of the south into the Pueblo of Isleta, where the lieutenant-governor was stationed, and those

* A general term for all the *Catholic Indians* of N. Mexico, and their *villages*.

of the north and adjacent districts into Santa Fé. A considerable number collected in the fortifications of Isleta, and many families from the surrounding jurisdictions were able to reach the capital; yet great numbers were massacred on the way; for the Indians, perceiving their plot discovered, did not await the appointed time, but immediately commenced their work of destruction.

General hostilities having commenced, every possible preparation was made for a vigorous defence of the capital. The population of the suburbs had orders to remove to the centre, and the streets were all barricaded. On the evening of the 10th two soldiers arrived from Taos, having with much difficulty escaped the vigilance of the Indians. They brought intelligence that the Pueblos of Taos had all risen; and that on arriving at La Cañada, they had found the Spaniards well fortified, although a great number of them had been assassinated in the vicinity. The governor now sent out a detachment of troops to reconnoitre, instructing them to bring away the citizens who remained at La Cañada. They returned on the 12th, with the painful information that they had found many dead bodies on their way—that the temples had been plundered, and all the stock driven off from the *ranchos*.

The massacre of the Spaniards in many neighboring Pueblos, was now unreservedly avowed by the Indians themselves; and as those who remained in Santa Fé appeared in the most imminent danger, the government buildings were converted into a fortification. By this time two friendly Indians who had been dispatched in the direction of Galisteo, came in with the intelligence that 500 warriors of the tribe called *Tagnos*,* were marching towards the city, being even then only about a league distant. By conversing with the enemy the spies had been able to ascertain their temper and their projects. They seemed confident of success—"for the God of the Christians is dead," said they, " but our god, which is the sun, never dies;" adding that they were only waiting the arrival of the *Teguas*,† Taosas and Apaches, in order to finish their work of extermination.

Next morning the savages were seen approaching from the south. On their arrival they took up their quarters in the deserted houses of the suburbs, with the view of waiting for their expected allies, before they laid siege to the city. A parley was soon afterwards held with the chief leaders, who told the Spaniards that they had brought two crosses, of which they might have their choice: one was red, denoting war, the other was white and professed peace, on the condition of their immediately evacuating the province. The governor strove to conciliate them by offering to pardon all the crimes they had com-

---

* The *Pecos* and several other populous *Pueblos* to the southward of Santa Fé were *Tagnos*.

† These embraced nearly all the *Pueblos* between Santa Fé and Taos.

mitted, provided they would be good Christians and loyal subjects thereafter. But the Indians only made sport of him and laughed heartily at his propositions. He then sent a detachment to dislodge them; but was eventually obliged to turn out in person, with all the efficient men he had. The battle continued the whole day, during which a great number of Indians and some Spaniards were killed. But late in the evening, the Teguas, Taosas and others, were seen pouring down upon the city from the north, when the troops had to abandon the advantages they had gained, and fly to the defence of the fortifications.

The siege had now continued for nine days, during which the force of the Indians had constantly been on the increase. Within the last forty-eight hours they had entirely deprived the city of water by turning off the stream which had hitherto supplied it; so that the horses and other stock were dying of thirst. The want of water and provisions becoming more and more insupportable every moment, and seeing no chance of rescue or escape, Governor Otermin resolved to make a sortie the next morning, and die with sword in hand, rather than perish so miserably for want of supplies. At sunrise he made a desperate charge upon the enemy, whom, notwithstanding the inferiority of his forces, he was soon able to dislodge. Their ranks becoming entirely disordered, more than three hundred were slain, and an abundance of booty taken, with forty-seven prisoners, who, after some examination as to the origin of the conspiracy, were all shot. The Spaniards, according to their account of the affair, only had four or five men killed, although a considerable number were wounded—the governor among the rest.

The city of Santa Fé, notwithstanding a remaining population of at least a thousand souls, could not muster above a hundred able-bodied men to oppose the multitude that beset them, which had now increased to about three thousand. Therefore Governor Otermin, with the advice of the most intelligent citizens in the place, resolved to abandon the city. On the following day (August 21), they accordingly set out, the greater portion afoot, carrying their own provisions; as there were scarcely animals enough for the wounded. Their march was undisturbed by the Indians, who only watched their movements till they passed Isleta, when nothing more was seen of them. Here they found that those who had been stationed at Isleta had also retreated to the south a few days before. As they passed through the country, they found the Pueblos deserted by the Indians, and the Spaniards who pertained to them all massacred.

They had not continued on their march for many days, when the caravan became utterly unable to proceed; for they were not only without animals, but upon the point of starvation—the Indians having removed from the route everything that could have afforded them relief. In this emergency, Otermin dispatched an express to the lieutenant-governor, who was considerably in advance, and received from his party a few carts, with a supply of provisions. Towards the latter end of September, the Governor and his companions in misfortune reached Paso del Norte (about 320 miles south of Santa Fé), where they found the advance party.

The Governor immediately sent an account of the disaster to the Viceroy at Mexico, soliciting reinforcements for the purpose of recovering the lost province, but none arrived till the following year. Meanwhile the refugees remained where they were, and founded, according to the best traditions, the town of *el Paso del Norte*, so called in commemoration of this retreat, or *passage from the north*. This is in an extensive and fertile valley, over which were scattered several Pueblos, all of whom remained friendly to the Spaniards, affording them an asylum with provisions and all the necessaries of life.

The following year Governor Otermin was superseded by Don Diego de Vargas Zapata, who commenced the work of reconquering the country. This war lasted for ten years. In 1688, Don Pedro Petrir de Cruzate entered the province and reduced the Pueblo of Zia, which had been famous for its brave and obstinate resistance. In this attack more than six hundred Indians of both sexes were slain, and a large number made prisoners. Among the latter was a warrior named Ojeda, celebrated for valor and vivacity, who spoke good Spanish. This Indian gave a graphic account of all that had transpired since the insurrection.

He said that the Spaniards, and especially the priests, had been everywhere assassinated in the most barbarous manner; and particularly alluded to the murder of the curate of Zia, whose fate had been singularly cruel. It appears that on the night of the outbreak, the unsuspecting *padre* being asleep in the convent, the Indians hauled him out, and having stripped him naked, mounted him upon a hog. Then lighting torches, they carried him in that state through the village, and several times around the church and cemetery, scourging him all the while most unmercifully! Yet, not even contented with this, they placed the weak old man upon all-fours, and mounting upon his back by turns, spurred him through the streets, lashing him without cessation till he expired!

The discord which soon prevailed among the different Pueblos, greatly facilitated their second subjugation, which closely followed their emancipation. These petty feuds reduced their numbers greatly, and many villages were entirely annihilated, of which history only furnishes the names.

In 1698, after the country had been for some time completely subdued again by the Spaniards, another irruption took place in which many Pueblos were concerned; but through the energy of Governor Vargas Zapata it was soon quelled.

Since this last effort, the Indians have been treated with more humanity, each Pueblo being allowed a league or two of land, and permitted to govern themselves. Their rancorous hatred for their conquerors, however, has never entirely subsided, yet no further outbreak took place till 1837, when they joined the Mexican insurgents in another bloody conspiracy. Some time before these tragic events took place, it was prophesied among them that a new race was about to appear from the east, to redeem them from the Spanish yoke. I heard this spoken of several months before the subject of the insurrection had been seriously agitated. It is probable that the Pueblos built their hopes upon the Americans, as they seemed as yet to have no knowledge of the Texans. In fact, they have always appeared to look upon foreigners as a superior people, to whom they could speak freely of their discontent and their grievances. The truth is, the Pueblos, in every part of Mexico, have always been ripe for insurrection. It is well known that the mass of the revolutionary chief Hidalgo's army was made up of this class of people. The immediate cause of the present outbreak in the north, however, had its origin among the Hispano-Mexican population. This grew chiefly out of the change of the federal government to that of *Centralismo* in 1835. A new governor, Col. Albino Perez, was then sent from the city of Mexico, to take charge of this isolated department; which was not very agreeable to the 'sovereign people,' as they had previously been ruled chiefly by native governors. Yet while the new form of government was a novelty and did not affect the pecuniary interests of the people, it was acquiesced in; but it was now found necessary for the support of the new organization, to introduce a system of direct taxation, with which the people were wholly unacquainted; and they would sooner have paid a *doblon* through a tariff than a *real* in this way. Yet, although the conspiracy had been brewing for some time, no indications of violence were demonstrated, until, on account of some misdemeanor, an *alcalde* was imprisoned by the *Prefecto* of the northern district, Don Ramon Abreu. His honor of the staff was soon liberated by a mob; an occurrence which seemed as a watchword for a general insurrection.

These new movements took place about the beginning of August, 1837, and an immense rabble was soon gathered at La Cañada (a town some twenty-five miles to the north of Santa Fé), among whom were to be found the principal warriors of all the Northern Pueblos. Governor Perez issued orders to the alcaldes for the assembling of the militia; but all that could be collected together was about a hundred and fifty men, including the warriors of the Pueblo of Santo Domingo. With this inadequate force, the Governor made an attempt to march from the capital, but was soon surprised by the insurgents who lay in ambush near La Cañada; when his own men fled to the enemy, leaving him and about twenty-five trusty friends to make their escape in the best way they could. Knowing that they would not be safe in Santa Fé, the refugees pursued their flight southward, but were soon overtaken by the exasperated Pueblos; when the Governor was chased back to the suburbs of the city, and savagely put to death. His body was then stripped and shockingly mangled: his head was carried as a trophy to the camp of the insurgents, who made a foot-ball of it among themselves. I had left the city the day before this sad catastrophe took place, and beheld the Indians scouring the fields in pursuit of their victims, though I was yet ignorant of their barbarous designs. I saw them surround a house and drag from it the secretary of state, Jesus Maria Alarid. He and some other principal characters (including Prefect Abreu), who had also taken refuge among the ranchos, were soon afterwards stripped, and finally dispatched *á lanzadas*, that is, pierced through and through with lances, a mode of assassination very common among those demi-civilized savages.

Don Santiago Abreu (brother of the prefect), formerly governor and the most famed character of N. Mexico, was butchered in a still more barbarous manner. They cut off his hands, pulled out his eyes and tongue, and otherwise mutilated his body, taunting him all the while with the crimes he was accused of, by shaking the shorn members in his face. Thus perished nearly a dozen of the most conspicuous men of the obnoxious party, whose bodies lay for several days exposed to the beasts and birds of prey.

On the 9th of August about two thousand of the insurgent mob, including the Pueblo Indians, pitched their camp in the suburbs of the capital. The horrors of a *saqueo* (or plundering of the city) were now anticipated by every one. The American traders were particularly uneasy, expecting every instant that their lives and property would fall a sacrifice to the ferocity of the rabble. But to the great and most agreeable surprise of all, no outrage of any importance was committed upon either inhabitant or trader. A great portion of the insurgents remained in the city for about two days, during which one of their boldest leaders, José Gonzalez of Taos, a good honest hunter but a very ignorant man, was elected for governor.

The first step of the revolutionists was to seize all the property of their proscribed or murdered victims, which was afterwards distributed among the victors by a decree of the *Asamblea general*—that being the title by which a council summoned together by Governor Gonzalez, and composed of all the alcaldes and principal characters of the territory, was dignified. The families of the unfortunate victims of this revolutionary movement were thus left destitute of everything; and the foreign merchants who had given the officers credit to a large amount upon the strength of their reputed property and salaries, remained without a single resource with which to cover their demands. As these losses were chiefly experienced in consequence of a want of sufficient protection from the general government, the American merchants drew up a memorial setting forth their claims, which, together with a schedule of the various accounts due, was sent to the Hon. Powhattan Ellis, American Minister at Mexico. These demands were certainly of a far more equitable character than many of those which some time after occasioned the French blockade; yet our Government has given the unfortunate claimants no hope of redress. Even Mexico did not dispute the justness of these claims, but, on the contrary, she promptly paid to the order of General Armijo, a note given by the late Governor Perez to Mr. Sutton, an American merchant, which Armijo had purchased at a great discount.

In the South, the Americans were everywhere accused of being the instigators of this insurrection, which was openly pronounced another Texas affair. Their goods were confiscated or sequestered, upon the slightest pretexts, or for some pretended irregularity in the accompanying documents; although it was evident that these and other indignities were heaped upon them, as a punishment for the occurrence of events which it had not been in their power to prevent. Indeed, these ill-used merchants were not only innocent of any participation in the insurrectionary movements, but had actually furnished means to the government for the purpose of quelling the disturbances.

As I have observed before, the most active agents in this desperate affair were the Pueblo Indians, although the insurgent party was composed of all the heterogeneous ingredients that a Mexican population teems with. The *rancheros* and others of the lowest class, however, were only the instruments of certain discontented *ricos*, who, it has been said, were in hope of elevating themselves upon the wreck of their enemies. Among these was the present Governor Armijo, an ambitious and turbulent demagogue, who, for some cause or other, seemed anxious for the downfall of the whole administration.

As soon as Armijo received intelligence of the catastrophe, he hurried to the capital, expecting, as I heard it intimated by his own brother, to be elected governor; but, not having rendered any personal aid, the 'mobocracy' would not acknowledge his claim to their suffrages. He therefore retired, Santa-Anna-like, to his residence at Alburquerque, to plot, in imitation of his great prototype, some measures for counteracting the operation of his own intrigues. In this he succeeded so well, that towards September he was able to collect a considerable force in the Rio-Abajo, when he proclaimed a *contra-revolucion* in favor of the federal government. About the same time the disbanded troops of the capital under Captain Caballero, made a similar *pronunciamento*, demanding their arms, and offering their services gratis. The 'mobocratic' dynasty had gone so far as to deny allegiance to Mexico, and to propose sending to Texas for protection: although there had not been any previous understanding with that Republic.

Armijo now marched to Santa Fé with all his force, and Governor Gonzalez being without an army to support him, fled to the north. After his triumphal entrance into the capital, Armijo caused himself to be proclaimed Governor and *Comandante General*, and immediately dispatched couriers to Mexico with a highly colored account of his own exploits, which procured him a confirmation of those titles and dignities for eight years.

In the meanwhile news of the insurrection having reached Mexico, the *Escuadron de Vera Cruz*, from Zacatecas, consisting of about two hundred dragoons, with an equal number of regulars from the *Presidios* of Chihuahua, under the command of Colonel Justiniani, were ordered to New Mexico. Having arrived at Santa Fé, these troops, together with Governor Armijo's little army, marched in January, 1838, to attack the rebels, who, by this time, had again collected in considerable numbers at La Cañada.

The greatest uneasiness and excitement now prevailed at the Capital, lest the rabble should again prove victorious, in which case they would not fail to come and sack the city. Foreign merchants had as usual the greatest cause for fear, as vengeance had been openly vowed against them for having furnished the government party with supplies. These, therefore, kept up a continual watch, and had everything in readiness for a precipitate flight to the United States. But in a short time their fears were completely dispelled by the arrival of an express, with the welcome news of the entire defeat of the insurgents.

It appeared that, when the army arrived within view of the insurgent force, Armijo evinced the greatest perturbation. In fact, he was upon the point of retiring without venturing an attack, when Captain Muñoz, of the Vera Cruz dragoons, exclaimed, "What's to be done, General Armijo? If your Excellency will but permit me, I will oust that rabble in an instant with my little company alone." Armijo having given his consent, the gallant captain rushed upon the insurgents, who yielded at once, and fled precipitately—suffering a loss of about a dozen men, among whom was the deposed Governor Gonzalez, who, having been caught in the town after the skirmish had ended, was instantly shot, without the least form of trial.

CHAPTER VII.

Geographical Position of New Mexico—Absence of navigable Streams—The Rio del Norte—Romantic Chasm—Story of a sunken River—Mr. Stanley's Excursion to a famous Lake—Santa Fé and its Localities—El Valle de Taos and its Fertility—Soil of N. Mexico—The first Settler at Taos and his Contract with the Indians—Salubrity and Pleasantness of the Climate of New Mexico—Population—State of Agriculture—Staple Productions of the Country—Corn-fields and Fences—Irrigation and *Acequias*—*Tortillas* and *Tortilleras*—*Atole*, *Frijoles*, and *Chile*—Singular Custom—Culinary and Table Affairs—Flax and the Potato indigenous—Tobacco and *Punche*—Fruits—Peculiar Mode of cultivating the Grape—Forest Growths—*Piñon* and *Mezquite*—Mountain Cottonwood—*Palmilla* or Soap-plant—Pasturage.

NEW MEXICO possesses but few of those natural advantages, which are necessary to anything like a rapid progress in civilization. Though bounded north and east by the territory of the United States, south by that of Texas and Chihuahua, and west by Upper California, it is surrounded by chains of mountains and prairie wilds, extending to a distance of 500 miles or more, except in the direction of Chihuahua, from which its settlements are separated by an unpeopled desert of nearly two hundred miles—and without a single means of communication by water with any other part of the world.

The whole nominal territory, including those bleak and uninhabitable regions with which it is intersected, comprises about 200-000 square miles—considered, of course, according to its original boundaries, and therefore independently of the claims of Texas to the Rio del Norte. To whichsoever sovereignty that section of land may eventually belong, that portion of it, at least, which is inhabited, should remain united. Any attempt on the part of Texas to make the Rio del Norte the line of demarkation would greatly retard her ultimate acquisition of the territory, as it would leave at least one third of the population accustomed to the same rule, and bound by ties of consanguinity and affinity of customs, wholly at the mercy of the contiguous hordes of savages, that inhabit the Cordilleras on the west of them. This great chain of mountains which reaches the borders of the Rio del Norte, not far above El Paso, would, in my opinion, form the most natural boundary between the two countries, from thence northward.

There is not a single navigable stream to be found in New Mexico. The famous Rio del Norte is so shallow, for the most part of the year, that Indian canoes can scarcely float in it. Its navigation is also obstructed by frequent shoals and rippling sections for a distance of more than a thousand miles below Santa Fé. Opposite Taos, especially, for an uninterrupted distance of nearly fifteen miles, it runs pent up in a deep *cañon*, through which it rushes in rapid torrents. This frightful chasm is absolutely impassable; and, viewed from the top, the scene is imposing in the extreme. None but the boldest hearts and firmest nerves can venture to its brink, and look down its almost perpendicular precipice, over projecting crags and deep crevices, upon the foaming current of the river, which, in some places, appears like a small rippling brook; while in others it winds its serpentine course silently but majestically along, through a narrow little valley; with immense plains bordering and expanding in every direction, yet so smooth and level that the course of the river is not perceived till within a few yards of the verge. I have beheld this *cañon* from the summit of a mountain, over which the road passes some twenty miles below Taos, from whence it looks like the mere fissure of an insignificant ravine.

Baron Humboldt speaks of an extraordinary event as having occurred in 1752, of which he says the inhabitants of Paso del Norte still preserved the recollection in his day. "The whole bed of the river," says the learned historian, "became dry all of a sudden, for more than thirty leagues above and twenty leagues below the Paso: and the water of the river precipitated itself into a newly formed chasm, and only made its reappearance near the *Presidio* of San Eleazeario. . . . . . At length, after the lapse of several weeks, the water resumed its course, no doubt because the chasm and the subterraneous conductors had filled up." This, I must confess, savors considerably of the marvellous, as not the least knowledge of these facts appears to have been handed down to the present generation. During very great droughts, however, this river is said to have entirely disappeared in the sand, in some places, between San *Elceario* and the Presidio del Norte.

Notwithstanding the numerous tributary streams which would be supposed to pour their contents into the Rio del Norte, very few reach their destination before they are completely exhausted. Rio Puerco, so called from the extreme muddiness of its waters, would seem to form an exception to this rule. Yet this also, although at least a hundred miles in length, is dry at the mouth for a portion of the year. The creek of Santa Fé itself, though a bold and dashing rivulet in the immediate vicinity of the mountains, sinks into insignificance, and is frequently lost altogether before it reaches the main river. Pecos and Conchos, its most important inlets, would scarcely be entitled to a passing remark, but for the geographical error of Baron Humboldt, who set down the former as the head branch of 'Red River of Natchitoches.' These streams may be considered the first constant-flowing inlets which the Rio del Norte receives from Santa Fé south—say for the distance of five hundred miles! It is then no wonder that this 'Great River of the North' decreases in volume of water as it descends. In fact, above the region of tide-water, it is almost everywhere fordable during most of the year, being seldom over knee-deep, except at the time of freshets. Its banks are generally very low, often less than ten feet above low-water mark; and yet, owing to the disproportioned width of the channel (which is for the most part some four hundred yards), it is not subject to inundations. Its only important rises are those of the annual freshets, occasioned by the melting of the snow in the mountains.

This river is only known to the inhabitants of Northern Mexico as *Rio del Norte*, or North river, because it descends from that direction; yet in its passage southward, it is in some places called *Rio Grande*, on account of its extent; but the name of *Rio Bravo* (Bold or Rapid river), so often given to it on maps, is seldom if ever heard among the people. Though its entire length, following its meanders from its source in the Rocky Mountains to the Gulf of Mexico, must be considerably over two thousand miles, it is hardly navigable to the extent of two hundred miles above its mouth.

The head branch of Pecos, as well as the creeks of Santa Fé and Tezuque, are said to be fed from a little lake which is located on the summit of a mountain about ten miles east of Santa Fé. Manifold and marvellous are the stories related of this lake and its wonderful localities, which although believed to be at least greatly exaggerated, would no doubt induce numbers of travellers to visit this snow-bound elysium, were it not for the laboriousness of the ascent. The following graphic account of a 'pleasure excursion' to this celebrated 'watering place,' is from the memoranda of Mr. E. Stanley, who spent many years in the New Mexican capital.

"The snow had entirely disappeared from the top of the highest mountains, as seen from Santa Fé before the first of May, and on the eighteenth we set off on our trip. All were furnished with arms and fishing-tackle—well prepared to carry on hostilities both by land and water. Game was said to be abundant on the way—deer, turkeys, and even the formidable grizzly bear, ready to repel any invasion of his hereditary domain. Santa Fé creek, we knew, abounded with trout, and we were in hopes of finding them in the lake, although I had been told by some Mexicans, that there were no fish in it, and that it contained no living thing, except a certain nondescript and hideously misshapen little animal. We travelled up the course of the creek about eight miles, and then began to climb the mountain. Our journey now became laborious, the ascent being by no means gradual—rather a succession of hills—some long, others short—some declivitous, and others extremely precipitous. Continuing in this way for six or seven miles, we came to a grove of aspen, thick as cottonwoods in the Missouri bottoms. Through this grove, which extended for nearly a mile, no sound met the ear; no sign of life—not even an insect was to be seen; and not a breath of air was stirring. It was indeed a solitude to be felt. A mile beyond the grove brought us near the lake. On this last level, we unexpectedly met with occasional snow-banks, some of them still two or three feet deep. Being late, we sought out a suitable encampment, and fixed upon a little marshy prairie, east of the lake. The night was frosty and cold, and ice was frozen nearly an inch thick. Next morning we proceeded to the lake; when, lo—instead of beholding a beautiful sheet of water, we found an ugly little pond, with an area of two or three acres—frozen over, and one side covered with snow several feet deep. Thus all our hope of trout and monsters were at an end; and the *tracks* of a large bear in the snow, were all the *game* we saw during the trip."

SANTA FÉ, the capital of New Mexico, is the only town of any importance in the province. We sometimes find it written *Santa Fé de San Francisco* (Holy Faith of St. Francis), the latter being the patron, or tutelary saint. Like most of the towns in this section of country it occupies the site of an ancient Pueblo or Indian village, whose race has been extinct for a great many years. Its situation is twelve or fifteen miles east of the Rio del Norte, at the western base of a snow-clad mountain, upon a beautiful stream of small mill-power size, which ripples down in icy cascades, and joins the river some twenty miles to the southwestward. The population of the city itself but little exceeds 3000; yet, including several surrounding villages which are embraced in its corporate jurisdiction, it amounts to nearly 6,000 souls.*

The town is very irregularly laid out, and most of the streets are little better than common highways traversing scattered settlements which are interspersed with corn-fields nearly sufficient to supply the inhabitants with grain. The only attempt at anything like architectural compactness and precision, consists in four tiers of buildings, whose fronts are shaded with a fringe of *portales* or *corredores* of the rudest possible description. They stand around the public square, and comprise the *Palacio*, or Governor's house, the Custom-house, the Barracks (with which is connected the fearful *Calabozo*), the *Casa Consistorial* of the *Alcaldes*, the *Capilla de los Soldados* or Military Chapel, besides several private residences, as well as most of the shops of the American traders.

The population of New Mexico is almost exclusively confined to towns and villages, the suburbs of which are generally farms. Even most of the individual *ranchos* and *haciendas* have grown into villages,—a result al-

* The latitude of Santa Fé, as determined by various observations, is 35° 41' (though it is placed on most maps nearly a degree further north); and the longitude about 106° west from Greenwich. Its elevation above the ocean is nearly 7000 feet; that of the valley of Taos is no doubt over a mile and a half. The highest peak of the mountain (which is covered with perennial snow) some ten miles to the northeast of the capital, is reckoned about 5,000 feet above the town. Those from Taos northward rise still to a much greater elevation.

most indispensable for protection against the marauding savages of the surrounding wilderness. The principal of these settlements are located in the valley of the Rio del Norte, extending from nearly one hundred miles north to about one hundred and forty south of Santa Fé.* The most important of these, next to the capital, is *El Valle de Taos*,† so called in honor of the *Taosa* tribe of Indians, a remnant of whom still forms a *Pueblo* in the north of the valley. No part of New Mexico equals this valley in amenity of soil, richness of produce and beauty of appearance. Whatever is thrown into its prolific bosom, which the early frosts of autumn will permit to ripen, grows to a wonderful degree of perfection.

Wheat especially has been produced of a superlative quality, and in such abundance, that, as is asserted, the crops have often yielded over a hundred fold. I would not have it understood, however, that this is a fair sample of New Mexican soil; for, in point of fact, though many of the bottoms are of very fertile character, the uplands must chiefly remain unproductive; owing, in part, to the sterility of the soil, but as much, no doubt, to want of irrigation; hence nearly all the farms and settlements are located in those valleys which

---

* The settlements *up the river* from the capital are collectively known as *Rio-Arriba*, and those *down the river* as *Rio-Abajo*. The latter comprise over a third of the population, and the principal wealth of New Mexico.

† 'The *Valley of Taos*,' there being no *town* of this name. It includes several villages and other settlements, the largest of which are Fernandez and Los Ranchos, four or five miles apart.

may be watered by some constant-flowing stream.*

The first settler of the charming valley of Taos, since the country was reconquered from the Indians, is said to have been a Spaniard named Pando, about the middle of the eighteenth century. This pioneer of the North, finding himself greatly exposed to the depredations of the Comanches, succeeded in gaining the friendship of that tribe, by promising his infant daughter, then a beautiful child, to one of their chiefs in marriage. But the unwilling maiden having subsequently refused to ratify the contract, the settlement was immediately attacked by the savages, and all were slain except the betrothed damsel who was led into captivity. After living some years with the Comanches on the great prairies, she was bartered away to the Pawnees, of whom she was eventually purchased by a Frenchman of St. Louis. Some very respectable families in that city are descended from her; and there are many people yet living who remember with what affecting pathos the old lady was wont to tell her tale of wo. She died but a few years ago.

Salubrity of climate is decidedly the most interesting feature in the character of New

---

* For the generally barren and desolate appearance which the uplands of New Mexico present, some of them have possessed an extraordinary degree of fertility; as is demonstrated by the fact that many of the fields on the undulating lands in the suburbs of Santa Fé, have no doubt been in constant cultivation over two hundred years, and yet produce tolerable crops, without having been once renovated by manure.

Mexico. Nowhere—not even under the much boasted Sicilian skies, can a purer or a more wholesome atmosphere be found. Bilious diseases—the great scourge of the valley of the Mississippi—are here almost unknown. Apart from a fatal epidemic fever of a typhoid character, that ravaged the whole province from 1837 to 1839, and which, added to the small-pox that followed in 1840, carried off nearly ten per cent. of the population, New Mexico has experienced very little disease of a febrile character; so that as great a degree of longevity is attained there, perhaps, as in any other portion of the habitable world. Persons withered almost to mummies, are to be encounterered occasionally, whose extraordinary age is only to be inferred from their recollection of certain notable events which have taken place in times far remote.

A sultry day, from Santa Fé north, is of very rare occurrence. The summer nights are usually so cool and pleasant that a pair of blankets constitutes an article of comfort seldom dispensed with. The winters are long, but not so subject to sudden changes as in damper climates; the general range of the thermometer, throughout the year, being from 10 to 75° above zero, of Fahrenheit. Baron Humboldt was led into as great an error with respect to the climate of New Mexico as to the rivers; for he remarks, that near Santa Fé and a little further north, "the Rio del Norte is sometimes covered for a succession of several years, with ice thick enough to admit the passage of horses and carriages:" a circumstance which would be scarcely less astounding to the New Mexicans, than would the occurrence of a similar event in the harbor of New York be to her citizens.

The great elevation of all the plains about the Rocky Mountains, is perhaps the principal cause of the extraordinary dryness of the atmosphere. There is but little rain throughout the year, except from July to October—known as the *rainy season;* and as the Missouri traders usually arrive about its commencement, the coincidence has given rise to a superstition, quite prevalent among the vulgar, that the Americans bring the rain with them. During seasons of drought, especially, they look for the arrival of the annual caravans as the harbinger of speedy relief.

There has never been an accurate census taken in New Mexico. Of the results of one which was attempted in 1832, the Secretary of State at Santa Fé speaks in the following terms: "At present (1841) we may estimate the Spanish or white population at about 60,000 souls or more, being what remains of 72,000, which the census taken eight or nine years ago showed there then existed in New Mexico." He supposes that this great diminution resulted from the ravages of the frightful diseases already alluded to. The decrease of population from these causes, however, is thus greatly overrated. The discrepancy must find its explanation in the original inaccuracy of the census referred to.

If we exclude the unsubjugated savages, the entire population of New Mexico, including the Pueblo Indians, cannot be set down, according to the best estimates I have been able to obtain, at more than 70,000 souls. These may be divided as follows: white creoles, say 1,000; Mestizos, or mixed creoles, 59,000, and Pueblos, 10,000. Of naturalized citizens, the number is inconsiderable —scarcely twenty; and if we except transient traders, there are not over double as many alien residents. There are no negroes in New Mexico, and consequently neither mulattoes nor *zambos*. In 1803, Baron Humboldt set down the population of this province at 40,200, so that according to this the increase for forty years has barely exceeded one per cent. per annum.

Agriculture, like almost everything else in New Mexico, is in a very primitive and unimproved state. A great portion of the peasantry cultivate with the hoe alone—their ploughs (when they have any) being only used for mellow grounds, as they are too rudely constructed to be fit for any other service. Those I have seen in use are mostly fashioned in this manner:—a section of the trunk of a tree, eight or ten inches in diameter, is cut about two feet long, with a small branch left projecting upwards, of convenient length for a handle. With this a beam is connected to which oxen are yoked. The block, with its fore end sloped downwards to a point, runs flat, and opens a furrow similar to that of the common shovel-plough. What is equally worthy of remark is, that these ploughs are often made exclusively of wood, without one particle of iron, or even a nail to increase their durability.

The *labores* and *milpas* (cultivated fields) are often, indeed most usually, without any enclosure. The owners of cattle are obliged to keep herdsmen constantly with them, else graze them at a considerable distance from the farms; for if any trespass is committed upon the fields by stock, the proprietor of the latter is bound to pay damages: therefore, instead of the cultivator's having to guard his crop from the cattle as with us, the owners of these are bound to guard them from the crops. Only a chance farm is seen fenced with poles scattered along on forks, or a loose hedge of brush. Mud-fences, or walls of very large *adobes*, are also occasionally to be met with.

The necessity of irrigation has confined, and no doubt will continue to confine agriculture principally to the valleys of the constant-flowing streams. In some places the crops are frequently cut short by the drying up of the streams. Where water is abundant, however, art has so far superseded the offices of nature in watering the farms, that it is almost a question whether the interference of nature in the matter would not be a disadvantage. On the one hand the husbandman need not have his grounds overflowed if he administers the water himself, much less need he permit them to suffer from drought. He is therefore more sure of his crop than if it were subject to the caprices of the weather in more favored agricultural regions.

One *acequia madre* (mother ditch) suffices generally to convey water for the irrigation of an entire valley, or at least for all the fields of one town or settlement. This is made and kept in repair by the public, under the supervision of the alcaldes; laborers being allotted to work upon it as with us upon our county roads. The size of this principal ditch is of course proportioned to the quantity of land to be watered. It is conveyed over the highest part of the valley, which, on these mountain streams, is, for the most part, next to the hills. From this, each proprietor of a farm runs a minor ditch, in like manner, over the most elevated part of his field. Where there is not a superabundance of water, which is often the case on the smaller streams, each farmer has his day, or portion of a day allotted to him for irrigation; and at no other time is he permitted to extract water from the *acequia madre*. Then the cultivator, after letting the water into his minor ditch, dams this, first at one point and then at another, so as to overflow a section at a time, and with his hoe, depressing eminences and filling sinks, he causes the water to spread regularly over the surface. Though the operation would seem tedious, an expert irrigator will water in one day his five or six acre field, if level, and everything well arranged; yet on uneven ground he will hardly be able to get over half of that amount.*

All the *acequias* for the valley of the Rio del Norte are conveyed from the main stream, except where a tributary of more convenient water happens to join it. As the banks of the river are very low, and the descent considerable, the water is soon brought upon the surface by a horizontal ditch along an inclined bank, commencing at a convenient point of constant-flowing water—generally without dam, except sometimes a wing of stones to turn the current into the canal.

The staple productions of the country are emphatically Indian corn and wheat. The former grain is most extensively employed for making *tortillas*—an article of food greatly in demand among the people, the use of which has been transmitted to them by the aborigines. The corn is boiled in water with a little lime: and when it has been sufficiently softened, so as to strip it of its skin, it is ground into paste upon the *metate*,† and formed into a thin cake. This is afterwards spread on a small sheet of iron or copper, called

---

* There is no land measure here correspondent to our acres. Husbandmen rate their fields by the amount of wheat necessary to sow them; and thus speak of a *fanega* of land—*fanega* being a measure of about two bushels—meaning an extent which two bushels of wheat will suffice to sow. Tracts are usually sold by the number of *leguas* (leagues), or *varas* front of irrigable lands; for those back from the streams are considered worthless. The *vara* is very nearly 33 English inches, 5,000 of which constitute the Mexican league—under two miles and two-thirds.

† From the Indian word *metatl*, a hollowed oblong stone, used as a grinding-machine.

A KITCHEN SCENE.

comal (*comalli*, by the Indians), and placed over the fire, where, in less than three minutes, it is baked and ready for use. The thinness of the tortilla is always a great test of skill in the maker, and much rivalry ensues in the art of preparation. The office of making tortillas has, from the earliest times, pertained chiefly to the women, who appear to be better adapted to this employ than the other sex, both as regards skill and dexterity, in preparing this particular food for the table. I perfectly agree with the historian Clavigero, however, in the opinion that "although this species of corn-bread may be very wholesome and substantial, and well-flavored when newly made, it is unpleasant when cold."

A sort of thin mush, called *atole*, made of

Indian meal, is another article of diet, the preparation of which is from the aborigines; and such is its nationality, that in the North it is frequently called *el café de los Mexicanos* (the coffee of the Mexicans). How general soever the use of coffee among Americans may appear, that of *atole* is still more so among the lower classes of Mexicans. They virtually 'breakfast, dine and sup' upon it. Of this, indeed, with *frijoles* and *chile* (beans and red pepper), consists their principal food. The extravagant use of red pepper among the Mexicans has become truly proverbial. It enters into nearly every dish at every meal, and often so predominates as entirely to conceal the character of the viands. It is likewise ground into a sauce, and thus used even more abundantly than butter. *Chile verde* (green pepper), not as a mere condiment, but as a salad, served up in different ways, is reckoned by them one of the greatest luxuries. But however much we may be disposed to question their taste in this particular, no one can hesitate to do homage to their incomparable chocolate, in the preparation of which the Mexicans surely excel every other people.

Besides these, many other articles of diet peculiar to the country, and adopted from the aborigines, are still in use—often of rich and exquisite flavor, and though usually not much relished at first by strangers, they are for the most part highly esteemed after a little use.

The rancheros, and all the humbler classes

of people, very seldom use any table for their meals, an inconvenience which is very little felt, as the dishes are generally served out from the kitchen in courses of a single plate to each guest, who usually takes it upon his knees. Knives and forks are equally dispensed with, the viands being mostly hashed or boiled so very soft as to be eaten with a spoon. This is frequently supplied by the *tortilla*, a piece of which is ingeniously doubled between the fingers, so as to assist in the disposal of anything, be it ever so rare or liquid. Thus it may well be said, as in the story of the Oriental monarch, that these rancheros employ a new spoon for every mouthful: for each fold of the tortilla is devoured with the substance it conveys to the mouth.

The very singular custom of abstaining from all sorts of beverage during meals, has frequently afforded me a great deal of amusement. Although a large cup of water is set before each guest, it is not customary to drink it off till the repast is finished. Should any one take it up in his hand while in the act of eating, the host is apt to cry out, " Hold, hold! there is yet more to come." I have never been able to ascertain definitely the meaning of this peculiarity; but from the strictness with which it is observed, it is natural to suppose, that the use of any kind of drink whilst eating, is held extremely unwholesome.*

* What also strikes the stranger as a singularity in that country, is that the females rarely ever eat with the males—at least in the presence of strangers—but usually take their food in the kitchen by themselves.

The New Mexicans use but little wine at meals, and that exclusively of the produce of the Paso del Norte.

But to return to the productions of the soil. *Cotton* is cultivated to no extent, although it has always been considered as indigenous to the country; while the ancient manufactures of the aborigines prove it to have been especially so in this province. *Flax* is entirely neglected, and yet a plant resembling in every respect that of the *linum usitatissimum*, is to be found in great abundance in many of the mountain valleys. The potato (*la papa*), although not cultivated in this country till very lately, is unquestionably an indigenous plant, being still found in a state of nature in many of the mountain valleys—though of small size, seldom larger than filberts: whence it appears that this luxury had not its exclusive origin in South America, as is the current opinion of the present day. Universal as the use of tobacco is among these people, there is very little of it grown, and that chiefly of a light and weak species, called by the natives *punche*, which is also indigenous, and still to be met with growing wild in some places. What has in a great measure contributed to discourage people from attending to the cultivation of the tobacco plant, is the monopoly of this *indispensable* by the federal government; for although the tobacco laws are not enforced in New Mexico (there being no *Estanquillo*, or public store-house), yet the people cannot carry it anywhere else in the republic for sale, without risk of its being immediately confiscated. A still more powerful cause operating against this, as well as every other branch of agriculture in New Mexico, is the utter want of navigable streams, as a cheap and convenient means of transportation to distant markets.

Famous as the republic of Mexico has been for the quality and variety of its fruits, this province, considering its latitude, is most singularly destitute in this respect. A few orchards of apples, peaches and apricots, are occasionally met with, but even these are of very inferior quality, being only esteemed in the absence of something better. A few small vineyards are also to be found in the valley of the Rio del Norte, but the grape does not thrive as at El Paso. The mode of cultivating the grape in these parts is somewhat peculiar, and might, I have no doubt, be practised to great advantage in other countries. No scaffold or support of any kind is erected for the vines, which are kept pruned so as to form a sort of shrubbery. Every fall of the year, these are completely covered with earth, which protects them during the winter. Upon the opening of spring the dirt is scraped away, and the vines pruned again. This being repeated from year to year, the shrubs soon acquire sufficient strength to support the heavy crops of improved and superiorly-flavored grapes which they finally produce.

Indigenous wild fruits are not quite so scarce; a clear evidence that the lack of cultivated fruit is not so much the fault of nature, as the result of indolence and neglect on the part of the people. The prickly pear is found in greatest abundance, and of several varieties: and though neither very wholesome nor savory, it is nevertheless frequently eaten.

There is but little timber in New Mexico, except in the mountains and along the watercourses; the table-plains and valleys are generally all open prairie. The forest growths, moreover, of all the north of Mexico, present quite a limited variety of timber, among which a species of pitch-pine mostly predominates. The tree which appears to be most peculiar to the country, is a kind of scrub pine called *piñon*, which grows generally to the height of twenty or thirty feet, with leaves ever-green and pine-like, but scarcely an inch long. From the surface of this tree exudes a species of turpentine resembling that of the pitch-pine, but perhaps less resinous. The wood is white and firm, and much used for fuel. The most remarkable appendage of this tree is the fruit it bears, which is also known by the same name. This is a little nut about the size of a kidney-bean, with a rich oily kernel in a thin shell, enclosed in a chestnut-like bur. It is of pleasant flavor and much eaten by the natives, and considerable quantities are exported annually to the southern cities. It is sometimes used for the manufacture of a certain kind of oil, said to be very good for lamps.

The *mezquite* tree, vulgarly called *muskeet*

in Texas, where it has attained some celebrity, grows in some of the fertile valleys of Chihuahua to the height of thirty and forty feet, with a trunk of one to two feet in diameter. The wood makes excellent fuel, but it is seldom used for other purposes, as it is crooked, knotty, and very coarse and brittle, more resembling the honey-locust (of which it might be considered a scrubby species) than the mahogany, as some people have asserted. The fruit is but a diminutive honey-locust in appearance and flavor, of the size and shape of a flattened bean-pod, with the seeds disposed in like manner. This pod, which, like that of the honey-locust, encloses a glutinous substance, the Apaches and other tribes of Indians grind into flour to make their favorite *pinole*. The mezquite seems undoubtedly of the *Acacia Arabica* species; as some physicians who have examined the gum which exudes from the tree, pronounce it genuine Arabic.

On the water-courses there is little timber to be found except cottonwood, scantily scattered along their banks. Those of the Rio del Norte are now nearly bare throughout the whole range of the settlements, and the inhabitants are forced to resort to the distant mountains for most of their fuel. But nowhere, even beyond the settlements, are there to be seen such dense cottonwood bottoms as those of the Mississippi valley. Besides the common cottonwood there is another to be found upon the mountain streams of New Mexico, which has been called willow-leaf or bitter cottonwood (*populus angustifolia?*) and has been reckoned by some a species of cinchona, yet for no other reason perhaps than that the bark possesses efficacious tonic qualities. Attached to the seeds of this tree is also a cotton similar to that of the sweet cottonwood, or *populus angulata*.

Among the wild productions of New Mexico is the *palmilla*—a species of palmetto, which might be termed the *soap-plant*—whose roots, as well as those of another species known as *palma* (or palm), when bruised, form a saponaceous pulp called *amole*, much used by the natives for washing clothes, and is said to be even superior to soap for scouring woollens.

But by far the most important indigenous product of the soil of New Mexico is its pasturage. Most of the high table-plains afford the finest grazing in the world, while, for want of water, they are utterly useless for most other purposes. That scanty moisture which suffices to bring forth the natural vegetation, is insufficient for agricultural productions, without the aid of irrigation. The high prairies of all Northern Mexico differ greatly from those of our border in the general character of their vegetation. They are remarkably destitute of the gay flowering plants for which the former are so celebrated, being mostly clothed with different species of a highly nutritious grass called *grama*, which is of a very short and curly quality. The highlands, upon which alone this sort of grass is produced, being seldom verdant till after the rainy season sets in, the *grama* is only in perfection from August to October. But being rarely nipt by the frost until the rains are over, it cures upon the ground and remains excellent hay—equal if not superior to that which is cut and stacked from our western prairies. Although the winters are rigorous, the feeding of stock is almost entirely unknown in New Mexico; nevertheless, the extensive herds of the country, not only of cattle and sheep, but of mules and horses, generally maintain themselves in excellent condition upon the dry pasturage alone through the cold season, and until the rains start up the green grass again the following summer.

CHAPTER VIII.

The Mines of New Mexico—Supposed Concealment of them by the Indians—Indian Superstition and Cozenage—Ruins of *La Gran Quivira*—Old Mines—*Placeres* or Mines of Gold Dust—Speculative Theories as to the original Deposites of the Gold—Mode of Working the *Placeres*—Manners and Customs of the Miners—Arbitrary Restrictions of the Mexican Government upon Foreigners—Persecution of a Gachupin—Disastrous Effects of official Interference upon the Mining Interest—Disregard of American Rights and of the U. States Government—*Gambucinos* and their System—Gold found throughout N. Mexico—Silver Mines—Copper, Zinc and Lead—Sulphurous Springs—Gypsum, and Petrified Trees.

TRADITION speaks of numerous and productive mines having been in operation in New Mexico before the expulsion of the Spaniards in 1680; but that the Indians, seeing that the cupidity of the conquerors had been the cause of their former cruel oppressions, determined to conceal all the mines by filling them up, and obliterating as much as possible every trace of them. This was done so effectually, as is told, that after the second conquest (the Spaniards in the mean time not having turned their attention to mining pursuits for a series of years), succeeding generations were never able to discover them again. Indeed it is now generally credited by the Spanish population, that the Pueblo Indians, up to the present day, are acquainted with the *locales* of a great number of these wonderful mines, of which they most sedulously preserve the secret. Rumor further asserts that the old men and sages of the Pueblos periodically lecture the youths on this subject, warning them against discovering the mines to the Spaniards, lest the cruelties of the original conquest be renewed towards them, and they be forced to toil and suffer in those mines as in days of yore. To the more effectual preservation of secrecy, it is also stated that they have called in the aid of superstition, by promulgating the belief that the Indian who reveals the location of these hidden treasures, will surely perish by the wrath of their gods.

Playing upon the credulity of the people, it sometimes happens that a roguish Indian will amuse himself at the expense of his reputed superiors in intelligence, by proffering to disclose some of these concealed treasures. I once knew a waggish savage of this kind to propose to show a valley where virgin gold could be 'scraped up by the basket-full.' On a bright Sunday morning, the time appointed for the expedition, the chuckling Indian set out with a train of Mexicans at his heels, provided with mules and horses, and a large quantity of meal-bags to carry in the golden stores; but, as the shades of evening were closing around the party, he discovered —— that he couldn't find the place.

It is not at all probable, however, that the

aborigines possess a tenth part of the knowledge of these ancient fountains of wealth, that is generally attributed to them; but that many valuable mines *were* once wrought in this province, not only tradition but authenticated records and existing relics sufficiently prove. In every quarter of the territory there are still to be seen vestiges of ancient excavations, and in some places, ruins of considerable towns evidently reared for mining purposes.

Among these ancient ruins the most remarkable are those of *La Gran Quivira*, about 100 miles southward from Santa Fé. This appears to have been a considerable city, larger and richer by far than the present capital of New Mexico has ever been. Many walls, particularly those of churches, still stand erect amid the desolation that surrounds them, as if their sacredness had been a shield against which Time dealt his blows in vain. The style of architecture is altogether superior to anything at present to be found north of Chihuahua—being of hewn stone, a building material wholly unused in New Mexico. What is more extraordinary still, is, that there is no water within less than some ten miles of the ruins; yet we find several stone cisterns, and remains of aqueducts eight or ten miles in length, leading from the neighboring mountains, from whence water was no doubt conveyed. And, as there seem to be no indications whatever of the inhabitants' ever having been engaged in agricultural pursuits, what could have induced the rearing of a city in such an arid, woodless plain as this, except the proximity of some valuable mine, it is difficult to imagine. From the peculiar character of the place and the remains of the cisterns still existing, the object of pursuit in this case would seem to have been a *placer*, a name applied to mines of gold-dust intermixed with the earth. However, other mines have no doubt been worked in the adjacent mountains, as many spacious pits are found, such as are usually dug in pursuit of ores of silver, etc.; and it is stated that in several places heaps of scoria are still to be seen.

By some persons these ruins have been supposed to be the remains of an ancient Pueblo or aboriginal city. That is not probable, however; for though the relics of aboriginal temples might possibly be mistaken for those of Catholic churches, yet it is not to be presumed that the Spanish coat of arms would be found sculptured and painted upon their façades, as is the case in more than one instance. The most rational accounts represent this to have been a wealthy Spanish city before the general massacre of 1680, in which calamity the inhabitants perished—all except one, as the story goes; and that their immense treasures were buried in the ruins. Some credulous adventurers have lately visited the spot in search of these long lost coffers, but as yet none have been found.*

* In the same vicinity there are some other ruins of a similar character, though less extensive; the principal of which are those of Abó, Tagique and Chililí. The last of these is now being resettled by the Mexicans.

The mines of *Cerrillos*, twenty miles southward of Santa Fé, although of undoubted antiquity, have, to all appearance, been worked to some extent within the present century; indeed, they have been reopened within the recollection of the present generation; but the enterprise having been attended with little success, it was again abandoned. Among numerous pits still to be seen at this place, there is one of immense depth cut through solid rock, which it is believed could not have cost less than $100,000. In the mountains of Sandía, Abiquiú, and more particularly in those of Picuris and Embudo, there are also numerous excavations of considerable depth. A few years ago an enterprising American undertook to reopen one of those near Picuris; but after having penetrated to the depth of more than a hundred feet, without reaching the bottom of the original excavation (which had probably been filling up for the last hundred and fifty years), he gave it up for want of means. Other attempts have since been made, but with as little success. Whether these failures have been caused by want of capital and energy, or whether the veins of ore were exhausted by the original miners, remains for future enterprise to determine.

The only successful mines known in New Mexico at the present day, are those of gold, the most important one of which is that originally incorporated as *El Real de Dolores*, but generally known by the significant name of

El Placer. This mine lies in a low detached spur of mountains, at a distance of twenty-seven miles south of the capital. In 1828, a *Sonoreño* who was in the habit of herding his mules in that vicinity, being one day in pursuit of some that had strayed into the mountains, happened to pick up a stone, which he soon identified as being of the same class that was to be found in the gold regions of Sonora. Upon a little further examination, he detected sundry particles of gold, which did not fail to occasion some degree of excitement in the country. Although the amount procured from these mines, was, for the first two or three years, very insignificant, yet it answered the purpose of testing the quality of the metal, which was found to be of uncommon purity. A market was therefore very soon opened with foreign merchants.

The quantity of gold extracted between the years 1832 and '35 could not have amounted to less than from $60,000 to $80,000 per annum. Since this time, however, there has been a considerable falling off, some seasons producing but $30,000 or $40,000. It is believed, notwithstanding, that the entire aggregate yield since the first discovery has exceeded half a million of dollars. The reduction in profit during the last few years has been caused more by want of energy and enterprise, than by exhaustion of the precious metal, as only a very small portion of the 'gold region' has as yet been dug; and experience has shown that the 'dust' is about as likely to be found in one part of it as in another. All the best 'diggings' in the immediate vicinity of the water, however, seem pretty well excavated: in some places the hills and valleys are literally cut up like a honey-comb.

It has been the impression of some persons, that the gold of this region was originally accumulated in some particular deposit, and that it has thus been spread over the surface of the country by some volcanic eruption.

The dust and grains obtained at this mine, are virgin gold, and, as before remarked, of very fine quality, producing at the United States Mint an average of at least $19 70 to the ounce troy after melting, or about $19 30 gross. It was at first bought by the traders at the rate of fifteen dollars per ounce, but in consequence of the competition which was afterwards excited among the dealers, its price was raised for a short time above its maximum at the Mint, although it has since settled down at about $17 30 per ounce troy.

During the process of these excavations, when such a depth has been reached as to render a ladder indispensable, a pole ten or fifteen feet long is cut full of notches for that purpose, and set diagonally in the orifice. In proportion as the pit becomes deeper, others are added, forming a somewhat precarious zigzag staircase, by which the agile miner descends and ascends without even using his hands to assist himself, although with a large

GOLD-WASHING.

load of earth upon his shoulders. It is in this way that most of the rubbish is extracted from these mines, as windlasses or machinery of any kind are rarely used.

The winter season is generally preferred by the miners, for the facilities it affords of supplying the gold-washers with water in the immediate neighborhood of their operations; for the great scarcity of water about the mining regions is a very serious obstacle at other seasons to successful enterprise. Water in winter is obtained by melting a quantity of snow thrown into a sink, with heated stones. Those employed as washers are very frequently the wives and children of the miners. A round wooden bowl called *batea*, about eighteen inches in diameter, is the washing vessel, which they fill with the earth, and then immerse it in the pool, and stir it with their hands; by which operation the loose dirt floats off, and the gold settles to the bottom. In this manner they continue till nothing remains in the bottom of the *batea* but a little heavy black sand mixed with a few grains of gold, the value of which (to the trayful) varies from one to twelve cents, and sometimes, in very rich soils, to twenty-five or more. Some attempts have been made to wash with machinery, but as yet without success; partly owing to the scarcity of water, but as much perhaps to a lack of perseverance, and to the arbitrary restrictions imposed upon foreigners, who, after all, are the only persons that have ever attempted any improvements of the kind. An instance or two will fully illustrate the embarrassments and disadvantages to which foreigners are subject, in embarking capital in mining enterprises in this country.

When the Placer was in its greatest *bonanza*—yielding very large profits to those engaged in the business—the 'mining fever' rose to such a tremendous pitch among the New Mexicans, particularly the government officers, that every one fancied he saw a door opened for the accumulation of a princely fortune.

About the commencement of this gold mania, a very arbitrary and tyrannical measure was adopted in order to wrest from a persecuted *Gachupin** his interest in a mine, in

---
* A term used to designate European Spaniards in America.

which he had made a very propitious commencement. This mine, different from the rest of the *Placer*, consisted of a vein of gold in a stratum of rock, which it was necessary to grind and separate with quicksilver; and as it belonged to a native named Ortiz who knew nothing of this operation, the latter formed a partnership with Don Dámaso Lopez, the Gachupin before alluded to, who had some experience and skill in mining operations and the extraction of metals. The partners went vigorously to work, and at the close of the first month found that their net profits amounted to several hundred dollars, consisting in a few balls of gold. At the sight of these, Ortiz was so overjoyed that he must needs exhibit his valuable acquisitions to the governor and other officers and magnates of the capital, who, with characteristic cupidity, at once begrudged the Gachupin his prospective fortune. A compact was thereupon entered into between the *oficiales* and the acquiescent Ortiz, to work the mine on their joint account, and to exclude Lopez altogether. This they effected by reviving the old decree of expulsion (spoken of in another place), which had virtually become obsolete. The unfortunate victim of this outrageous conspiracy was accordingly ordered to the frontier, as the patriotic officers alleged that they "could no longer connive at his residence so near the capital in contravention of the laws."

The new company now commenced operations with additional zeal and earnestness.

But they were destined to expiate their ill conduct in a way they had least anticipated. The ores collected during the first month, had been ground and impregnated with quicksilver, and the amalgamation being supposed complete, all the partners in the concern were summoned to witness the splendid results of the new experiments. Yet, after the most diligent examination, not a grain of gold appeared! The fact is, that they were all ignorant of mining operations, and knew nothing of the art of separating the metals from the ores. The mine had therefore soon to be abandoned, and Ortiz found himself prostrated by his losses—a victim to the unprincipled rapacity of his new associates.

Lest foreigners generally should share the wealth which was being developed in these mountains, an order was subsequently issued prohibiting all except natives from working at the mines. Some who had commenced operations at the Placer, and incurred considerable expense, were compelled suddenly to break up, with an entire loss of all their labor and outlays.

Acts of political oppression like these have discouraged Americans from making any further attempts, although the decree of prohibition has ceased to be enforced. Could any dependence be placed in the integrity of the government, I have no doubt that, with sufficient capital and the aid of machinery (such as is used in the mines of Georgia and Carolina), the old mines of this province might be reopened, and a great number of the *placeres* very extensively and profitably worked. But as New Mexico is governed at present, there is no security in an enterprise of the kind. The progress of a foreign adventurer is always liable to be arrested by the jealousy of the government, upon the first flattering *bonanza*, as the cited instances abundantly demonstrate. Americans in particular would have little to hope for in the way of redress; for our government has shown itself so tardy in redressing or revenging injuries done its citizens by foreign states, that they would be oppressed, as they have been, with less scruple because with more impunity than the subjects of any other nation.

The gold regions are, for the most part, a kind of common property, and have been wrought chiefly by an indigent class of people, known familiarly as *gambucinos*, a name applied to petty miners who work 'on their own hook.' Among these one very seldom finds any foreigners; for according to the present simple method of working, the profit is too small and too precarious to entice the independent American laborer, who is seldom willing to work for less than a dollar a day, clear of all expenses; while the Mexican *gambucino* is content with two or three *reales*, most of which is required to furnish him food. Therefore these poor miners lead a miserable life after all. When short of means they often support themselves upon only a *real* each per day, their usual food consisting of bread and a kind of coarse cake-sugar called *piloncillo*, to which is sometimes added a little crude ranchero cheese; yet they seem perfectly satisfied.

To prevent collisions among such heterogeneous multitudes as are to be found at the mining places, some municipal provisions have been established, in pursuance of which any person may open a *labor* or pit on unoccupied ground not nearer than ten paces to another, and is entitled to the same extent in every direction, not interfering with prior claims—his *labor* being confirmed for a small fee by application to the alcalde. But if the proprietor abandon his *labor* for a certain time, any one that chooses may take possession.

Besides the Placer of which I have already spoken, others have lately been discovered in the same ledge of mountains towards the south, one of which is now extensively worked, being already filled with retail shops of every description, where all the gold that is extracted, is either sold or bartered. The *gambucinos* being generally destitute of all other resources, are often obliged to dispose of their gold daily—and very frequently in driblets of but a few cents value. *Placeres* of gold have also been discovered in the mountains of Abiquiú, Taos and elsewhere, which have been worked to some extent. In truth, as some of the natives have justly remarked, New Mexico is almost one continuous *placer;* traces of gold being discoverable over nearly the whole surface of the country. The opinion formerly entertained that gold is only to be found in southern climates, seems fully confuted here; for at a point called Sangre de Cristo, considerably north of Taos, (above the 37th degree of latitude), and which from its location among the snowy mountains of that region, is ice-bound over half the year, a very rich *placer* has been discovered; yet owing to the peculiarly exposed situation in which it lies, it has been very little worked.

For the last century no *silver* mines have been in successful operation in New Mexico. A few years ago there was discovered near the village of Manzano, in the mountains of Tomé, a vein of silver which bid fair to prove profitable; but when the ore came to be tested, the rock was found to be so hard that the pursuit has been entirely abandoned.

In addition to gold and silver, there are also to be found, in many isolated spots, ores of copper, zinc, and lead; although the latter is so mixed up with copper and other hard metals, as to be almost unfit for ordinary purposes. The copper obtained in the province has frequently been found to contain a slight mixture of the precious metals, well worth extracting. Iron is also abundant.

Besides the mines of metals which have been discovered, or yet remain concealed in the mountains of New Mexico, those of *Salt* (or *salt lakes*, as they would perhaps be called), the *Salinas*, are of no inconsiderable importance. Near a hundred miles southward from the capital, on the high table land between the Rio del Norte and Pecos, there are some extensive salt ponds, which afford an inexhaustible supply of this indispensable commodity, not only for the consumption of this province, but for portions of the adjoining departments. The largest of these *Salinas* is five or six miles in circumference. The best time to collect the salt is during the dry season, when the lakes contain but little water; but even when flooded, salt may be scooped up from the bottom, where it is deposited in immense beds, in many places of unknown depth; and, when dried, much resembles the common alum salt. The best, however, which is of superior quality, rises as a scum upon the water. A great many years ago, a firm causeway was thrown up through the middle of the principal lake, upon which the *carretas* and mules are driven, and loaded with salt still dripping with water. The *Salinas* are public property, and the people resort to them several times a year,—in caravans, for protection against the savages of the desert in which they are situated. Although this salt costs nothing but the labor of carrying it away, the danger from the Indians and the privations experienced in an expedition to the *Salinas* are such, that it is seldom sold in the capital for less than a dollar per bushel. On the same great plain still a hundred miles further south, there is another *Salina* of the same character.

While I am on this subject, I cannot forbear a brief notice of the mineral springs of New Mexico. There are several warm springs (*ojos calientes*), whose waters are generally sulphurous, and considered as highly efficacious in the cure of rheumatisms and other chronic diseases. Some are bold springs, and of a very agreeable temperature for bathing; but there is one in the west of the province, which does not flow very freely, but merely escapes through the crevices of the rocks, yet it is hot enough to cook any article of food. It is a curious phenomenon, that, within a few paces of it, as in the case of the hot springs of Arkansas, there is another spring perfectly cold.

New Mexico affords many interesting geological productions, of which the most useful to the natives is *yeso* or gypsum, which abounds in many places. Being found in foliated blocks, composed of laminæ, which are easily separated with a knife into sheets from the thickness of paper to that of window-glass, and almost as transparent as the latter, it is used to a great extent in the ranchos and villages for window-lights, for which indeed it is a tolerable substitute.

In several places about the borders of the *mesas* are to be found some beautiful specimens of petrified trees. One lies between Santa Fé and the Placer, broken into blocks since its petrifaction, which shows every knot, crack and splinter almost as natural as in its ligneous state. It is said that there are some of these arboreous petrifactions in the vicinity of Galisteo, still standing erect.

CHAPTER IX.

Domestic Animals and their Condition—Indifference on the subject of Horse-breeding—*Caballos de Silla*—Popularity and Usefulness of the Mule—Mode of harnessing and lading Mules for a Journey—*Arrieros* and their System—The *Mulera* or Bell-mare—Surprising feats of the Muleteers and *Vaqueros*—The *Lazo* and its uses—Ridiculous Usages of the country in regard to the Ownership of Animals—Anecdote of a Mexican Colonel—The *Burro* or domestic ass and its Virtues—Shepherds and their Habits—The Itinerant Herds of the Plains—Sagacity of the Shepherds' Dogs—The Sheep Trade—Destruction of Cattle by the Indians—Philosophical notions of the Marauders—Excellent Mutton—Goats and their Utility—Wild Animals and their Character—A 'Bear Scrape'—Wolves, Panthers, Wild Birds and Reptiles—The Honey-bee, etc.

NOTHING that has come within my sphere of observation in New Mexico, has astonished me more than the little attention that is paid to the improvement of domestic animals. While other nations have absolutely gone mad in their endeavors to better their breeds of horses, and have ransacked the four quarters of the world for the best blood and purest pedigrees, the New Mexicans, so justly celebrated for skilful horsemanship, and so much devoted to equestrian exercise, that they have been styled a race of centaurs, leave the propagation of their horses exclusively to chance; converting their best and handsomest steeds into saddle-horses.

Their race of *horses* is identical with that which is found running wild on the Prairies, familiarly known by the name of *mustang*. Although generally very small, they are quick, active and spirited: and were they not commonly so much injured in the breaking, they would perhaps be as hardy and long-lived as any other race in existence. Some of their *caballos de silla* or saddle-horses are so remarkably well trained, that they will stop suddenly upon the slightest check, charge against a wall without shrinking, and even attempt to clamber up its sides. In addition to this, a complete riding horse should have a peculiar up-and-down gait, affording all the exercise of the most violent trotter, while he gets over the ground so slowly as to enable the *caballero* to enjoy the 'pleasures' of a fatiguing ride of hours, without losing sight of his mistress's balcony.

The little attention paid to the breeding of horses in New Mexico, may perhaps be accounted for from the fact that, until lately, when the continued depredations of the hostile Indians discouraged them from their favorite pursuit, the people of the country had bestowed all their care in the raising of *mules*. This animal is in fact to the Mexican, what the camel has always been to the Arab—invaluable for the transportation of freight over sandy deserts and mountainous roads, where no other means of conveyance could be used to

such advantage. These mules will travel fo ＿
hundreds of miles with a load of the most
bulky and unwieldy articles, weighing frequently three or four hundred pounds.

The *Aparejo* (or pack-saddle, if it can be so
styled), is a large pad, consisting of a leathern
case stuffed with hay, which covers the back
of the mule and extends half way down on
both sides. This is secured with a wide sea-
grass bandage, with which the poor brute is
so tightly laced as to reduce the middle of its
body to half its natural size. During the
operation of lacing, the corseted quadruped
stands trembling in perfect agony, not an inapt
emblem of some fashionable exquisites who
are to be met with lounging on tip-toe, in all
the principal thoroughfares of large cities.

The muleteers contend that a tightly laced
beast, will travel, or at least support burdens,
with greater ease; and though they carry this
to an extreme, still we can hardly doubt that
a reasonable tension supports and braces the
muscles. It is necessary too for the *aparejo* to
be firmly bound on to prevent its slipping
and chafing the mule's back; indeed, with all
these precautions, the back, withers and sides
of the poor brute are often horribly mangled—
so much so that I have seen the rib-bones bare,
from day to day, while carrying a usual load
of three hundred pounds! The *aparejo* is also
furnished with a huge crupper, which often
lacerates the tail most shockingly. It is this
packing that leaves most of the lasting cica-
trices and marks so common upon Mexican
mules.

The *carga*, if a single package, is laid across the mule's back, but when composed of two, they are placed lengthwise, side by side; and being coupled with a cord, they are bound upon the aparejo with a long rope of sea-grass or raw-hide, which is so skilfully and tensely twined about the packages as effectually to secure them upon the animal. The mule is at first so tightly bound that it seems scarcely able to move; but the weight of the pack soon settles the aparejo, and so loosens the girths and cords as frequently to render it necessary to tighten them again soon after getting under way. It keeps most of the muleteers actively employed during the day, to maintain the packs in condition; for they often lose their balance and sometimes fall off. This is done without detaining the *atajo* (drove of pack-mules), the rest of which travel on while one is stopped to adjust its disordered pack. Indeed it is apt to occasion much trouble to stop a heavily laden *atajo;* for, if allowed a moment's rest, the mules are inclined to lie down, when it is with much difficulty they can rise again with their loads. In their efforts to do so they sometimes so strain their loins as to injure them ever after. The day's travel is made without a nooning respite; for the consequent unloading and reloading would consume too much time: and as a heavily-packed atajo should rarely continue *en route* more than five or six hours, the *jornada de recua* (day's journey of a pack-drove) is usually but twelve or fifteen miles.

It is truly remarkable to observe with what dexterity and skill the *Arrieros*, or muleteers, harness and adjust the packs of merchandise upon their beasts. Half a dozen usually suffice for forty or fifty mules. Two men are always engaged at a time in the dispatch of each animal, and rarely occupy five minutes in the complete adjustment of his *aparejo* and *carga*. In this operation they frequently demonstrate a wonderful degree of skill in the application of their strength. A single man will often seize a package, which, on a 'dead lift,' he could hardly have raised from the ground, and making a fulcrum of his knees and a lever of his arms and body, throw it upon the mule's back with as much apparent ease as if the effort cost him but little exertion. At stopping-places the task of unpacking is executed with still greater expedition. The packages are piled in a row upon the ground, and in case of rain the *aparejos* are laid upon them, over which is stretched a covering of *mantas de guangoche* (sheets of sea-grass texture), which protects the goods against the severest storms; a ditch also being cut around the pile, to prevent the water from running underneath. In this way freights are carried from point to point, and over the most rugged mountain passes at a much cheaper rate than foreigners can transport their merchandise in wagons, even through a level country. The cheapness of this mode of transportation arises from the very low wages paid to the *arrieros*, and the little expense incurred to feed

MEXICAN ARRIEROS WITH AN ATAJO OF PACK-MULES.

both them and the mules. The salary of the muleteer ranges from two to five dollars per month; and as their food seldom consists of anything else except corn and *frijoles*, it can be procured at very little cost. When the *arrieros* get any meat at all, it is generally at their own expense.

An *atajo* is conducted in a very systematic manner, each *arriero* having his appropriate sphere of action allotted to him. They have also their regulations and technicalities, which, if not as numerous, are about as unintelligible to the uninitiated as sailors' terms. One person, called the *savanero*, has the charge of the mules at night, which are all turned loose without tether or hopple, with the *mulera* or bell-mare, to prevent them from straying abroad. Although the attachment of the mules to the *mulera* appears very great, it seems to be about as much for the bell as for the animal. What the queen-bee is to a hive, so is the *mulera* to an *atajo*. No matter what may be the temper of a mule, it can seldom be driven away from her; and if she happen to be taken from among her associates, the latter immediately become depressed and melancholy, and ramble and whinny in every direction, as if they were completely lost. In addition to preparing food for the party, it is the office of the *madre* (or mother, as the cook of the company is facetiously called) to lead the *mulera* ahead, during the journey, after which the whole pack follows in orderly procession.

The muleteers, as well as the *vaqueros* (cow-herds), are generally mounted upon swift and well-trained horses, and in their management of the animals will often perform many surprising feats, which would grace an equestrian circus in any country; such, for instance, as picking up a dollar from the ground at every pass with the horse at full gallop. But the greatest display of skill and agility consists in their dextrous use of the *lazo* or *lareat*,* which is usually made of horse-hair, or sea-grass tightly twisted together, with a convenient noose at one end. Their aim is always more sure when the animal to be caught is running at full speed, for then it has no time to dodge the *lareat*. As soon as the noose is cast, the *lazador* fetches the end of his *lazo* a turn round the high pommel of his saddle, and by a quick manœuvre the wildest horse is brought up to a stand or topsy-turvy at his pleasure. By this process, the head of the animal is turned towards his subduer, who, in order to obtain the mastery over him more completely, seldom fails to throw a *bozal* (or half-hitch, as boatmen would say) around the nose, though at full rope's length.

If the object of pursuit happens to be a cow or an ox, the *lazo* is usually thrown about the horns instead of the neck. Two *vaqueros*,

---

* *Lasso* and *lariat*, as most usually written, are evidently corruptions of the Spanish *lazo* and *la reata* (the latter with the article *la* compounded), both meaning kinds of rope. I have therefore preferred retaining the orthography indicated by their etymology.

each with his rope to the horns, will thus subject the wildest and most savage bull, provided they are mounted upon well-trained steeds. While the infuriated animal makes a lunge at one of his pursuers, the other wheels round and pulls upon his rope, which always brings the beast about in the midst of his career; so that between the two he is jerked to and fro till he becomes exhausted and ceases to make any further resistance. The use of the lazo is not confined to the *arrieros* and *vaqueros*, although these generally acquire most skill in that exercise: it prevails in every rank of life; and no man, especially among the rancheros, would consider his education complete until he had learned this national accomplishment. They acquire it in fact from infancy; for it forms one of the principal rural sports of children, who may daily be seen with their *lazitos*, noosing the dogs and chickens about the yards, in every direction.

The lazo is often employed also as a 'weapon' both offensive and defensive. In skirmishes with the Indians, the mounted *vaquero*, if haplessly without arms, will throw this formidable object round the neck or the body of his enemy, who, before he has time to disencumber himself, is jerked to the ground and dragged away at full speed; when, if his brains are not beaten out against the stones, roots, or trees, he becomes at least so stunned and disabled that the *lazador* can dispatch him at his leisure. The panther, the bear, and other ferocious animals of the mountains and prairies, are also successfully attacked in this manner.

The laws and customs of the country with regard to the ownership of animals are very annoying to the inexperienced foreign traveller. No matter how many proprietors a horse or mule may have had, every one marks him with a huge hieroglyphic brand, which is called the *fierro*, and again, upon selling him, with his *venta*, or sale-brand; until at last these scars become so multiplied as to render it impossible for persons not versed in this species of 'heraldry,' to determine whether the animal has been properly *vented* or not: yet any *fierro* without its corresponding *venta* lays the beast liable to the claim of the brander. Foreigners are the most frequently subjected to this kind of imposition; and when a party of *estrangeros* enters any of the southern towns, they are immediately surrounded by a troop of loungers, who carefully examine every horse and mule; when, should they by chance discover any *unvented* brand, they immediately set to work to find some one with a branding-iron of the same shape, by which the beast is at once claimed and taken; for in all legal processes the only proof required of the claimant is his *fierro*, or branding-iron, which, if found to assimilate in shape with the mark on the animal, decides the suit in his favor. A colonel in Chihuahua once claimed a mule of me in this manner, but as I was convinced that I had bought it of the legitimate owner, I refused to give it up. The officer, unwilling to lose his prize, started immediately for the alcalde, in hopes of inducing that functionary to lend him the aid of the law; but during his absence I caused the shoulder of the animal to be shorn, so that the *venta* became distinctly visible. As soon as the discovery was made known to the colonel and his judge, they made a precipitate exit, as though conscious of detected fraud.

But while I fully acknowledge the pretensions of the mule, as an animal of general usefulness, I must not forget paying a passing tribute to that meek and unostentatious member of the brute family, the 'patient ass;' or, as it is familiarly called by the natives, *el burro*. This docile creature is here emphatically the 'poor man's friend,' being turned to an infinite variety of uses, and always submissive under the heaviest burdens. He is not only made to carry his master's grain, his fuel, his water, and his luggage, but his wife and his children. Frequently the whole family is stowed away together upon one diminutive donkey. In fact, the chief riding animal of the peasant is the *burro*, upon which saddle, bridle, or halter, is seldom used. The rider, seated astride his haunches instead of his back, guides the docile beast with a bludgeon which he carries in his hand.

Nothing, perhaps, has been more systematically attended to in New Mexico than the raising of *sheep*. When the territory was at the zenith of its prosperity, *ranchos* were to be met with upon the borders of every stream, and in the vicinity of every mountain where water was to be had. Even upon the arid and desert plains, and many miles away from brook or pond, immense flocks were driven out to pasture, and only taken to water once in two or three days. On these occasions it is customary for the shepherds to load their burros with *guages* filled with water, and return again with their folds to the plains. The *guage* is a kind of gourd, of which there are some beautiful specimens with two bulbs; the intervening neck serving to retain the cord by which it is carried.

These itinerant herds of sheep generally pass the night wherever the evening finds them, without cot or enclosure. Before nightfall the principal shepherd sallies forth in search of a suitable site for his *hato*, or temporary sheep-fold; and building a fire on the most convenient spot, the sheep generally draw near it of their own accord. Should they incline to scatter, the shepherd then seizes a torch and performs a circuit or two around the entire fold, by which manœuvre, in their efforts to avoid him, the heads of the sheep are all turned inwards; and in that condition they generally remain till morning, without once attempting to stray. It is unnecessary to add that the flock is well guarded during the night by watchful and sagacious dogs against prowling wolves or other animals of prey. The well-trained shepherd's dog of this country is indeed a prodigy: two or three of them will follow a flock of sheep for a dis tance of several miles as orderly as a shepherd, and drive them back to the pen again at night, without any other guidance than their own extraordinary instincts.

In former times there were extensive proprietors who had their *ranchos* scattered over half the province, in some cases amounting to from three to five hundred thousand head of sheep. The custom has usually been to farm out the ewes to the rancheros, who make a return of twenty per cent. upon the stock in merchantable *carneros*—a term applied to sheep generally, and particularly to wethers fit for market.

Sheep may be reckoned the staple production of New Mexico, and the principal article of exportation. Between ten and twenty years ago, about 200,000 head were annually driven to the southern markets; indeed, it is asserted, that, during the most flourishing times, as many as 500,000 were exported in one year. This trade has constituted a profitable business to some of the *ricos* of the country. They would buy sheep of the poor rancheros at from fifty to seventy-five cents per head, and sell them at from one to two hundred per cent. advance in the southern markets. A large quantity of wool is of course produced, but of an inferior quality. Inconsiderable amounts have been introduced into the United States *via* Missouri, which have sometimes been sold as low as fifteen cents per pound. It is bought, however, at the New Mexican ranchos at a very low rate—

three or four cents per pound, or (as more generally sold) per fleece, which will average, perhaps, but little over a pound. Yet, from the superiority of the pasturage and climate, New Mexico might doubtless grow the finest wool in the world. In conformity with their characteristic tardiness in improvement, however, the natives have retained their original stocks, which are wretchedly degenerate. They formerly sheared their flocks chiefly for their health, and rarely preserved the fleece, as their domestic manufactures consumed but a comparatively small quantity.

But the *ganado menor*, or small beasts of pasture (that is, sheep and goats in general), have of late been very much reduced in quantity; having suffered to a deplorable extent from the frequent inroads of the aboriginal 'lords of the soil,' who, every now and then, whenever hunger or caprice prompts them, attack the ranchos, murder the shepherds, and drive the sheep away in flocks of thousands. Indeed, the Indians have been heard to observe, that they would long before this have destroyed every sheep in the country, but that they prefer leaving a few behind for breeding purposes, in order that their Mexican shepherds may raise them new supplies!

The sheep of New Mexico are exceedingly small, with very coarse wool, and scarcely fit for anything else than mutton, for which, indeed, they are justly celebrated. Their flesh has a peculiarly delicious flavor, and is reckoned by epicures to be far superior to our best venison; owing probably in part to the excellence of the grass upon which they feed. The flesh of the sheep is to the New Mexican what that of the hog is to the people of our Western States,—while pork is but seldom met with in Northern Mexico. The sheep there are also remarkable for horny appendages, which frequently branch out in double or triple pairs, giving the head a very whimsical and grotesque appearance. I have seen some of them with at least six separate horns, each pointing in a different direction.

Although the raising of *goats* has not been made so much of a business as the raising of sheep, the former are nevertheless to be found in great abundance. Their milk is much more generally used than that of the cow, not only because it is sweeter and richer, but because the goat, like the *burro*, sustains itself upon the mere rubbish that grows in the mountain passes, and on the most barren hills, where cows could not exist without being regularly fed. The flesh of the goat is coarse, but wholesome, and being cheaper than mutton or beef, it is very freely used by the poor. That of the kid is hardly surpassed for delicacy and sweetness.

With regard to domestic *fowls*, it may be worthy of remark, that there is not to be found, as I believe, in all New Mexico, a single species (saving half a dozen turkeys perhaps, and a few pigeons), except the common hen, of which, however, there is a sufficient abundance. The goose, the duck, the peacock, etc., are altogether unknown.

Of wild animals there is not so great a variety as in the southern districts of the republic, where they are found in such abundance. The *black* and *grizzly bear*, which are met with in the mountains, do not appear to possess the great degree of ferocity, however, for which the latter especially is so much famed further north. It is true they sometimes descend from the mountains into the corn-fields, and wonderful stories are told of dreadful combats between them and the *labradores;* but judging from a little adventure I once witnessed, with an old female of the grizzly species, encountered by a party of us along the borders of the great prairies, I am not disposed to consider either their ferocity or their boldness very terrible.

Our company had just halted at noon, to take refreshments, when we perceived a group of these interesting animals,—a dam with a few cubs fully as large as common wolves,—busily scratching among the high grass in an adjacent valley, as if in search of roots or insects. Some of our party immediately started after the brutes, in hopes of getting a shot at them, in which, however, they were disappointed. One or two 'runners,' who had followed on horseback, then made a desperate charge upon the enemy, but the old monster fled to the thickets, without even so much as turning once upon her pursuers, although one of her cubs was killed, and the remainder were scattered in different directions, during the general scamper.

The sequel of the adventure served to confirm me in the opinion I had of the exaggerated stories in regard to these much dreaded animals. We had in our company a giant blacksmith and general repairer of wagons, named Campbell, who measured full six feet eight in his stockings, and was besides, elegantly proportioned. Independently of his universal utility as 'Jack-of-all-trades,' our colossal friend was in such constant requisition, that he might well have given origin to the western phrase of one's being 'a whole team;' for if a wagon happened to be in the mire, he was worth more than the whole team to extract it. He was, in short, the most appropriate subject for a regular grizzly-bear scrape. On the occasion I speak of, Campbell had laid himself down under the shade of a bush, upon the brink of a precipice about ten feet high, and was taking a comfortable snooze, while his companions were sporting in the neighborhood. During the chase, one of the young bears, which had been scared from its mother, was perceived loping down the trail towards our camp, apparently heedless of the company. Several of us seized our guns, and as it sprang across the ravine through a break near the spot where Campbell lay, we gave it a salute, which caused it to tumble back wounded into the branch, with a frightful yell. Campbell being suddenly roused by the noise, started up with the rapidity of lightning, and tumbled over the precipice upon the bear. "Whauh!" growled master bruin—"Murder!" screamed the giant—"Clinch it, Campbell, or you're gone!" exclaimed his comrades; for no one could venture to shoot for fear of killing the man. The latter, however, had no notion of closing clutches with his long-clawed antagonist, but busied himself in vain attempts to clamber up the steep bank; while the bear rising upon his hinder legs, and staring a moment at the huge frame of the blacksmith, soon made up his mind as to the expediency of 'turning tail,' and finally succeeded in making his escape, notwithstanding a volley of shot that were fired after him.

The large *gray wolf* of the Prairies is also to be found in great abundance in Northern Mexico. They sometimes make dreadful havoc among the cattle, frequently killing and devouring even mules and horses; but they never extend their rapacity so far as to attack human beings, unless urged by starvation. There are other animals of prey about the mountains, among which the panther is most conspicuous.

Elk and deer are also to be met with, but not in large quantities. Of the latter, the species known as the *black-tailed* deer is the most remarkable. It differs but little from the common buck, except that it is of darker color and its tail is bordered with black, and that, though its legs are shorter, its body is larger. The *carnero cimarron* or bighorn of the Rocky Mountains—the *berrendo* or antelope and the *tuza* or prairie dog of the plains—hares, polecats, and other animals of lesser importance, may also be considered as denizens of these regions.

Of wild *birds*, the water fowls are the most numerous; the ponds and rivers being literally lined at certain seasons of the year with myriads of geese, ducks, cranes, etc. In some of the mountains, wild turkeys are very numerous; but partridges and quails are scarce. There is to be found in Chihuahua and other southern districts a very beautiful bird called *paisano* (literally 'countryman'), which, when domesticated, performs all the offices of a cat in ridding the dwelling-houses of mice and other vermin. It is also said to kill and devour the rattlesnake; a reptile, however, which seems much less vicious here than elsewhere. Scorpions, tarantulas and centipedes also, although found in this province, are almost harmless, and very little dreaded by the natives. Another indigenous reptile is the horned-frog of the Prairies, known here by the name of *camaleon* (or chameleon), of which it is probably a species, as its color has been observed to vary a little in accordance with the character of the soil it inhabits.

The *honey-bee* would appear to have originated exclusively from the east, as its march has been observed westward, but none have yet reached this portion of the Mexican dominion. According to ancient historians, different species were indigenous to the south of the republic; but in the north, the only insect of the kind more resembles the bumble-bee than that of our hives; and builds in rocks and holes in the ground, in some parts of the mountains. They unite in but small numbers (some dozens together), and seldom make over a few ounces of honey, which is said, however, to be of agreeable flavor.

As to *flies*, like the high plains, this dry climate is but little infested—particularly with the more noxious kinds. Fresh meats are preserved and dried in mid-summer without difficulty, as there are very few blow-flies. Horse-flies are not seen except sometimes in the mountains: the prairie-fly, so tormenting to stock with us in the West, is unknown.

CHAPTER X.

Condition of the Arts and Sciences in New Mexico—Neglect of Education—Primary Schools—Geographical Ignorance—Female Accomplishments—Imported Refinements—Peculiarities of Language, etc.—Condition of the Public Press—State of Medical Science—The Mechanical Arts—Carpentry and Cabinet Work—State of Architecture—Dwelling Houses and their Peculiarities—Rustic Furniture—Curiously constructed Vehicles—Manufacture of Blankets—Other Fabrics—Want of Machinery.

THERE is no part of the civilized globe, perhaps, where the Arts have been so much neglected, and the progress of Science so successfully impeded as in New Mexico. Reading and writing may fairly be set down as the highest branches of education that are taught in the schools; for those pedants who occasionally pretend to teach arithmetic, very seldom understand even the primary rules of the science of numbers. I should perhaps make an exception in favor of those ecclesiastics, who have acquired their education abroad; and who, from their vocation, are necessarily obliged to possess a smattering of Latin. Yet it is a well known fact that the majority of this privileged class, even, are lamentably deficient in the more important branches of familiar science. I have been assured by a highly respectable foreigner, who has long resided in the country, that the questions were once deliberately put to him by a curate—whether Napoleon and Washington were not *one* and the *same* person, and whether Europe was not a province of Spain!

From the earliest time down to the secession of the colonies, it was always the policy of the Spanish Government as well as of the papal hierarchy, to keep every avenue of knowledge closed against their subjects of the New World; lest the lights of civil and religious liberty should reach them from their neighbors of the North. Although a system of public schools was afterwards adopted by the republic, which, if persevered in, would no doubt have contributed to the dissemination of useful knowledge, yet its operations had to be suspended about ten years ago, for want of the necessary funds to carry out the original project. It is doubtful, however, whether the habitual neglect and utter carelessness of the people, already too much inured to grope their way in darkness and in ignorance, added to the inefficiency of the teachers, would not eventually have neutralized all the good that such an institution was calculated to effect. The only schools now in existence, are of the lowest primary class, supported entirely by individual patronage, the liberal extension of which, may be inferred from the fact, that at least three-fourths of the present population can neither read nor write.

To illustrate the utter absence of geographical information among the humbler classes, it is only necessary to mention that I have been asked by persons, who have enjoyed a long intercourse with Americans, whether the United States was as large a place as the town of Santa Fé!

Female education has, if possible, been more universally neglected than that of the other sex; while those who have received any instruction at all, have generally been taught in private families. Indeed, until very lately, to be able to read and write on the part of a woman, was considered an indication of very extraordinary talent; and the fair damsel who could pen a billet-doux to her lover, was looked upon as almost a prodigy. There is, however, to be found among the higher classes a considerable sprinkling of that superficial refinement which is the bane of fashionable society everywhere, and which consists, not in superiority of understanding, not in acquired knowledge, but in that peculiar species of assumption, which has happily been styled "the flowing garment with which Ignorance decks herself."

Yet, notwithstanding this dreadful state of ignorance on all those subjects which it behooves man to be acquainted with, it is truly astonishing to notice the correctness with which the common people speak their mother tongue, the Spanish. The application of words out of their classical sense may occasionally occur, but a violation of the simple grammatical rules (which is so common among the illiterate who use the English language), is extremely rare. In pronunciation, the only material difference between them and the Castilian race, consists in the adoption of certain provincialisms, which can hardly be ranked as defects. Thus, instead of giving *c* before *e* and *i*, and *z* in all cases, the Castilian lisp of *th* as in *thin*, they sound both like *s* in *sin;* and instead of pronouncing *ll* as the Italian liquid *gl* in *seraglio*, they sound this double letter precisely like *y* in *yes;* and in writing, frequently confound the *ll* and *y* indiscriminately together. These may be considered as their only peculiarities of pronunciation, and they prevail through most sections of the republic. In fact, this point of difference is looked upon by many with national pride, as distinguishing their language from that of their former oppressors. They have also adopted many significant Indian words from their aboriginal predecessors and neighbors, which serve to embellish and amplify this already beautiful and copious language.

In nothing is the deplorable state of things already noticed made more clearly manifest, than in the absence of a public press. There has never been a single newspaper or periodical of any kind published in New Mexico, except in the year 1834, when a little foolscap sheet (entitled *El Crepúsculo*) was issued weekly, for about a month, to the tune of fifty subscribers, and was then abandoned, partially for want of patronage and partially because the editor had accomplished his object of procuring his election to Congress. Indeed, the only printing press in the country is a small affair which was brought the same year across the prairies from the United States, and is now employed occasionally in printing billets, primers and Catholic catechisms. This literary negligence is to be attributed, not more to the limited number of reading people, than to those injudicious restrictions upon that freedom of the press, which is so essential to its prosperity. An editor attempting to arraign the conduct of public functionaries, or to oppose 'the powers that be,' is sure to subject himself to persecution, and most probably suspension, a tyrannical course of proceeding which has checked the career of two or three papers even among the more enlightened inhabitants of Chihuahua; where a miserable organ of the Government is still occasionally issued from the office of the *Imprenta del Gobierno,* or Government Press. No wonder then that the people of Northern Mexico are so much behind their neighbors of the United States in intelligence, and that the pulse of national industry and liberty beats so low!

Medical science is laboring under similar disadvantages; there being not a single native physician in the province*; although a great multitude of singular cures are daily performed with indigenous roots and herbs that grow

---

* Neither is there a professed lawyer in New Mexico: a fact which at least speaks favorably of the state of litigation in the country.

in abundance all over the country. But lest a knowledge of this scarcity of doctors should induce some of the Esculapian faculty to strike for Santa Fé in quest of fortune, I would remark that the country affords very poor patronage. Foreign physicians who have visited New Mexico, have found the practice quite unprofitable; not more for the want of patients, than on account of the poverty of the people. Nine-tenths of those who are most subject to disease, are generally so destitute of means, that the only return they can make, is, "*Dios se lo pague*" (May God pay you!) Even the more affluent classes do not hesitate sometimes to liquidate their bills in the same currency. A French doctor of Santa Fé, who had been favored with too many payments of this description, was wont to rebuke their "*Dios se lo pague*" with a "*No, señor, su bolsa me lo pagará*"—No, sir, your purse shall pay me!

The mechanical arts have scarcely risen above the condition they were found in among the aborigines. Gold and silversmiths are perhaps better skilled in their respective trades than any other class of artisans whatever; as the abundance of precious metals in former days, and the ruling passion of the people for ostentatious show, gave a very early stimulus to the exercise of this peculiar talent. Some mechanics of this class have produced such singular specimens of ingenious workmanship, that on examining them, we are almost unwilling to believe that rude art could accomplish so much. Even a bridle-bit or a pair of spurs it would no doubt puzzle the 'cutest' Yankee to fashion after a Mexican model—such as I have seen manufactured by the commonest blacksmiths of the country.

In carpentry and cabinet-work the mechanic has to labor to great disadvantage, on account of a want of tools and scarcity of suitable timber. Their boards have to be hewed out with the axe—sawed lumber being absolutely unknown throughout New Mexico, except what is occasionally cut by foreigners. The axe commonly used for splitting and hewing is formed after the model of those clumsy hatchets known as 'squaw-axes' among Indian traders. Yet this is not unfrequently the only tool of the worker in wood: a cart or a plough is often manufactured without even an auger, a chisel, or a drawing-knife.

In architecture, the people do not seem to have arrived at any great perfection, but rather to have conformed themselves to the clumsy style which prevailed among the aborigines, than to waste their time in studying modern masonry and the use of lime. The materials generally used for building are of the crudest possible description; consisting of unburnt bricks, about eighteen inches long by nine wide and four thick, laid in mortar of mere clay and sand. These bricks are called *adobes*, and every edifice, from the church to the *palacio*, is constructed of the same stuff. In fact, I should remark, perhaps, that though all

Southern Mexico is celebrated for the magnificence and wealth of its churches, New Mexico deserves equal fame for poverty-stricken and shabby-looking houses of public worship.

The general plan of the Mexican dwellings is nearly the same everywhere. Whether from motives of pride, or fear of the savages, the wealthier classes have adopted the style of Moorish castles; so that all the larger buildings have more the appearance of so many diminutive fortifications, than of private family residences. Let me add, however, that whatever may be the roughness of their exterior, they are extremely comfortable inside. A tier of rooms on each side of a square, comprising as many as the convenience of the occupant may require, encompass an open *patio* or court, with but one door opening into the street,—a huge gate, called *la puerta del zaguan*, usually large enough to admit the family coach. The back tier is generally occupied with the *cocina, dispensa, granero* (kitchen, provision-store, and granary), and other offices of the same kind. Most of the apartments, except the winter rooms, open into the *patio;* but the latter are most frequently entered through the *sala* or hall, which, added to the thickness of their walls and roofs, renders them delightfully warm during the cold season, while they are perfectly cool and agreeable in summer. In fact, hemmed in as these apartments are with nearly three feet of earth, they may be said to possess all the pleasant properties of cellars, with a freer circulation of air, and nothing of the dampness which is apt to pervade those subterranean regions.

The roofs of the houses are all flat *azoteas* or terraces, being formed of a layer of earth two or three feet in thickness, and supported by stout joists or horizontal rafters. These roofs, when well packed, turn the rain off with remarkable effect, and render the houses nearly fire-proof.* The *azotea* also forms a pleasant promenade, the surrounding walls rising usually so high as to serve for a balustrade, as also a breast-work, behind which, in times of trouble, the combatants take their station, and defend the premises.

The floors are all constructed of beaten earth 'slicked over' with soft mortar, and covered generally with a coarse carpet of domestic manufacture. A plank floor would be quite a curiosity in New Mexico; nor have I met with one even in Chihuahua, although the best houses in that city are floored with brick or squares of hewn stone. The interior of each apartment is roughly plastered over with a clay mortar unmixed with lime, by females who supply the place of trowels with their hands. It is then white washed with

---

* During a residence of nearly nine years in the country, I never witnessed but one fire, and that was in the mining town of Jesus Maria. There a roof of pine clap-boards is usually extended over the *azotea*, to protect it against the mountain torrents of rain. This roof was consumed, but the principal damage sustained, in addition, was the burning of a huge pile of corn and some bags of flour, which were in the garret: the body of the building remained nearly *in statu quo*.

calcined *yeso* or gypsum, a deleterious stuff, that is always sure to engraft its affections upon the clothing of those who come in contact with it. To obviate this, the parlors and family rooms are usually lined with wall-paper or calico, to the height of five or six feet. The front of the house is commonly plastered in a similar manner, although not always whitewashed. In the suburbs of the towns, and particularly in the villages and ranchos, a fantastic custom prevails of painting only a portion of the fronts of the houses, in the shape of stripes, which imparts to the landscape a very striking and picturesque appearance.

Wood buildings of any kind or shape are utterly unknown in the north of Mexico, with the exception of an occasional picket-hut in some of the ranchos and mining-places. It will readily be perceived, then, what a flat and uncouth appearance the towns of New Mexico present, with houses that look more like so many collections of brick-kilns prepared for burning than human abodes.

The houses of the villages and ranchos are rarely so spacious as those of the capital, yet their construction is much the same. Some very singular subterrene dwellings are to be found in a few places. I was once passing through the village of Casa Colorada, when I observed some noisy urchins just before me, who very suddenly and mysteriously disappeared. Upon resorting to the spot, I perceived an aperture under a hillock, which, albeit considerably larger, was not very unlike the habitations of the little prairie dogs.

The immense expense attending the purchase of suitable furniture and kitchen-ware, indeed, the frequent impossibility of obtaining these articles at any price, caused the early settlers of Northern Mexico to resort to inventions of necessity, or to adopt Indian customs altogether, many of which have been found so comfortable and convenient, that most of those who are now able to indulge in luxuries, feel but little inclination to introduce any change. Even the few pine-board chairs and settees that are to be found about the houses are seldom used; the prevailing fashion being to fold mattrasses against the walls, which, being covered over with blankets, are thus converted into sofas. Females, indeed, most usually prefer accommodating themselves, *à l'Indienne*, upon a mere blanket spread simply upon the floor.

Wagons of Mexican manufacture are not to be found; although a small number of American-built vehicles, of those introduced by the trading caravans, have grown into use among the people. Nothing is more calculated to attract the curiosity of strangers than the unwieldy *carretas* or carts of domestic construction, the massive wheels of which are generally hewed out of a large cottonwood. This, however, being rarely of sufficient size to form the usual diameter, which is about five feet, an additional segment or felloe is pinned upon each edge, when the whole is fashioned into an irregular circle. A crude pine or cottonwood pole serves for the axle-tree, upon which is tied a rough frame of the same material for a body. In the construction of these *carretas* the use of iron is, for the most part, wholly dispensed with; in fact, nothing is more common than a cart, a plough, and even a mill, without a particle of iron or other metal about them. To this huge truckle it is necessary to hitch at least three or four yokes of oxen; for even a team of six would find it difficult to draw the load of a single pair with an ordinary cart. The labor of the oxen is much increased by the Mexican mode of harnessing, which appears peculiarly odd to a Yankee. A rough pole serves for a yoke, and, with the middle tied to the cart-tongue, the extremities are placed across the heads of the oxen behind the horns, to which they are firmly lashed with a stout rawhide thong. Thus the head is maintained in a fixed position, and they pull, or rather push by the force of the neck, which, of course, is kept continually strained upwards.

Rough and uncouth as these *carretas* always are, they constitute nevertheless the 'pleasure-carriages' of the rancheros, whose families are conveyed in them to the towns, whether to market, or to *fiestas*, or on other joyful occasions. It is truly amusing to see these rude vehicles bouncing along upon their irregularly rounded wheels, like a limping bullock, and making the hills and valleys around vocal with the echo of their creaking and frightful sounds.

The New Mexicans are celebrated for the manufacture of coarse blankets, which is an article of considerable traffic between them and the southern provinces, as also with the neighboring Indians, and on some occasions with the United States. The finer articles are curiously woven in handsome figures of various colors. These are of different qualities, the most ordinary being valued at about two dollars apiece, while those of the finest texture, especially their imitations of the *Sarape Navajó*, will sell for twenty dollars or more. There have also been made in New Mexico a few imitations of the *Sarape Saltillero*,—the blanket of Saltillo, a city of the south celebrated for the manufacture of the most splendid fancy blankets, singularly figured with all the colors of the rainbow. These are often sold for more than fifty dollars each. What renders the weaving of the fancy blankets extremely tedious, is, that the variegation of colors is all effected with the shuttle, the texture in other respects being perfectly plain, without even a twill. An additional value is set upon the fine *sarape* on account of its being a fashionable substitute for a cloak. Indeed, the inferior sarape is the only overdress used by the peasantry in the winter.

Besides blankets, the New Mexicans manufacture a kind of coarse twilled woollen stuff, called *gerga*, which is checkered with black and white, and is used for carpets, and also by the peasantry for clothing, which, in fact, with some other similar domestic stuffs, together with buckskin, constituted almost the only article of wear they were possessed of, till the trade from Missouri furnished them with foreign fabrics at more reasonable prices than they had been in the habit of paying to the traders of the southern provinces. Their domestic textures are nearly all of wool, there being no flax or hemp* and but little cotton spun. The manufacture even of these articles is greatly embarrassed for want of good spinning and weaving machinery. Much of the spinning is done with the *huso* or *malacate* (the whirligig spindle), which is kept whirling in a bowl with the fingers while the thread is drawn. The dexterity with which the females spin with this simple apparatus is truly astonishing.

* Hemp is unknown in this province, and flax, as has before been remarked, though indigenous, is nowhere cultivated. "The court of Spain (as Clavigero tells us, speaking of Michuacan, New Mexico, and Quivira, where he says flax was to be found in great abundance), informed of the regions adapted to the cultivation of this plant, sent to those countries, about the year 1778, twelve families from the valley of Granada, for the purpose of promoting so important a branch of agriculture." The enterprise seems never to have been prosecuted, however—at least in New Mexico.

CHAPTER XI.

Style of Dress in New Mexico—Riding-dress of the Caballero—Horse Trappings—The *Rebozo*—Passion for Jewelry—Apparel of the Female Peasantry—'Wheeled Tarantulas'—General Appearance of the People—Tawny Complexion—Singular Mode of Painting the Human Face—Striking Traits of Character—Alms-giving—Beggars and their Tricks—Wonderful Cure of Paralysis—Lack of Arms and Officers—Traits of Boldness among the Yeomanry—Politeness and Suavity of the Mexicans—Remarks of Mr. Poinsett—Peculiarities observed in epistolary Intercourse—Salutations—*La Siesta*.

THE best society in the interior of New Mexico is fast conforming to European fashion, in the article of dress, with the exception of the peculiar riding costume, which is still worn by many *caballeros*. This generally consists of a *sombrero*—a peculiarly shaped low crowned hat with wide brim, covered with oil-cloth and surmounted with a band of tinsel cord nearly an inch in diameter: a *chaqueta* or jacket of cloth gaudily embroidered with braid and fancy barrel-buttons: a curiously shaped article called *calzoneras*, intended for pantaloons, with the outer part of the legs open from hip to ankle—the borders set with tinkling filigree buttons, and the whole fantastically trimmed with tinsel lace and cords of the same materials. As suspenders do not form a component part of a regular Mexican costume, the nether garment is supported by a rich sash which is drawn very tightly around the body, and contributes materially to render the whole appearance of the *caballero* extremely picturesque. Then there are the *botas* which somewhat resemble the leggins worn by the bandits of Italy, and are made of embossed leather, embroidered with fancy silk and tinsel thread and bound around the knee with curiously tasselled garters. The *sarape saltillero* (a fancy blanket) completes the picture. This peculiarly useful as well as ornamental garment is commonly carried dangling carelessly across the pommel of the saddle, except in bad weather, when it is drawn over the shoulders, after the manner of a Spanish cloak, or as is more frequently the case, the rider puts his head through a slit in the middle, and by letting it hang loosely from the neck, his whole person is thus effectually protected.

The steed of the caballero is caparisoned in the same pompous manner, the whole of the saddle trappings weighing sometimes over a hundred pounds. First of all we have the high pommel of the saddle-tree crowned with silver, and the 'hinder tree' garnished with the same, and a quilted cushion adjusted to the seat. The *coraza* is a cover of embossed leather embroidered with fancy silk and tinsel, with ornaments of silver, and is thrown loose over the cushion and *fuste* or saddle-tree, the

extremities of which protrude through appropriate apertures. Then comes the *cola de pato*, literally 'duck's tail' (it were more appropriately called 'peacock's tail'), a sort of leathern housing, also gaudily ornamented to correspond with the *coraza*, attached to the hind-tree, and covering the entire haunches of the animal. The *estribos* or stirrups are usually made either of bent or mortised wood, fancifully carved, over which are fastened the *tapaderas* or coverings of leather to protect the toes. Formerly the stirrups constituted a complete slipper, mortised in a solid block of wood, which superseded the use of *tapaderas*. But one of the most costly articles of the saddle-suit is perhaps the bridle, which is sometimes of entire silver, or otherwise heavily ornamented with silver buckles, slides and stars. To this is appended a massive bit, sometimes of pure silver, but more commonly of iron, most singularly wrought. The spurs are generally of iron, though silver spurs are very frequent. The shanks of the *vaquero* spurs are three to five inches long, with rowels sometimes six inches in diameter. I have in my possession a pair of these measuring over ten inches from one extremity to another, with rowels five and three-fourths inches in diameter, weighing two pounds and eleven ounces. Last, not least, there are the *armas de pelo*, being a pair of shaggy goat skins (richly trimmed across the top with embroidered leather), dangling from the pommel of the saddle for the purpose of being drawn over the legs in case of rain, or as a protection against brush and brambles. The *corazas* of travelling saddles are also provided with several pockets called *coginillos*—a most excellent contrivance for carrying a lunch or bottle, or anything to which convenient access may be desired.

In former times there was a kind of harness of leather attached to the saddle behind, covering the hinder parts of the horse as low as mid-thighs, with its lower border completely fringed with jingling iron tags, but these are now seldom met with in the North. Even without this noisy appendage, however, a Mexican caballero of the present day, with full equestrian rigging, his clink and his rattle, makes altogether a very remarkable appearance.

Though the foregoing description refers par

ticularly to the chivalrous caballero of the South—the *rico* of the country, yet similar modes of costume and equipage, but of coarser material, are used by the lower classes. Nor are they restricted among these to the riding-dress, but are very generally worn as ordinary apparel. Common velveteens, fustians, blue drillings and similar stuffs, are very much in fashion among such rancheros and *villageois* as are able to wear anything above the ordinary woollen manufactures of the country. Coarse wool hats, or of palm-leaf (*sombreros de petate*), all of low crowns, are the kind generally worn by the common people.

As I have already observed, among the better classes the European dress is now frequently worn; although they are generally a year or two behind our latest fashions. The ladies, however, never wear either hat, cap or bonnet, except for riding; but in lieu of it, especially when they walk abroad, the *rebozo* (or scarf), or a large shawl, is drawn over the head. The *rebozo* is by far the most fashionable: it is seven or eight feet in length by nearly a yard in width, and is made of divers stuffs—silk, linen or cotton, and usually variegated and figured in the warp by symmetrically disposed threads waved in the dying. It is certainly a beautiful specimen of domestic manufacture. The finest articles are valued at fifty to a hundred dollars in the North; but the ordinary cotton *rebozo* ranges at from one to five dollars, and is generally worn by the lower classes. A Mexican female is scarcely ever seen without her rebozo or shawl, except when it is laid aside for the dance. In-doors, it is loosely thrown about her person, but in the promenade it is coquettishly drawn over the head, and one end of it brought round, and gracefully hooked over the opposite shoulder. As a favorite modern authoress justly remarks, however, in speaking of the rebozo and the sarape, an important objection to their use, in this unsettled society, is the facility they afford for the concealment of the person, as well as secret weapons of the wearer. Pistols, knives, and even swords are carried unsuspected under the sarape, while a lady fashionably muffled with a rebozo, may pass a crowd of familiar acquaintances without being recognized.

The ordinary apparel of the female peasantry and the *rancheras*, is the *enaguas* or petticoat of home-made flannel; or, when they are able to procure it, of coarse blue or scarlet cloth, connected to a wide list of some contrasting-colored stuff, bound around the waist over a loose white chemise, which is the only covering for the body, except the rebozo. Uncouth as this costume may appear at first, it constitutes nevertheless a very graceful sort of undress—in which capacity it is used even by ladies of rank.

The New Mexican ladies are all passionately fond of jewelry; and they may commonly be seen, with their necks, arms and fingers loaded with massive appendages of a valuable description. But as there has been so much imposition with regard to foreign jewelry, articles of native manufacture, some of which are admirably executed, without alloy or counterfeit, are generally preferred.

In New Mexico, *coches de paseo* of any kind are very rare; occasionally, however, one of those huge, clumsy, old-fashioned vehicles of Mexican manufacture, so abundant in the southern cities, and often nick-named 'wheeled tarantulas,' by strangers, may be seen. Such an apparition in a Yankee city would excite as much curiosity as a caravan of the rarest animals. The coach alone is a load for two mules, therefore the vehicle is usually drawn by four and sometimes six, and invariably driven by postillions.

The stature of both sexes in New Mexico is commonly below medium: but they are mostly well proportioned, of athletic make, and sound, healthy constitutions. Their complexion is generally dark; but every variety of shade is found among them, from the lightest European tint to the swarthiest hue. Their darkness has resulted partly from their original Moorish blood, but more from intermarriages with the aborigines. An occasional Indian, and sometimes an entire village, have abandoned their wonted seclusion, and become identified with their conquerors. In the North, the system of Indian slavery has contributed still more to the same result. They buy the captive children of both sexes of the wild tribes, taken prisoners among each other, or by the Pueblos in their petty wars with the former—and indeed by the Mexicans themselves—who are generally held in bondage to the age of twenty-one years, and some, from ignorance, their whole lives. Such as resume their liberty, intermarry with the race of their masters, becoming Mexican citizens, often undistinguishable from many of the already dark-hued natives. The present race of New Mexicans has thus become an amalgam, averaging about equal parts of the European and aboriginal blood. The peasantry, as well from a more general intermixture with the Indian, as from exposure, are the darkest; yet the tawny complexion pervades all classes —the rich as well as the poor.

The females, although many of them are about as broad-featured as the veriest Indian, not unfrequently possess striking traits of beauty. They are remarkable for small feet and handsome figures, notwithstanding their profound ignorance of the 'refined art' of lacing. The belles of the ranchos and villages have a disgusting habit of besmearing their faces with the crimson juice of a plant or fruit called *alegría*, which is not unlike blood; as also with clay and starch. This is not intended, as some travellers have supposed, as a beautifying appendage, but for the purpose of protecting the skin from the sun. A country beauty will often remain in this filthy condition for a whole fortnight, in order to appear to advantage at some favorite feast or ball; when, by washing off the paint, the cheeks look as fresh and ruddy as the natural darkness of their skin will permit.

The New Mexicans appear to have inherited much of the cruelty and intolerance of their ancestors, and no small portion of their bigotry and fanaticism. Being of a highly imaginative temperament and of rather accommodating moral principles—cunning, loquacious, quick of perception and sycophantic, their conversation frequently exhibits a degree of tact—a false glare of talent, eminently calculated to mislead and impose. They have no stability except in artifice; no profundity except for intrigue: qualities for which they have acquired an unenviable celebrity. Systematically cringing and subservient while out of power, as soon as the august mantle of authority falls upon their shoulders, there are but little bounds to their arrogance and vindictiveness of spirit. While such are the general features of the character of the Northern Mexicans, however, I am fain to believe and acknowledge, that there are to be found among them numerous instances of uncompromising virtue, good faith and religious forbearance.

But taking the Northern Mexicans without distinction of class or degree, there is scarcely a race of people on the face of the earth more alive to the dictates of charity—that is, almsgiving; which is more owing perhaps to the force of religious instruction than to real sympathy for the sufferings of the indigent and the helpless. The law making no provision for paupers, there is no country perhaps more infested with beggars, especially from Chihuahua south. In the large cities, Saturday is the alms-giving day by custom; and on such occasions the *limosneros* (as the mendicant race is called), may be seen promenading the streets in gangs of thirty or forty, or in smaller numbers, performing genuflections at every nook and corner of the town, each croaking aloud his favorite set of orisons and inviting the blessings of heaven upon every man, woman or child, who may have been so fortunate as to propitiate the benison by casting a few *clacos* into his outstretched hand. In some sections of the country, this system of begging has proved so successful that parents have actually been known to maim and deform their children, during the earliest stages of infancy, in order to fit them for the trade, and thereby secure to themselves a constant source of emolument for the remainder of their lives. Persons affecting disease and frequently malformation for the purpose of exciting the commiseration of the wayfarer, are also extremely numerous. I had often observed in Chihuahua a robust-looking fellow, who, to all appearance, had partially lost the use of his lower extremities, sliding about the streets from door to door upon a sort of cushion, asking alms. One fine day, a furious bull, pursued by some *vaqueros*, came plunging down in the direction where he sat, moaning and grieving most piteously; when, forgetting his physical disabilities, he sprang to his feet with the agility of a dancing master, and incontinently betook himself to his heels.

The Northern Mexicans have often been branded with cowardice: a stigma which may well be allowed to rest upon the wealthier classes, and the city-bred caballeros, from whose ranks are selected the military leaders who decide the fate of battles. But the rancheros, or as they might be still more appropriately styled—the yeomanry of the country, inured as they are from their peculiar mode of life to every kind of fatigue and danger, possess a much higher calibre of moral courage. Their want of firmness in the field, is partially the result of their want of confidence in their commanders; while the inefficacy and worthlessness of their weapons are alone sufficient to inspire even a valiant heart with dismal forebodings. It is true that most of the regular troops are provided with English muskets, which, by the way, they are generally too ignorant to keep in order; but a great portion of the militia are obliged to use the clumsy old-fashioned *escopeta*, or firelock of the sixteenth century; while others have nothing but the bow and arrow, and sometimes the lance, which is in fact a weapon very much in use throughout the country. I have seen persons of the lower class do things, however, which would really seem to indicate a superlative degree of courage. Some of them will often perform journeys alone through wildernesses teeming with murderous savages; but as they not unfrequently embark upon these perilous jaunts unarmed, it is evident they depend greatly upon good luck and swiftness of limbs, and still more upon the protection of their favorite saint, *la Virgen de Guadalupe.*

The Mexicans, like the French, are remarkable for their politeness and suavity of manners. You cannot visit a friend but he assures you that, "*Está V. en su casa, y puede mandar,*" etc. (You are in your own house, and can command, etc.), or, "*Estoy enteramente á su disposicion*" (I am wholly at your disposal), without, however, meaning more than an expression of ordinary courtesy. Nor can you speak in commendation of any article, let its value be what it may; but the polite owner immediately replies, "*Tómelo, V. Señor; es suyo* (Take it, sir; it is yours), without the slightest intention or expectation that you should take him at his word.—Mr. Poinsett observes, "Remember, when you take leave of a Spanish grandee, to bow as you leave the room, at the head of the stairs, where the host accompanies you; and after descending the first flight, turn round and you will see him expecting a third salutation, which he returns with great courtesy, and remains until you are out of sight; so that as you wind down the stairs, if you catch a glimpse of him, kiss your hand, and he will think you a most accomplished cavalier." Graphic as this short sketch is, it hardly describes the full measure of Mexican politeness; for in that country, when the visitor reaches the street, another tip of the hat, and another inclination of the head, will be expected by the attentive host, who gently waves, with his hand, a final '*á dios*' from a window.

In epistolary correspondence, the ratio of respect is generally indicated by the width of the left margin. If the letter is addressed to an equal, about one-fourth of the page is occupied for that purpose; but when extraordinary respect is intended to be shown to a superior, nearly one-half of the page is left a blank. There are other marks of civility and respect peculiar to the country, which among us would be accounted absolute servility.

In their salutations, the ancient custom of close embrace, not only between individuals of the same sex, but between those of different sexes, is almost universal. It is quite a luxury to meet a pretty señorita after some absence. The parties approach, shake hands in a cordial manner, and without loosening the grasp, the left arm of each is brought about the other's waist; and while a gentle embrace brings their persons closer to each other, the contact of the cheeks becomes inevitable—without admitting a kiss, however, which would be held as decidedly indelicate. In short, it is worth while absenting oneself, for the gratification of a first meeting with the prettier of one's female friends upon the return.

Among the least unpleasant customs of this country is that of the *siesta* or afternoon nap; a species of indulgence in which all classes are prone to share. The stores, private and public offices, are, by common consent, generally closed at one o'clock (that being the usual dinner hour), and not reopened till three. During that interval nearly every kind of business and labor is suspended. The streets are comparatively deserted; the rich and the poor retire to their respective couches, and remain wrapped in slumber, or 'thinking o' nothing,' till the loud peal of the three o'clock bell warns them to resume their occupations.

CHAPTER XII.

Government of New Mexico—The Administration of Justice—Judicial Corruption—Prejudices against Americans—Partiality for the English—Anecdote of Governor Armijo and a Trapper—Outrage upon an American Physician—Violence suffered by the American Consul and others—Arbitrary Impositions upon Foreigners—*Contribucion de Guerra*—The Alcaldes and their System—The *Fueros*—Mode of punishing Delinquents and Criminals—Mexican System of Slavery—Thieves and Thieveries—Outrage upon an American Merchant—Gambling and Gambling-houses—Game of *Monte*—Anecdote of a Lady of Fashion—*Chuza*—Cockpits—*Correr el gallo*—*El Coleo*—Fandangoes—*Cigarritos*.

PRIOR to the adoption of the *Sistema Central* in the Mexican republic, the province of New Mexico was under a territorial government. The executive was called *Gefe Político* (political chief), and the *Diputacion Provincial* very inefficiently supplied the place of a legislature. Under the present system, however, New Mexico being a *department*, the names of these powers have been changed. but their functions remain very nearly the same. The *Gobernador* (governor) is appointed by the President for eight years. The legislative power is nominally vested in a *Junta Departamental*, a kind of state council, with very circumscribed powers, somewhat analogous to, and certainly not more extensive than, those of a board of aldermen with us. But even this shadow of popular representation was 'prorogued' by Gov. Armijo soon after his accession to power (five or six years ago), and has never since been convened; so that its functions have been arbitrarily exercised by the governor ever since.

The administration of the laws in Northern Mexico constitutes one of the most painful features of her institutions. Justice, or rather judgments, are a common article of traffic; and the hapless litigant who has not the means to soften the claws of the alcalde with a 'silver unction,' is almost sure to get severely scratched in the contest, no matter what may be the justice of his cause, or the uprightness of his character. It is easy to perceive, then, that the poor and the humble stand no chance in a judicial contest with the wealthy and consequential, whose influence, even apart from their facilities for corrupting the court and suborning witnesses, is sufficient to neutralize any amount of plebeian testimony that might be brought against them.

The evil consequences arising from mal-administration of justice in New Mexico are most severely felt by foreigners, against whom a strong prejudice prevails throughout the South. Of these, the citizens of the United States are by far the most constant sufferers; an inevitable result of that sinister feeling with which the 'rival republic' views the advancement and superiority of her more industrious neighbors. It is a notorious fact, that while the English are universally treated with comparative consideration and respect, the Americans residing in the southern parts of the republic are frequently taunted with the effeminacy of their government and its want of decision. So openly has this preference for British subjects been manifested, and so thoroughly conscious have the Americans become of the humiliating fact, that when a mercantile firm, consisting of an American and an Englishman, has occasion to present a memorial of any description, or to sue either for an act of favor or of justice from the nation, the application is sure to be made in the name of the latter, knowing it will thus be more likely to command proper attention.

Few men, perhaps, have done more to jeopard the interests of American traders, or to bring the American character itself into contempt, than Armijo, the present arbitrary governor of New Mexico. I am happy to say, however, that in the midst of his many oppressions, he was once at least obliged to 'knock under' to one of those bold and daring spirits of the Rocky Mountains whom obstacles rather energize than subdue. This was about the year 1828, during Armijo's previous governorship. A law was then in existence which had been enacted by the general Congress prohibiting foreigners from trapping beaver in the Mexican territory, under penalty of confiscation, etc.; but as there were no native trappers in New Mexico, Gov. Baca and his successor (Narbona) thought it expedient to extend licenses to foreigners, in the name of citizens, upon condition of their taking a certain proportion of Mexicans to learn the art of trapping. In pursuance of this disposition, Gov. Narbona extended a license to one Ewing Young, who was accompanied by a Mr. Sublette, brother of Capt. Wm. Sublette, and almost equally celebrated for his mountain adventures. Previous to the return of this party from their trapping expedition, Armijo had succeeded Narbona in office, and they were informed that it was his intention to seize their furs. To prevent this, they deposited them at a neighboring village, where they were afterwards discovered, seized, and confiscated. The furs being damp, they were spread out in the sun before the *Guardia*, in Santa Fé, when Sublette, perceiving two packs of beaver which had been his own property, got by honest labor, instantly seized them and carried them away before the eyes of the whole garrison, and concealed both them and his own person in a house opposite. The entire military force was immediately put in requisition, and a general search made for the offender and his prize; but in vain: indeed, if the truth must be spoken, the troops seemed to have as little desire to find Sublette as the latter had of being found; for his character was too well known to leave any room for hope that his capture could be effected without a great deal of trouble. In the meanwhile, Armijo raved, and threatened the Americans for not ferreting out their countryman and delivering him over to justice. Failing to produce any impression by blustering, however, he caused a couple of cannons to be pointed at the house where the offender was supposed to be concealed, declaring at the same time that he would batter it down; but all to no purpose. Mr. Sublette finally conveyed his furs in safety to the frontier, and thence to the United States.

The following anecdote affords another illustration of Armijo's summary mode of dealing with Americans. In the fall of 1840, a gross outrage was committed upon a physician from Massachusetts (said to be a gentleman of unexceptionable deportment), who was travelling through the country for his health. He had loaned nine hundred dollars to a person of the name of Tayon, who afterwards borrowed the same amount of another foreigner and repaid this debt. The doctor then left for the South, where he intended to pass the winter, being afflicted with a pulmonary disease. But the individual who had lent Tayon the money, being informed that he was insolvent, applied to Gov. Armijo for an order to compel the doctor to return, expecting thereby to make him reimburse the money. The order overtook him at the village of Algodones, near forty miles from Santa Fé, where he was at once arrested by the alcalde, and detained some time, ignorant even of the offence for which he was doing penance.

In the meantime, the American Consul at Santa Fé, having been informed of what had taken place, procured a counter-order from the governor for the release of the prisoner. When the alcalde of Algodones received this document, he determined at once that so extraordinary an act of justice should cost the foreigner some trifle. Accordingly, another order was forged on the spot, commanding that he should be taken to the capital—yet a 'gentle hint' was given, that his liberty might be purchased by the payment of two hundred dollars. Being in a land of strangers, among whom he had but little hope of receiving fair play, the doctor resolved to pay the amount demanded, and fly to Chihuahua, where he would at least be safe from Armijo's clutches. Having been informed, however, of the fraud practised by the alcalde, before he had proceeded far on his journey, he returned and made an attempt to bring the delinquent officer to justice, but altogether without success.

But perhaps the most glaring outrages upon American citizens were committed in 1841, upon the occasion of the capture of the Texan Santa Fé Expedition. In Taos, a poor deaf and dumb U. S. creole Frenchman was beaten to death in open day. In San Miguel, the alcalde, at the head of a mob, entered the store of a Mr. Rowland, whom he robbed of a considerable amount of merchandise. At the same time, the greatest excitement raged in Santa Fé against Americans, whose lives appeared in imminent danger; and a most savage attack was made upon our excellent Consul, Manuel Alvarez, Esq., who had always taken an active interest in the welfare of American citizens.

A few minutes after the governor had departed for San Miguel, to encounter the Texans, a fellow named Martin, his nephew and confidential agent, aided by a band of ferocious *sans culottes*, and armed with a large knife, secretly entered the house of the Consul, who perceived him in time, however, to avert the blow; yet he received a severe wound in the face during the scuffle that ensued: the rabble running in at the same time, and vociferating, "*Sáquenlo afuera! mátenlo!*"—Drag him out! kill him! Mr. Alvarez doubtless owed his preservation partially to the consternation with which the failure of their clandestine attempt at his life inspired the cowardly ruffians. Instead of being punished for this diabolical act, the principal assassin, on the contrary, was soon after promoted in the army.

The outrage did not end here, however; for on the Consul's demanding his passport for the United States, it was refused for nearly a month; thus detaining him until the cold season had so far advanced, that, of his party (about fifteen in number), two perished from the cold; and not one arrived without being more or less frost-bitten—some very severely—besides suffering a loss of about fifty animals from the same cause.

Although these and other daring outrages have been duly represented to our Government, it does not appear that any measures of redress have yet been taken.

With a view of oppressing our merchants, Gov. Armijo had, as early as 1839, issued a decree exempting all the natives from the tax imposed on store-houses, shops, etc., throwing the whole burden of impost upon foreigners and naturalized citizens; a measure clearly and unequivocally at variance with the treaties and stipulations entered into between the United States and Mexico. A protest was presented without effect; when our Consul, finding all remonstrances useless, forwarded a memorial to the American Minister at Mexico, who, although the vital interests of American citizens were at stake, deemed the affair of too little importance, perhaps, and therefore appears to have paid no attention to it. But this system of levying excessive taxes upon foreigners, is by no means an original invention of Gov. Armijo. In 1835, the government of Chihuahua having levied a *contribucion de guerra* for raising means to make war upon the savages, who were laying waste the surrounding country, foreign merchants, with an equal disregard for their rights and the obligations of treaties, were taxed twenty-five dollars each per month; while the native merchants, many of whom possessed large haciendas, with thousands of stock, for the especial protection of which these taxes were chiefly imposed, paid only from five to ten dollars each. Remonstrances were presented to the governor, but in vain. In his official reply, that functionary declared, "*que el gobierno cree arreglado el reparto de sus respectivas contribuciones,*"—the government believes your respective contributions in accordance with justice—which concluded the correspondence, and the Americans paid their twenty-five dollars per month.

The only tribunals of 'justice' in New Mexico are those of the ordinary *alcaldes* or justices of the peace; and an appeal from them is carried to the Supreme Court in the department of Chihuahua. The course of litigation is exceedingly simple and summary. The plaintiff makes his verbal complaint or demand before the alcalde, who orders him to summon the defendant, which is done by simply saying, "*Le llama el alcalde*" (the alcalde calls you) into his presence, the applicant acting thus in the double capacity of constable and complainant. The summons is always verbal, and rarely for a future time —instant attendance being expected. Should the defendant refuse to obey this simple mandate (which, by the bye, is a very rare occurrence), the alcalde sends his *baston de justicia*, his staff of justice, an ordinary walking-cane, distinguished only by a peculiar black silk tassel. This never fails to enforce compliance, for a refusal to attend after being shown the staff, would be construed into a contempt of court, and punished accordingly. The witnesses are sometimes sworn upon a cross cut on the *baston de justicia*, or more frequently, perhaps, upon a cross formed with the finger and thumb. Generally speaking, however, the process of examination is gone through without a single oath being administered; and in the absence of witnesses, the alcalde often proceeds to sentence upon the simple statements of the contending parties. By a species of mutual agreement, the issue of a suit is sometimes referred to *hombres buenos* (arbitrators), which is the nearest approximation that is made to trial by jury. In judicial proceedings, however, but little, or rather no attention is paid to any code of laws; in fact, there is scarcely one alcalde in a dozen who knows what a law is, or who ever saw a law-book. Their decisions, when not influenced by corrupt agencies, are controlled by the prevailing customs of the country.

In the administration of justice, there are three distinct and privileged jurisdictions, known as *fueros:* the *eclesiástico*, which provides that no member of the clergy, at least of the rank of curate and upwards, shall ever be arraigned before a civil tribunal, but shall be tried by their superiors in the order; the *militar*, which makes a similar provision in favor not only of commissioned officers, but of every common soldier from the ranks; and the *civil* or ordinary courts, for all cases in which the defendants are laymen. These *fueros* have hitherto maintained the ecclesiastical and military classes in perfect independence of the civil authorities. The *civil*, in fact, remains in some degree subordinate to the other two *fueros;* for it can, under no circumstances, have any jurisdiction whatever over them; while the lay plaintiff, in the privileged tribunals of these, may, if unsuccessful, have judgment entered up against him: a consequence that can never follow the suits of the ecclesiastical or military orders before the civil tribunals. The judgments of the latter, in such cases, would be void. It is no wonder, then, that the cause of freedom in Mexico has made so little progress.

Imprisonment is almost the only sort of punishment resorted to in the North. For debt, petit larceny, highway robbery, and murder, the usual sentence is "*A la cárcel*" (to jail), where a person is likely to remain about as long for inability to pay *dos reales*, as for the worst of crimes: always provided he has not the means to pacify the offended majesty of the law. I never heard of but one execution for murder in New Mexico, since the declaration of independence. The most desperate and blood-stained criminals escape with impunity, after a few weeks of incarceration, unless the prosecutor happens to be a person of great influence; in which case, the prisoner is detained in the *calabozo* at will, even when the offence committed has been of a trivial character. Notwithstanding this laxity in the execution of the laws, there are few murders of any kind commited.

In case of debt, as before remarked, the delinquent is sent to jail—provided the creditor will not accept his services. If he will, however, the debtor becomes *nolens volens* the servant of the creditor till the debt is satisfied; and, serving, as he does, at very reduced wages, his expenses for clothing, and other necessaries, but too often retain him in perpetual servitude. This system does not operate, however, upon the higher classes, yet it acts with terrible severity upon the unfortunate poor, whose condition is but little better, if not worse indeed than that of the slaves of the South. They labor for fixed wages, it is true; but all they can earn is hardly sufficient to keep them in the coarsest clothing and pay their contingent expenses. Men's wages range from two to five dollars a month, and those of women from fifty cents to two dollars; in payment of which, they rarely receive any money; but instead thereof, articles of apparel and other necessaries at the most exorbitant prices. The consequence is that the servant soon accumulates a debt which he is unable to pay—his wages being often engaged for a year or two in advance. Now, according to the usages, if not the laws of the country, he is bound to serve his master until all arrearages are liquidated; and is only enabled to effect an exchange of masters, by engaging another to pay his debt, to whom he becomes in like manner bound.

As I have already remarked, capital crimes and highway robberies are of comparatively rare occurrence in the North, but in smaller delinquencies, such as pilfering and petty rogueries of every shade and description, the common classes can very successfully compete with any other people. Nothing indeed can be left exposed or unguarded without great danger of its being immediately stolen. No husbandman would think of leaving his axe or his hoe, or anything else of the slightest value, lying out over night. Empty wagons are often pillaged of every movable piece of iron, and even the wheels have been carried away. Pieces of merchandise are frequently purloined from the shelves, when they happen to be in reach. In Chihuahua, goods have actually been snatched from the counter while being exposed to the inspection of a pretended purchaser. I once had a trick of this kind played upon me by a couple of boys, who made their escape through a crowd of spectators with their booty exposed. In vain I cried "*Agarren á los ladrones!*" (catch the thieves!) not a single individual moved to apprehend them. I then proffered the goods stolen, to any person who might succeed in bringing the rogues to me, but to no purpose. In fact there seems to exist a great deal of repugnance, even among the better classes, to apprehending thieves; as if the mere act of informing against them was considered dishonorable. I heard a very respectable caballero once remark that he had seen a man purloin certain articles of merchandise, but he could not be induced to give up his name; observing, "O, I can't think of exposing the poor fellow!"

The impunity with which delinquencies of this description are every day committed is perhaps in some degree, the consequence of those severe enactments, such as the *Leyes de las Indias* (the laws of the Indies), which rendered many thefts and robberies punishable with death. The magistracy contracted the habit of frequently winking at crime, rather than resort to the barbarous expedients prescribed by the letter of the law. The utmost that can be gained now by public prosecution, is the recovery of the stolen property, if that be anywhere to be found, and occasionally a short period of imprisonment for the culprit. This is more particularly the case when the prosecutor happens to be a foreigner; while on the other hand, if he be the party accused, he is likely to be subjected to very severe treatment. A remarkable circumstance of this kind occurred in Chihuahua in the year 1835. One of our most respectable Missouri merchants had bought a mule of a stranger, but the animal was soon after claimed by a third person, who proved that it had been stolen from him. The Missourian would have been perfectly satisfied to lose the mule, and end the matter there; but to the surprise of all, he was directly summoned before an alcalde, and forthwith sentenced to jail: the partial judge having labored to fix the theft upon the innocent purchaser, while the real culprit, who was a native, was permitted to go at large.

The love of gambling also deserves to be noticed as a distinguishing propensity of these people. Indeed it may well be said, without any undue stretch of imagination, that shoplifting, pocket-picking, and other elegant pastimes of the same kindred, are the legitimate offspring, especially among the lower classes, of that passion for gaming, which in Mexico more than anywhere else—to use Madame Calderon's language—"is impregnated with the constitution—in man, woman, and child." It prevails in the lowly hut, as well as in the glittering saloon; nor is the sanctity of the gown nor the dignity of station sufficient proof against the fascinations of this exciting vice. No one considers it a degradation to be seen frequenting a *monte bank:* the governor himself and his lady, the grave magistrate and the priestly dignity, the gay caballero and the titled señora may all be seen staking their doubloons upon the turn of a card; while the humbler ranchero, the hired domestic and the ragged pauper, all press with equal avidity to test their fortune at the same shrine. There are other games at cards practised among these people, depending more upon skill; but that of *el monte*, being one exclusively of chance, seems to possess an all-absorbing attraction, difficult to be conceived by the uninitiated spectator.

The following will not only serve to show the light in which gambling is held by all classes of society, but to illustrate the purifying effects of wealth upon character. Some twelve or fifteen years ago there lived (or rather roamed) in Taos a certain female of very loose habits, known as *La Tules*. Finding it difficult to obtain the means of living in that district, she finally extended her wanderings to the capital. She there became a constant attendant on one of those pandemoniums where the favorite game of *monte* was dealt *pro bono publico*. Fortune, at first, did not seem inclined to smile upon her efforts, and for some years she spent her days in lowliness and misery. At last her luck turned, as gamblers would say, and on one occasion she left the bank with a spoil of several hundred dollars! This enabled her to open a bank of her own, and being favored by a continuous run of good fortune, she gradually rose higher and higher in the scale of affluence, until she found herself in possession of a very handsome fortune. In 1843, she sent to the United States some ten thousand dollars to be invested in goods. She still continues her favorite 'amusement,' being now considered the most expert 'monte dealer' in all Santa Fé. She is openly received in the first circles of society: I doubt, in truth, whether there is to be found in the city a lady of more fashionable reputation than this same Tules, now known as Señora Doña Gertrudes Barceló.

Among the multitude of games which seem to constitute the real business of life in New Mexico, that of *chuza* evidently presents the most attractions to ladies; and they generally lay very heavy wagers upon the result. It is played with little balls, and bears some faint resemblance to what is called *roulette*. Bullbaiting and cock-fighting, about which so much has been said by every traveller in Mexico, are also very popular 'amusements' in the North, and generally lead to the same excesses and the same results as gaming. The cock-pit rarely fails to be crowded on Sundays and other feast days; on which occasions the church, the ball-room, the gambling-house, and the cock-pit look like so many opposition establishments; for nothing is more common than to see people going from one place to another by alternate fits, just as devotional feeling or love of pleasure happens to prompt them.

One of the most attractive sports of the rancheros and the peasantry, and that which, more than any other, calls for the exercise of skill and dexterity, is that called *correr el gallo*, practised generally on St. John's day. A common cock or hen is tied by the feet to some swinging limb of a tree, so as to be barely within the reach of a man on horseback: or the fowl is buried alive in a small pit in the ground leaving only the head above the surface. In either case, the racers, passing at full speed, grapple the head of the fowl, which being well greased, generally slips out of their fingers. As soon as some one, more dextrous than the rest, has succeeded in tearing it loose, he claps spurs to his steed, and endeavors to escape with the prize. He is hotly pursued, however, by the whole sporting crew, and the first who overtakes him tries to get possession of the fowl, when a strife ensues, during which the poor chicken is torn into atoms. Should the holder of the trophy be able to outstrip his pursuers, he carries it to a crowd of fair spectators and presents it to his mistress, who takes it to the fandango which usually follows, as a testimony of the prowess of her lover.

Among the vaqueros, and even among persons of distinction, *el coleo* (tailing) is a much nobler exercise than the preceding, and is also generally reserved for days of festivity. For this sport the most untractable ox or bull is turned loose upon a level common, when all the parties who propose to join in the amusement, being already mounted, start off in pursuit of him. The most successful rider, as soon as he gets near enough to the bull, seizes him by the tail, and with a sudden manœuvre, whirls him topsy-turvy upon the plain—to the no little risk of breaking his own neck, should his horse stumble or be tripped by the legs of the falling bull.

Respecting *fandangos*, I will observe that this term, as it is used in New Mexico, is never applied to any particular dance, but is the usual designation for those ordinary assemblies where dancing and frolicking are carried on; *baile* (or ball) being generally applied to those of a higher grade. The former especially are very frequent; for nothing is more general, throughout the country, and with all classes than dancing. From the gravest priest to the buffoon—from the richest nabob to the beggar—from the governor to the ranchero—from the soberest matron to the flippant belle—from the grandest *señora* to the *cocinera*—all partake of this exhilarating amusement. To judge from the quantity of tuned instruments which salute the ear almost every night in the week, one would suppose that a perpetual carnival prevailed everywhere. The musical instruments used at the *bailes* and *fandangos* are usually the fiddle and *bandolin*, or *guitarra*, accompanied in some villages by the *tombé* or little Indian drum. The musicians occasionally acquire considerable proficiency in the use of these instruments. But what most oddly greets, and really outrages most Protestant ears, is the accompaniment of divine service with the very same instruments, and often with the same tunes.

Of all the petty vices practised by the New Mexicans, the *vicio inocente* of smoking among ladies, is the most intolerable; and yet it is a habit of which the loveliest and the most refined equally partake. The *puro* or *cigarro** is seen in the mouths of all: it is handed round in the parlor, and introduced at the dinner table—even in the ball-room it is presented to ladies as regularly as any

---

* The *puro* is a common cigar of *pure* tobacco; but the term *cigarro* or *cigarrito* is applied to those made of cut tobacco rolled up in a strip of paper or corn-husk. The latter are by far in the most general use in New Mexico, even among the men, and are those only smoked by the females. In this province cigarros are rarely sold in the shops, being generally manufactured by every one just as they are needed. Their expertness in this 'accomplishment' is often remarkable. The mounted vaquero will take out his *guagito* (his little tobacco-flask), his packet of *hojas* (or prepared husks), and his flint, steel, etc.,—make his cigarrito, strike fire and commence smoking in a minute's time—all while at full speed: and the next minute will perhaps lazo the wildest bull without interrupting his smoke.

other species of 'refreshment;' and in the dance the señorita may often be seen whirling round with a lighted *cigarrito* in her mouth. The belles of the Southern cities are very frequently furnished with *tenazitas de oro* (little golden tongs), to hold the cigar with, so as to prevent their delicate fingers from being polluted either with the stain or scent of tobacco; forgetting at the same time its disagreeable effects upon the lips and breath.

Notwithstanding their numerous vices, however, I should do the New Mexicans the justice to say that they are but little addicted to inebriety and its attendant dissipations. Yet this doubtlessly results to a considerable degree from the dearness of spirituous liquors, which virtually places them beyond the reach of the lower classes.

CHAPTER XIII.

Military Hierarchy of Mexico—Religious Superstitions—Legend of *Nuestra Señora de Guadalupe*—A profane version of the Story—A curious Plan for manufacturing Water—Saints and Images—Processions—How to make it Rain—The Sacred Host—Fanaticism and Murder—Honors paid to a Bishop—Servility to Priests—Attendance at Public Worship—New Mexicans in Church—The Vesper Bells—Passion Week and the Ceremonies pertaining thereto—Ridiculous *Penitencia*—Whitewashing of Criminals—Matrimonial Connexions and Mode of Contracting them—Restrictions upon Lovers—Onerous Fees paid for Marriages and Burials—Anecdote of a *Ranchero*—Ditto of a Servant and a Widow, illustrative of Priestly Extortion—Modes of Burial, and Burial Ground of the Heretics.

The Mexicans seem the legitimate descendants of the subjects of 'His Most Catholic Majesty;' for the Romish faith is not only the religion established by law, but the only one tolerated by the constitution: a system of republican liberty wholly incomprehensible to the independent and tolerant spirits of the United States. Foreigners only of other creeds, in accordance with treaty stipulations, can worship privately within their own houses. The Mexicans, indeed, talk of a 'union of Church and State:' they should rather say a 'union of Church and Army;' for, as has already been shown, the civil authority is so nearly merged in the military and the ecclesiastical, that the government, if not a military hierarchy, is something so near akin that it is difficult to draw the distinction. As Mr. Mayer very appropriately remarks, you are warned of the double dominion of the army and the church "by the constant sound of the drum and the bell, which ring in your ears from morn to midnight, and drown the sounds of industry and labor."

In the variety and grossness of popular superstitions, Northern Mexico can probably compete with any civilized country in the world. Others may have their extravagant traditions, their fanatical prejudices, their priestly impostures, but here the popular creed seems to be the embodiment of as much that is fantastic and improbable in idolatrous worship, as it is possible to clothe in the garb of a christian faith. It would fill volumes to relate one-half of the wonderful miracles and extraordinary apparitions said to have occurred during and since the conquest of the Indian Pueblos and their conversion to the Romish faith. Their character may be inferred from the following national legend of *La Maravillosa Aparicion de Nuestra Señora de Guadalupe— anglicè*, the marvellous apparition of Our Lady of Guadalupe,—which, in some one of its many traditionary shapes, is generally believed throughout the republic. I have seen some half a dozen written versions of this celebrated tradition, and heard about as many oral ones; but no two agree in all the particulars. However, that which has received most currency informs us, that, on the 12th of December, 1531, an Indian called Juan Diego, while passing over the barren hill of Tepeyacac (about a league northward from the city of Mexico), in quest of medicinal herbs, had his attention suddenly arrested by the fragrance of flowers, and the sound of delightful music; and on looking up, he saw an angelic sort of figure directly before him. Being terrified he attempted to flee; but the apparition calling to him by name, " Juan Diego," said she, " go tell the bishop to have me a place of worship erected on this very spot." The Indian replied that he could not return, as he was seeking *remedios* for a dying relative. But the figure bade him to do as commanded, and have no further care about his relative—that he was then well. Juan Diego went to the city, but being unable to procure an audience from the bishop, he concluded he had been acting under a delusion, and again set off for his *remedios*. Upon ascending the same hill, however, the apparition again accosted him, and hearing his excuse, upbraided him for his want of faith and energy; and said, " Tell the bishop that it is Guadalupe, the Virgin Mary, come to dwell amongst and protect the Mexicans, who sends thee." The Indian, returning again to the city, forced his way into the presence of the bishop, who, like a good sensible man, received the messenger with jeers, and treated him as a maniac;

telling him finally to bring some sign, which, if really the Mother of God, his directress could readily furnish.

The perplexed Indian left the bishop's presence resolved to avoid further molestation from his spiritual acquaintance, by taking another route; yet, when near the place of his first meeting, he again encountered the apparition, who, hearing the result of his mission, ordered him to climb a naked rock hard by, and collect a bouquet of flowers which he would find growing there. Juan Diego, albeit without faith, obeyed, when, to his surprise he found the flowers referred to, and brought them to the Virgin, who, throwing them into his *tilma*, commanded him to carry them to the bishop; saying, " When he sees these he will believe, as he well knows that flowers do not bloom at this season, much less upon that barren rock." The humble messenger now with more courage sought the bishop's presence, and threw out the blooming credentials of his mission before him; when lo! to the astonishment of all, and to the entire conviction of his *Senoría ilustrísima*, the perfect image of the apparition appeared imprinted on the inside of the *tilma*.*

The reverend Prelate now fully acknowledged the divinity of the picture, and in a

---

* This is a kind of mantle or loose covering worn by the Indians, which, in the present instance, was made of the coarse filaments of a species of maguey, and a little resembled the common coffee sacks. The painting, as it necessarily must be on such a material, is said to be coarse, and represents the Virgin covered with a blue robe bespangled with stars.

conclave of ecclesiastics convened for the purpose, he pronounced it the image of *La verdadera Virgen* and protectress of Mexico. A splendid chapel was soon after erected upon the spot designated in the mandate, in which the miraculous painting was deposited, where it is preserved to the present day. In the suburbs of every principal city in the republic, there is now a chapel specially dedicated to *Nuestra Señora de Guadalupe*, where coarse resemblances of the original picture are to be seen. Rough paintings of the same, of various dimensions, are also to be met with in nearly every dwelling, from the palace to the most miserable hovel. The image, with an adapted motto, has also been stamped upon medals, which are swung about the necks of the faithful.*

* The accompanying cut represents both sides of a medal of "*Nuestra Señora de Guadalupe de Mexico*," of which, as I have been informed, 216,000 were struck at Birmingham in the year 1831, designed for the Mexican market. Similar medals are worn by nearly nine-tenths of the population of Northern Mexico. On one side, as will be seen, the Virgin is represented in her star-

As a further confirmation of the miracle, it is also told, that when Juan Diego returned to his home, he found his relative in good health—that he had suddenly risen from the last extremity about the time of the former's meeting with the Virgin.

Now comes the profane version of the story, which the skeptical have set afloat, as the most reasonable one; but against which, in the name of orthodoxy, I feel bound to enter my protest. To the better understanding of this 'explanatory tradition,' it may be necessary to premise that the name of Guadalupe was already familiar to the Spaniards, the Virgin Mary having, it is said, long before appeared in Spain, under the same title; on which occasion an order of monks, styled *Frailes Guadalupanos*, had been instituted. One of these worthy fathers who had been sent as a missionary to Mexico, finding the Indians rather stubborn and unyielding, conceived the plan of flattering their national vanity by fabricating a saint suited for the occasion. The Guadalupano had a poor friend who was an excellent painter, to whom he said, one day, "Take this tilma"—presenting him one of the coarsest and most slazy tex-

---

spangled robe, supported by a cherub and the moon under her feet: a design, which, it has been suggested, was most probably drawn from Revelation xii. 1. The date, "A. 1805," is that perhaps of some one of the innumerable miracles, which, according to fame in Mexico, have been wrought by the Virgin Guadalupe. The motto, "*Non fecit taliter omni nationi*" (She "hath not dealt so with any nation") which is found on the reverse of the medal, is extracted from Psalm cxlvii. 20.

ture (a sort of *manta de guangoche*); "paste it upon canvass, and paint me thereon the handsomest effigy of Nuestra Señora de Guadalupe that your fancy can portray." When this was done according to order, and the tilma separated from the canvass, the picture appeared somewhat miraculous. Viewed very closely, it showed exceedingly dim; but upon receding to some distance, so that the eye could embrace a larger field of the open texture, it appeared quite distinct and beautiful. This effect is often alluded to at the present day, and easily as it might be accounted for upon philosophical principles, I have heard many an ignorant Mexican declare, that *la Santisima Virgen* concealed herself from such as profaned her shrine by a too near approach, and only shone forth in all her brilliancy to those who kept at a respectful distance. But, in conclusion, the story relates, that a suitable damsel being selected and decked out to represent the Virgin, the affair was played off as it has been narrated.

As regards the miracle of the fresh flowers in December the *profanos* say, that there was nothing very wonderful about it, as flowers were known to bloom in the lowlands, and only a few leagues from the spot where the affair took place, at all seasons of the year; implying that these had been engrafted upon the rock for the occasion. There are some who go so far as to insinuate that the bishop and other ecclesiastics were privy to the whole affair, and that every precaution had been taken to see the Indian who played first fiddle in the matter, provided with a tiima, similar to the one on which the image of the Virgin was painted, and that this was artfully slipped in the place of the former, which the Indian had doffed when he climbed the rock after the flowers.—I have not seen the original portrait, but most of the copies and imitations I have met with, represent the Virgin with that peculiarly tawny complexion which was probably deemed indispensable to conciliate the prejudices of the aborigines.

The reader may reconcile the foregoing discrepancies in the best way he can: all that I have to add is, that the apparition having been canonized by the Pope, a belief in it now constitutes as much a part of the religious faith of the Mexicans, as any article of the Apostolic Creed. To judge from the blind and reverential awe in which the Virgin Guadalupe is held by the lowly and the ignorant, one would suppose her to be the first person in the Divinity; for to her their vows are directed, their prayers offered up, and all their confessions made.

Among the many traditions implicitly believed in by the people, and which tend to obstruct the advancement of knowledge, there is one equally as amusing and extravagant as the foregoing, which has been gravely recounted by the present Vicar of New Mexico and ex-delegate to Congress. During the memorable insurrection of 1680, the Pueblo of San Felipe was about the only one that remained faithful to the Spaniards in all the North. It was during that exciting period that the padre of another Pueblo took refuge among them. Being besieged by their neighbors and their communication with the water entirely cut off, they applied for advice to the reverend padre, who bade them not despair, as he had it in his power to supply them with water. He then began to pray very fervently, after which he opened a vein in each of his arms, from whence there flowed two such copious streams of water that all fears of being reduced by thirst were completely allayed!

It is a part of the superstitious blindness of these people to believe that every one of their legion of canonized saints possesses the power of performing certain miracles; and their aid is generally invoked on all occasions of sickness and distress. The kindest office, therefore, that the friends of a sick person can perform, is to bring forward the image of some of those saints whose healing powers have been satisfactorily tested. The efficacy of these superstitious remedies will not be difficult to account for, when the powerful influence of the imagination upon disease is taken into consideration.

The images of patron saints are never put in such general requisition, however, as in seasons of severe drought. The priests, being generally expert at guessing the approach of a pluvial period, take good care not to make confident promises till they have substantial reason to anticipate a speedy fulfilment of their prophecies. When the fitting season draws nigh, they carry out the image of Nuestra Señora de Guadalupe, or that of some other favorite saint, and parade about the streets, the fields and the meadows, followed by all the men, women, and children of the neighborhood, in solemn procession. Should the clouds condescend to vouchsafe a supply of rain within a week or two of this general humiliation, no one ever thinks of begrudging the scores of dollars that have been paid to the priests for bringing about so happy a result.

Speaking of processions, I am reminded of another peculiar custom so prevalent in Mexico, that it never fails to attract the attention of strangers. This is the passage of the Sacred Host to the residence of persons dangerously ill, for the purpose of administering to them the Extreme Unction. In New Mexico, however, this procession is not attended with so much ostentatious display as it is in the South, the paradise of ecclesiastics, where it is conveyed in a black coach drawn by a pair of black mules, accompanied by armed soldiers and followed by crowds of *léperos* of all sexes and ages. During the procession of the Host, two church-bells of different tones are kept sounding by alternate strokes. Also the carriage is always preceded by a bell-man tinkling a little bell in regular time, to notify all within hearing of its approach, that they may be prepared to pay it due homage. When this bell is heard, all those that happen to be within sight of the procession, though at ever so great a distance, instantly kneel and remain in that position till it has passed out of sight. On these occasions, if an American happens to be within hearing, he endeavors to avoid the *cortége*, by turning the corner of a street or entering a shop or the house of a friend; for although it may be expedient, and even rational, to conform with the customs and ceremonies of those countries we are sojourning in, very few Protestants would feel disposed to fall on their knees before a coach freighted with frail mortals pretending to represent the Godhead! I am sorry to say that non-compliants are frequently insulted and sometimes pelted with stones by the rabble. Even a foreign artisan was once massacred in the Mexican metropolis because he refused to come out of his shop, where he was kneeling, and perform the act of genuflexion in the street!

This abject idolatry sometimes takes a still more humiliating aspect, and descends to the worship of men in the capacity of religious rulers. On the occasion of the Bishop of Durango's visit to Santa Fé in 1833, an event which had not taken place for a great many years, the infatuated population hailed his arrival with as much devotional enthusiasm as if it had been the second advent of the Messiah. Magnificent preparations were made everywhere for his reception: the streets were swept, the roads and bridges on his route repaired and decorated; and from every window in the city there hung such a profusion of fancy curtains and rich cloths that the imagination was carried back to those glowing descriptions of enchanted worlds which one reads of in the fables of necromancers. I must observe, however, that there is a custom in all the towns of Mexico (which it would not be safe to neglect), providing that whenever a religious procession takes place, all the doors and windows facing the street along which it is to pass, shall be decorated with shawls, carpets, or fancy cloths, according to the means and capabilities of the proprietor. During the bishop's sojourn in Santa Fé, which, to the great joy of the inhabitants, lasted for several weeks, he never appeared in the streets but that 'all true Catholics' who were so fortunate as to obtain a glimpse of his *Señoría Ilustrísima* immediately dropped upon their knees, and never moved from that position till the mitred priest had either vouchsafed his benediction or had disappeared. Even the principal personages of the city would not venture to address him till they had first knelt at his feet and kissed his 'pastoral ring.' This, however, is only a heightened picture of what occurs every day in the intercourse between the rancheros and the common padres of the country. The slavish bsequiousness of the lower classes towards these pampered priests is almost incredible.

No people are more punctual in their attendance upon public worship, or more exact in the performance of the external rites of religion, than the New Mexicans. A man would about as soon think of venturing in twenty fathoms of water without being able to swim, as of undertaking a journey without hearing mass first. These religious exercises, however, partake but seldom of the character of true devotion; for people may be seen chattering or tittering while in the act of crossing themselves, or muttering some formal prayer. Indeed, it is the common remark of strangers, that they are wont to wear much graver countenances while dancing at a fandango than during their devotional exercises at the foot of the altar. In nothing, however, is their observance of the outward forms of religion more remarkable than in their deportment every day towards the close of twilight, when the large bell of the *Parroquia* peals for *la oracion*, or vespers. All conversation is instantly suspended—all labor ceases—people of all classes, whether on foot or on horseback, make a sudden halt—even the laden porter, groaning under the weight of an insupportable burden, stops in the midst of his career and stands still. An almost breathless silence reigns throughout the town, disturbed only by the occasional sibilations of the devout multitude: all of which, accompanied by the slow heavy peals of a large sonorous bell, afford a scene truly solemn and appropriate. At the expiration of about two minutes the charm is suddenly broken by the clatter of livelier-toned bells; and a *buenas tardes* (good evening) to those present closes the ceremony : when *presto*, all is bustle and confusion again—the colloquial chit-chat is resumed—the smith plies upon his anvil with redoubled energy—the clink of the hammer simultaneously resounds in every direction—the wayfarers are again in motion,—both pleasure and business, in short, assume their respective sway.

Although the Catholics have a saint for each day in the year, the number of canonized *fiestas* in which labor is prohibited has been somewhat reduced in Mexico. *La Semana Santa*, or Passion Week, is perhaps the period when the religious feeling, such as it is, is most fully excited : *Viernes Santo* (Good Friday), especially, is observed with great pomp and splendor. An image of Christ large as life, nailed to a huge wooden cross, is paraded through the streets, in the midst of an immense procession, accompanied by a glittering array of carved images, representing the Virgin Mary, Mary Magdalene, and several others ; while the most notorious personages of antiquity, who figured at that great era of the World's history,—the centurion with a band of guards, armed with lances, and apparelled in the costume supposed to have been worn in those days,—may be seen bestriding splendidly caparisoned horses, in the breathing reality of flesh and blood. Taking it all in all, this spectacle,—the ceremonies and manœuvres which attend its career through the densely crowded and ornamented streets,—are calculated to produce impressions of a most confused description, in which regret and melancholy may be said to form no inconsiderable share.

It has been customary for great malefactors to propitiate Divine forgiveness by a cruel sort of *penitencia*, which generally takes place during the *Semana Santa*. I once chanced to be in the town of Tomé on Good Friday, when my attention was arrested by a man almost naked, bearing, in imitation of Simon, a huge cross upon his shoulders, which, though constructed of the lightest wood, must have weighed over a hundred pounds. The long end dragged upon the ground, as we have seen it represented in sacred pictures, and about the middle swung a stone of immense dimensions, appended there for the purpose of making the task more laborious. Not far behind followed another equally destitute of clothing, with his whole body wrapped in chains and cords, which seemed buried in the muscles, and which so cramped and confined him that he was scarcely able to keep pace with the procession. The person who brought up the rear presented a still more disgusting aspect. He walked along with a patient and composed step, while another followed close behind belaboring him lustily with a whip, which he flourished with all the satisfaction of an amateur; but as the lash was pointed only with a tuft of untwisted sea-grass, its application merely served to keep open the wounds upon the penitent's back, which had been scarified, as I was informed, with the keen edge of a flint, and was bleeding most profusely. The blood was kept in perpetual flow by the stimulating juice of certain herbs, carried by a third person, into which the scourger frequently dipped his lash. Although the actors in this tragical farce were completely muffled, yet they were well known to many of the by-standers, one of whom assured me that they were three of the most notorious rascals in the country. By submitting to this species of penance, they annually received complete absolution of their past year's sins, and, thus 'purified,' entered afresh on the old career of wickedness and crime.

In New Mexico, the institution of marriage changes the legal rights of the parties, but it scarcely affects their moral obligations. It is usually looked upon as a convenient cloak for irregularities, which society less willingly tolerates in the lives of unmarried women. Yet when it is considered that the majority of matches are forced and ill-assorted, some idea may be formed of the little incitement that is given to virtue. There are very few parents who would stoop to consult a young lady's wishes before concluding a marriage contract, nor would maidens, generally, ever dream of a matrimonial connection unless proposed first by the father. The lover's proposals are, upon the same principle, made in writing direct to the parents themselves, and without the least deference to the wishes or inclinations of the young lady whose hand is thus sought in marriage. The tender emotions engendered between lovers during walks and rambles along the banks of silent streams, are never experienced in this country; for the sexes are seldom permitted to converse or be together alone. In short, instances have actually occurred when the betrothed couple have never seen each other till brought to the altar to be joined in wedlock.

Among the humbler classes, there are still more powerful causes calculated to produce irregularity of life; not the least of which is the enormous fee that must be paid to the curate for tying the matrimonial knot. This system of extortion is carried so far as to amount very frequently to absolute prohibition: for the means of the bridegroom are often insufficient for the exigency of the occasion; and the priests seldom consent to join people in wedlock until the money has been secured to them. The curates being without control, the marriage rates are somewhat irregular, but they usually increase in proportion to the character of the ceremonies and to the circumstances of the parties. The lowest (about twenty dollars) are adapted to the simplest form, solemnized in church at mass; but with the excuse of any extra service and ceremonies, particularly if performed at a private house, the fees are increased often as high as several hundred dollars: I have heard of $500 being paid for a marriage ceremony. The following communication, which appeared in a Chihuahua paper under the signature of "*Un Ranchero,*" affords some illustration of the grievances of the plebeians in this respect. Literally translated it runs thus:

"*Messrs. Editors of the Noticioso de Chihuahua:*

"Permit me, through your paper, to say a few words in print, as those of my pen have been unsuccessfully employed with the *curas* of Allende and Jimenez, to whom I applied the other day for the purpose of ascertaining their legal charge to marry one of my sons. The following simple and concise answer is all that I have been able to elicit from either of these ecclesiastics:—'*The marriage fees are a hundred and nineteen dollars.*' I must confess that I was completely suffocated when I heard this outrageous demand upon my poor purse; and did I not pride myself on being a true Apostolic Roman Catholic, and were it not that the charming graces of my intended daughter-in-law have so captivated my son that nothing but marriage will satisfy him, I would assuredly advise him to contrive some other arrangement with his beloved, which might not be so ruinous to our poor purse; for reflect that $119 are the life and all of a poor ranchero. If nothing else will do, I shall have to sell my few cows (*mis vaquitas*) to help my son out of this difficulty."—The 'Ranchero' then appeals to the Government to remedy such evils, by imposing some salutary restrictions upon the clergy; and concludes by saying, "If this is not done, I will never permit either of my remaining three sons to marry."

This article was certainly an effort of boldness against the priesthood, which may have cost the poor 'Ranchero' a sentence of excommunication. Few of his countrymen would venture on a similar act of temerity; and at least nine-tenths profess the most profound submission to their religious rulers. Being thus bred to look upon their priests as infallible and holy samples of piety and virtue, we should not be so much surprised at the excesses of the 'flock' when a large portion of the *pastores*, the padres themselves, are foremost in most of the popular vices of the country: first at the fandango—first at the gaming table—first at the cock-pit—first at bacchanalian orgies—and by no means last in the contraction of those *liaisons* which are so emphatically prohibited by their vows.

The baptismal and burial fees (neither of which can be avoided without incurring the charge of heresy) are also a great terror to the candidates for married life. "If I marry," says the poor yeoman, "my family must go unclad to baptize my children.; and if any of them should die, we must starve ourselves to pay the burial charges." The fee for baptism, it is true, is not so exorbitant, and in accordance to custom, is often paid by the *padrino* or sponsor; but the burial costs are almost equally extravagant with those of marriage, varying in proportion to the age and circumstances of the deceased. A faithful Mexican servant in my employ at Chihuahua, once solicited forty dollars to bury his mother. Upon my expressing some surprise at the exorbitancy of the amount, he replied—" That is what the cura demands, sir, and if I do not pay it my poor mother will remain unburied!" Thus this man was obliged to sacrifice several months' wages, to pamper the avarice of a vicious and mercenary priest. On another occasion, a poor widow in Santa Fé, begged a little medicine for her sick child: "Not," said the disconsolate mother, "that the life of the babe imports me much, for I know the *angelito* will go directly to heaven; but what shall I do to pay the priest for burying it? He will take my house and all from me—and I shall be turned desolate into the street!"—and so saying, she commenced weeping bitterly.

Indigent parents are thus frequently under the painful necessity of abandoning and disowning their deceased children, to avoid the responsibility of burial expenses. To this end the corpse is sometimes deposited in some niche or corner of the church during the night; and upon being found in the morning, the priest is bound to inter it gratis, unless the parent can be discovered, in which case the latter would be liable to severe castigation, besides being bound to pay the expenses.

Children that have not been baptized are destined, according to the popular faith, to a kind of negative existence in the world of spirits, called *Limbo*, where they remain forever without either suffering punishment or enjoying happiness. Baptized infants, on the other hand, being considered without sin, are supposed to enter at once into the joys of heaven. The deceased child is then denominated an *angelito* (a little angel), and is interred with joy and mirth instead of grief and wailing. It is gaudily bedecked with fanciful attire and ornaments of tinsel and flowers; and being placed upon a small bier, it is carried to the grave by four children as gaily dressed as their circumstances will allow; accompanied by musicians using the instruments and playing the tunes of the fandangos; and the little procession is nothing but glee and merriment.

In New Mexico the lower classes are very rarely, if ever, buried in coffins: the corpse being simply wrapped in a blanket, or some other covering, and in that rude attire consigned to its last home. It is truly shocking to a sensitive mind to witness the inhuman treatment to which the remains of the dead are sometimes subjected. There being nothing to indicate the place of the previous graves, it not unfrequently happens that the partially decayed relics of a corpse are dug up and forced to give place to the more recently deceased, when they are again thrown with the earth into the new grave with perfect indifference. The operation of filling up the grave especially, is particularly repulsive; the earth being pounded down with a large maul, as fast as it is thrown in upon the unprotected corpse, with a force sufficient to crush a delicate frame to atoms.

As the remains of heretics are not permitted to pollute either the church-yard or *Campo Santo*, those Americans who have died in Santa Fé, have been buried on a hill which overlooks the town to the northward. The corpses have sometimes been disinterred and robbed of the shroud in which they were enveloped; so that, on a few occasions, it has been deemed expedient to appoint a special watch for the protection of the grave.

CHAPTER XIV.

The Pueblos—Their Character for Sobriety, Honesty, and Industry—Traditional Descent from Montezuma—Their Languages—Former and present Population—The Pueblo of Pecos—Singular Habits of that ill-fated Tribe—Curious Tradition—Montezuma and the Sun—Legend of a Serpent—Religion and Government—Secret Council—Laws and Customs—Excellent Provisions against Demoralization—Primitive Pastimes of the Pueblos—Their Architecture—Singular Structures of Taos, and other novel Fortifications—Primitive state of the Arts among the Pueblos—Style of Dress, Weapons, etc.—Their Diet—The *Guayave*.

ALLUSION has so frequently been made to the aboriginal tribes of New Mexico, known as *Los Pueblos*, that I think I shall not be trespassing too much upon the patience of the reader, in glancing rapidly at some of the more conspicuous features of their national habits and character.

Although the term *Pueblo* in Spanish literally means the *people*, and their *towns*, it is here specifically applied to the *Christianized Indians* (as well as their villages)—to those aborigines whom the Spaniards not only subjected to their laws, but to an acknowledgment of the Romish faith, and upon whom they forced baptism and the cross in exchange for the vast possessions of which they robbed them. All that was left them was, to each Pueblo a league or two of land situated around their villages, the conquerors reserving to themselves at least ninety-nine hundredths of the whole domain as a requital for their generosity.

When these regions were first discovered it appears that the inhabitants lived in comfortable houses and cultivated the soil, as they have continued to do up to the present time. Indeed, they are now considered the best horticulturists in the country, furnishing most of the fruits and a large portion of the vegetable supplies that are to be found in the markets. They were until very lately the only people in New Mexico who cultivated the grape. They also maintain at the present time considerable herds of cattle, horses, etc. They are, in short, a remarkably sober and industrious race, conspicuous for morality and honesty, and very little given to quarrelling or dissipation, except when they have had much familiar intercourse with the Hispano-Mexican population.

Most of these Pueblos call themselves the descendants of Montezuma, although it would appear that they could only have been made acquainted with the history of that monarch, by the Spaniards; as this province is nearly two thousand miles from the ancient kingdom of Mexico. At the time of the conquest they must have been a very powerful people—numbering near a hundred villages, as existing ruins would seem to indicate; but they are now reduced to about twenty, which are scattered in various parts of the territory.

There are but three or four different languages spoken among them, and these, indeed, may be distantly allied to each other. Those of Taos, Picuris, Isleta, and perhaps some others, speak what has been called the *Piro* language. A large portion of the others, viz., those of San Juan, Santa Clara, Nambé, Pojuaque, Tezuque, and some others, speak *Tegua*, having all been originally known by this general name; and those of Cochití, Santo Domingo, San Felipe, and perhaps Sandía, speak the same tongue, though they seem formerly to have been distinguished as *Queres*. The numerous tribes that inhabited the highlands between Rio del Norte and Pecos, as those of Pecos, Ciénega, Galisteo, etc., were known anciently as *Tagnos*, but these are now all extinct; yet their language is said to be spoken by those of Jemez and others of that section. Those further to the westward*

* Of these, the Pueblo of Zuñi has been celebrated for honesty and hospitality. The inhabitants mostly profess the Catholic faith, but have now no curate. They cultivate the soil, manufacture, and possess considerable quantities of stock. Their village is over 150 miles west of the Rio del Norte, on the waters of the Colorado of the West, and is believed to contain between 1000 and 1500 souls. The "seven Pueblos of Moqui" (as they are called) are a similar tribe living a few leagues beyond. They formerly acknowledged the government and religion of the Spaniards, but have long since rejected both, and live in a state of independence and paganism. Their dwellings, however, like those of Zuñi, are similar to those of the interior Pueblos, and they are equally industrious and agricultural, and still more ingenious in their manufacturing. The language of the *Moquis* or *Moquinos* is said to differ but little from that of the Navajoes.

are perhaps allied to the Navajoes. Though all these Pueblos speak their native languages among themselves, a great many of them possess a smattering of Spanish, sufficient to carry on their intercourse with the Mexicans.

The population of these Pueblos will average nearly five hundred souls each (though some hardly exceed one hundred), making an aggregate of nine or ten thousand. At the time of the original conquest, at the close of the sixteenth century, they were, as has been mentioned, much, perhaps ten-fold, more numerous. Ancient ruins are now to be seen scattered in every quarter of the territory: of some, entire stone walls are yet standing, while others are nearly or quite obliterated, many of them being now only known by their names which history or tradition has preserved to us. Numbers were no doubt destroyed during the insurrection of 1680, and the petty internal strifes which followed.

Several of these Pueblos have been converted into Mexican villages, of which that of *Pecos* is perhaps the most remarkable instance. What with the massacres of the second conquest, and the inroads of the Comanches, they gradually dwindled away, till they found themselves reduced to about a dozen, comprising all ages and sexes; and it was only a few years ago that they abandoned the home of their fathers and joined the Pueblo of Jemez.

Many curious tales are told of the singular habits of this ill-fated tribe, which must no doubt have tended to hasten its utter annihilation. A tradition was prevalent among them that Montezuma had kindled a holy fire, and enjoined their ancestors not to suffer it to be extinguished until he should return to deliver his people from the yoke of the Spaniards. In pursuance of these commands, a constant watch had been maintained for ages to prevent the fire from going out; and, as tradition further informed them, that Montezuma would appear with the sun, the deluded Indians were to be seen every clear morning upon the terraced roofs of their houses, attentively watching for the appearance of the 'king of light,' in hopes of seeing him 'cheek by jowl' with their immortal sovereign. I have myself descended into the famous *estufas*, or subterranean vaults, of which there were several in the village, and have beheld this consecrated fire, silently smouldering under a covering of ashes, in the basin of a small altar. Some say that they never lost hope in the final coming of Montezuma until, by some accident or other, or a lack of a sufficiency of warriors to watch it, the fire became extinguished; and that it was this catastrophe that induced them to abandon their villages, as I have before observed.

The task of tending the sacred fire was, it is said, allotted to the warriors. It is further related, that they took the watch by turns for two successive days and nights, without partaking of either food, water, or sleep; while some assert, that instead of being restricted to two days, each guard continued with the same unbending severity of purpose until exhaustion, and very frequently death, left their places to be filled by others. A large portion of those who came out alive were generally so completely prostrated by the want of repose and the inhalation of carbonic gas that they very soon died; when, as the vulgar story asseverates, their remains were carried to the den of a monstrous serpent, which kept itself in excellent condition by feeding upon these delicacies. This huge snake (invented no doubt by the lovers of the marvellous to account for the constant disappearance of the Indians) was represented as the idol which they worshipped, and as subsisting entirely upon the flesh of his devotees: live infants, however, seemed to suit his palate best. The story of this wonderful serpent was so firmly believed in by many ignorant people, that on one occasion I heard an honest ranchero assert, that upon entering the village very early on a winter's morning, he saw the huge trail of the reptile in the snow, as large as that of a dragging ox.

This village, anciently so renowned, lies twenty-five miles eastward of Santa Fé, and near the *Rio Pecos*, to which it gave name. Even so late as ten years ago, when it contained a population of fifty to a hundred souls, the traveller would oftentimes perceive but a solitary Indian, a woman, or a child, standing here and there like so many statues upon the roofs of their houses, with their eyes fixed on the eastern horizon, or leaning against a wall or a fence, listlessly gazing at the passing stranger; while at other times not a soul was to be seen in any direction, and the sepulchral silence of the place was only disturbed by the occasional barking of a dog, or the cackling of hens.

No other Pueblo appears to have adopted this extraordinary superstition: like Pecos, however, they have all held Montezuma to be their perpetual sovereign. It would likewise appear that they all worship the sun; for it is asserted to be their regular practice to turn the face towards the east at sunrise. They profess the Catholic faith, however, of which, nevertheless, they cannot be expected to understand anything beyond the formalities; as but very few of their Mexican neighbors and teachers can boast of more.

Although nominally under the jurisdiction of the federal government, as Mexican citizens, many features of their ancient customs are still retained, as well in their civil rule as in their religion. Each Pueblo is under the control of a *cacique* or *gobernadorcillo*, chosen from among their own sages, and commissioned by the governor of New Mexico. The cacique, when any public business is to be transacted, collects together the principal chiefs of the Pueblo in an *estufa*, or cell, usually under ground, and there lays before them the subjects of debate, which are generally settled by the opinion of the majority. No Mexican is admitted to these councils, nor do the subjects of discussion ever transpire beyond the precincts of the cavern. The council has also charge of the interior police and tranquillity of the village. One of their regulations is to appoint a secret watch for the purpose of keeping down disorders and vices of every description, and especially to keep an eye over the young men and women of the village. When any improper intercourse among them is detected, the parties are immediately carried to the council, and the cacique intimates to them that they must be wedded forthwith. Should the girl be of bad character, and the man, therefore, unwilling to marry her, they are ordered to keep separate under penalty of the lash. Hence it is, that the females of these Pueblos are almost universally noted for their chastity and modest deportment.

They also elect a *capitan de guerra*, a kind of commander-in-chief of the warriors, whose office it is to defend their homes and their interests both in the field and in the council chamber. Though not very warlike, these Pueblos are generally valiant, and well skilled in the strategies of Indian warfare; and although they have been branded with cruelty and ferocity, yet they can hardly be said to surpass the Mexicans in this respect: both, in times of war, pay but little regard either to age or sex. I have been told that when the Pueblos return from their belligerent expeditions, instead of going directly to their homes, they always visit their council cell first. Here they undress, dance, and carouse, frequently for two days in succession before seeing their families.

Although the Pueblos are famous for hospitality and industry, they still continue in the rudest state of ignorance, having neither books nor schools among them, as none of their languages have been reduced to rules, and very few of their children are ever taught in Spanish. A degree of primitiveness characterizes all their amusements, which bear a strong similarity to those of the wilder tribes. Before the New Mexican government had become so much impoverished, there was wont to be held in the capital on the 16th of September of every year, a national celebration of the declaration of Independence, to which the Pueblos were invited. The warriors and youths of each nation with a proportionate array of dusky damsels would appear on these occasions, painted and ornamented in accordance with their aboriginal customs, and amuse the inhabitants with all sorts of grotesque feats and native dances. Each Pueblo generally had its particular uniform dress and its particular dance. The men of one village would sometimes disguise themselves as elks, with horns on their heads, moving on all-fours, and mimicking the animal they were attempting to personate. Others would appear in the garb of a turkey, with large heavy wings, and strut about in imitation of that bird. But the Pecos tribe, already reduced to seven men, always occasioned most diversion.

Their favorite exploit was, each to put on the skin of a buffalo, horns, tail, and all, and thus accoutred scamper about through the crowd, to the real or affected terror of all the ladies present, and to the great delight of the boys.

The Pueblo villages are generally built with more regularity than those of the Mexicans, and are constructed of the same materials as were used by them in the most primitive ages. Their dwelling-houses, it is true, are not so spacious as those of the Mexicans, containing very seldom more than two or three small apartments upon the ground floor, without any court-yard, but they have generally a much loftier appearance, being frequently two stories high and sometimes more. A very curious feature in these buildings, is, that there is most generally no direct communication between the street and the lower rooms, into which they descend by a trap-door from the upper story, the latter being accessible by means of ladders. Even the entrance to the upper stories is frequently at the roof. This style of building seems to have been adopted for security against their marauding neighbors of the wilder tribes, with whom they were often at war. When the family had all been housed at night, the ladder was drawn up, and the inmates were thus shut up in a kind of fortress, which bid defiance to the scanty implements of warfare used by the wild Indians.

Though this was their most usual style of architecture, there still exists a Pueblo of Taos, composed, for the most part, of but two edifices of very singular structure—one on each side of a creek, and formerly communicating by a bridge. The base-story is a mass of near four hundred feet long, a hundred and fifty wide, and divided into numerous apartments, upon which other tiers of rooms are built, one above another, drawn in by regular grades, forming a pyramidal pile of fifty or sixty feet high, and comprising some six or eight stories. The outer rooms only seem to be used for dwellings, and are lighted by little windows in the sides, but are entered through trap-doors in the *azoteas* or roofs. Most of the inner apartments are employed as granaries and store-rooms, but a spacious hall in the centre of the mass, known as the *estufa*, is reserved for their secret councils. These two buildings afford habitations, as is said, for over six hundred souls. There is likewise an edifice in the Pueblo of Picuris of the same class, and some of those of Moqui are also said to be similar.

Some of these villages were built upon rocky eminences deemed almost inaccessible: witness for instance the ruins of the ancient Pueblo of San Felipe, which may be seen towering upon the very verge of a precipice several hundred feet high, whose base is washed by the swift current of the Rio del Norte. The still existing Pueblo of Acoma also stands upon an isolated mound whose whole area is occupied by the village, being fringed all around by a precipitous *ceja* or cliff.

The inhabitants enter the village by means of ladders, and by steps cut into the solid rock upon which it is based.

At the time of the conquest, many of these Pueblos manufactured some singular textures of cotton and other materials; but with the loss of their liberty, they seem to have lost most of their arts and ingenuity; so that the finer specimens of native fabrics are now only to be met with among the Moquis and Navajoes, who still retain their independence. The Pueblos, however, make some of the ordinary classes of blankets and *tilmas*,* as well as other woollen stuffs. They also manufacture, according to their aboriginal art, both for their own consumption, and for the purposes of traffic, a species of earthenware not much inferior to the coarse crockery of our common potters. The pots made of this material stand fire remarkably well, and are the universal substitutes for all the purposes of cookery, even among the Mexicans, for the iron castings of this country, which are utterly unknown there. Rude as this kind of crockery is, it nevertheless evinces a great deal of skill, considering that it is made entirely without lathe or any kind of machinery. It is often fancifully painted with colored earths and the juice of a plant called *guaco*, which brightens by burning. They also work a singular kind of wicker-ware, of which some bowls (if they may be so called) are so closely plat-

---

* The *tilma* of the North is a sort of small but durable blanket, worn by the Indians as a mantle.

ted, that, once swollen by dampness, they serve to hold liquids, and are therefore light and convenient vessels for the purposes of travellers.

The dress of many of the Pueblos has become assimilated in some respects to that of the common Mexicans; but by far the greatest portion still retain most of their aboriginal costume. The Taosas and others of the north somewhat resemble the prairie tribes in this respect; but the Pueblos to the south and west of Santa Fé dress in a different style, which is said to be similar in many respects to that of the aboriginal inhabitants of the city of Mexico. The moccasin is the only part of the prairie suit that appears common to them all, and of both sexes. They mostly wear a kind of short breeches and long stockings, the use of which they most probably acquired from the Spaniards. The *saco*, a species of woollen jacket without sleeves, completes their exterior garment; except during inclement seasons, when they make use of the tilma. Very few of them have hats or headdress of any kind; and they generally wear their hair long—commonly fashioned into a *queue*, wrapped with some colored stuff. The squaws of the northern tribes dress pretty much like those of the Prairies; but the usual costume of the females of the southern and western Pueblos is a handsome kind of small blanket of dark color, which is drawn under one arm and tacked over the other shoulder, leaving both arms free and naked. It is generally worn with a cotton chemise underneath and is bound about the waist with a girdle. We rarely if ever see a thorough-bred Pueblo woman in Mexican dress.

The weapons most in use among the Pueblos are the bow and arrow, with a long-handled lance and occasionally a fusil. The rawhide shield is also much used, which, though of but little service against fire-arms, serves to ward off the arrow and lance.

The aliment of these Indians is, in most respects, similar to that of the Mexicans; in fact, as has been elsewhere remarked, the latter adopted with their utensils numerous items of aboriginal diet. The *tortilla*, the *atole*, the *pinole*,* and many others, together with the use of *chile*, are from the Indians. Some of the wilder tribes make a peculiar kind of *pinole*, by grinding the bean of the mezquite tree into flour, which is then used as that of corn. And besides the tortilla they make another singular kind of bread, if we may so style it, called *guayave*, a roll of which so much resembles a 'hornets' nest,' that by strangers it is often designated by this title. It is usually made of Indian corn prepared and ground as for tortillas, and diluted into a thin paste.

---

* *Pinole* is in effect the cold-*flour* of our hunters. It is the meal of parched Indian corn, prepared for use by stirring it up with a little cold water. This food seems also to have been of ancient use among the aborigines of other parts of America. Father Charlevoix, in 1721, says of the savages about the northern lakes, that they "reduce [the maize] to Flour which they call *Farine froide* (cold Flour), and this is the best Provision that can be made for Travellers."

I once happened to enter an Indian hut where a young girl of the family was baking *guayaves*. She was sitting by a fire, over which a large flat stone was heating, with a crock of prepared paste by her side. She thrust her hand into the paste, and then wiped it over the heated stone. What adhered to it was instantly baked and peeled off. She repeated this process at the rate of a dozen times or more per minute. Observing my curiosity, the girl handed me one of the 'sheets,' silently; for she seemed to understand but her native tongue. I found it pleasant enough to the taste; though when cold, as I have learned by experience, it is, like the cold tortilla, rather tough and insipid. They are even thinner than wafers; and some dozens, being folded in a roll, constitute the laminate composition before mentioned. Being thus preserved, they serve the natives for months upon their journeys.

CHAPTER XV.

The wild Tribes of New Mexico—Speculative Theories—Clavi gero and the *Azteques*—Pueblo Bonito and other Ruins—Probable Relationship between the *Azteques* and tribes of New Mexico—The several Nations of this Province—*Navajóes* and *Azteques*—Manufactures of the former—Their Agriculture, Religion, etc.—Mexican Cruelty to the Indians and its Consequences—Inroads of the Navajóes—Exploits of a Mexican Army—How to make a Hole in a Powder-keg—The *Apaches* and their Character—Their Food—Novel Mode of settling Disputes—Range of their marauding Excursions—Indian Traffic and imbecile Treaties—Devastation of the Country—Chihuahua Rodomontades—Juan José, a celebrated Apache Chief, and his tragical End, etc.—Massacre of Americans in Retaliation—A tragical Episode—*Proyecto de Guerra* and a 'gallant' Display—The *Yutas* and their Hostilities—A personal Adventure with them, but no blood shed—Jicarillas.

ALL the Indians of New Mexico not denominated Pueblos—not professing the Christian religion—are ranked as *wild tribes*, although these include some who have made great advances in arts, manufactures and agriculture. Those who are at all acquainted with the ancient history of Mexico, will recollect that, according to the traditions of the aborigines, all the principal tribes of Anahuac descended from the North: and that those of Mexico, especially the Azteques, emigrated from the north of California, or northwest of New Mexico. Clavigero, the famous historian heretofore alluded to, speaking of this emigration, observes, that the *Azteques*, or Mexican Indians, who were the last settlers in the country of Anahuac, lived until about the year 1160 of the Christian era in Aztlan, a country situated to the north of the Gulf of California; as is inferred from the route of their peregrinations, and from the information afterwards acquired by the Spaniards in their expeditions through those countries. He then proceeds to show by what incentives they were probably induced to abandon their native land; adding that whatever may have been the motive, no doubt can possibly exist as to the journey's having actually been performed. He says that they travelled in a southeastwardly direction towards the Rio Gila, where they remained for some time—the ruins of their edifices being still to be seen, upon its banks. They then struck out for a point over two hundred and fifty miles to the northwest of Chihuahua in about 29° of N. latitude, where they made another halt. This place is known by the name of *Casas Grandes* (big houses), on account of a large edifice which still stands on the spot, and which, according to the general tradition of those regions, was erected by the Mexican Indians, during their wanderings. The building is constructed after the plan of those in New Mexico, with three stories, covered with an *azotea* or terrace, and without door or entrance into the lower story. A hand ladder is also used as a means of communication with the second story.

Even allowing that the traditions upon which Clavigero founded his theoretical deductions are vague and uncertain, there is sufficient evidence in the ruins that still exist to show that those regions were once inhabited by a far more enlightened people than are now to be found among the aborigines. Of such character are the ruins of *Pueblo Bonito*, in the direction of Navajó, on the borders of the Cordilleras; the houses being generally built of slabs of fine-grit sand-stone, a material utterly unknown in the present architecture of the North. Although some of these structures are very massive and spacious, they are generally cut up into small, irregular rooms, many of which yet remain entire, being still covered, with the *vigas* or joists remaining nearly sound under the *azoteas* of earth; and yet their age is such that there is no tradition which gives any account of their origin. But there have been no images or sculptured work of any kind found about them. Besides these, many other ruins (though none so perfect) are scattered over the plains and among the mountains. What is very remarkable is, that a portion of them are situated at a great distance from any water; so that the inhabitants must have depended entirely upon rain, as is the case with the Pueblo of Acoma at the present day.

The general appearance of Pueblo Bonito,

as well as that of the existing buildings of Moqui in the same mountainous regions, and other Pueblos of New Mexico, resembles so closely the ruins of Casas Grandes, that we naturally come to the conclusion that the founders of each must have descended from the same common stock. The present difference between their language and that of the Indians of Mexico, when we take into consideration the ages that have passed away since their separation, hardly presents any reasonable objection to this hypothesis.

The principal wild tribes which inhabit or extend their incursions or peregrinations upon the territory of New Mexico, are the *Navajóes*, the *Apaches*, the *Yutas*, the *Caiguas* or Kiawas, and the *Comanches*. Of the latter I will speak in another place. The two first are from one and the same original stock, there being, even at the present day, no very important difference in their language. The Apaches are divided into numerous petty tribes, of one of which an insignificant band, called Jicarillas, inhabiting the mountains north of Taos, is an isolated and miserable remnant.

The *Navajóes* are supposed to number about 10,000 souls, and though not the most numerous, they are certainly the most important, at least in a historical point of view, of all the northern tribes of Mexico. They reside in the main range of Cordilleras, 150 to 200 miles west of Santa Fé, on the waters of Rio Colorado of California, not far from the region, according to historians, from whence the

Azteques emigrated to Mexico; and there are many reasons to suppose them direct descendants from the remnant, which remained in the North, of this celebrated nation of antiquity. Although they mostly live in rude *jacales*, somewhat resembling the wigwams of the Pawnees, yet, from time immemorial, they have excelled all others in their original manufactures: and, as well as the Moquis, they are still distinguished for some exquisite styles of cotton textures, and display considerable ingenuity in embroidering with feathers the skins of animals, according to their primitive practice. They now also manufacture a singular species of blanket, known as the *Sarape Navajó*, which is of so close and dense a texture that it will frequently hold water almost equal to gum-elastic cloth. It is therefore highly prized for protection against the rains. Some of the finer qualities are often sold among the Mexicans as high as fifty or sixty dollars each.

Notwithstanding the present predatory and somewhat unsettled habits of the Navajoes, they cultivate all the different grains and vegetables to be found in New Mexico. They also possess extensive herds of horses, mules, cattle, sheep and goats of their own raising, which are generally celebrated as being much superior to those of the Mexicans; owing, no doubt, to greater attention to the improvement of their stocks.

Though Baron Humboldt tells us that some missionaries were established among this tribe prior to the general massacre of 1680, but few attempts to christianize them have since been made. They now remain in a state of primitive paganism—and not only independent of the Mexicans, but their most formidable enemies.

After the establishment of the national independence, the government of New Mexico greatly embittered the disposition of the neighboring savages, especially the Navajoes, by repeated acts of cruelty and ill-faith well calculated to provoke hostilities. On one occasion, a party consisting of several chiefs and warriors of the Navajoes assembled at the Pueblo of Cochití, by invitation of the government, to celebrate a treaty of peace; when the New Mexicans, exasperated no doubt by the remembrance of former outrages, fell upon them unawares and put them all to death. It is also related, that about the same period, three Indians from the northern mountains having been brought as prisoners into Taos, they were peremptorily demanded by the Jicarillas, who were their bitterest enemies; when the Mexican authorities, dreading the resentment of this tribe, quietly complied with the barbarous request, suffering the prisoners to be butchered in cold blood before their very eyes! No wonder, then, that the New Mexicans are so generally warred upon by their savage neighbors.

About fifteen years ago, the Navajoes were subjected by the energy of Col. Vizcarra, who succeeded in keeping them in submission for some time; but since that officer's departure from New Mexico, no man has been found of sufficient capacity to inspire this daring tribe either with respect or fear; so that for the last ten years they have ravaged the country with impunity, murdering and destroying just as the humor happened to prompt them. When the spring of the year approaches, terms of peace are generally proposed to the government at Santa Fé, which the latter never fails to accept. This amicable arrangement enables the wily Indians to sow their crops at leisure, and to dispose of the property stolen from the Mexicans during their marauding incursions, to advantage; but the close of their agricultural labors is generally followed by a renewal of hostilities, and the game of rapine and destruction is played over again.

Towards the close of 1835, a volunteer corps, which most of the leading men in New Mexico joined, was raised for the purpose of carrying war into the territory of the Navajoes. The latter hearing of their approach, and anxious no doubt to save them the trouble of so long a journey, mustered a select band of their warriors, who went forth to intercept the invaders in a mountain pass, where they lay concealed in an ambuscade. The valiant corps, utterly unconscious of the reception that awaited them, soon came jogging along in scattered groups, indulging in every kind of boisterous mirth; when the war-whoop, loud and shrill, followed by several shots, threw them all into a state of speechless consternation. Some tumbled off their horses with fright, others fired their muskets at random: a terrific panic had seized everybody, and some minutes elapsed before they could recover their senses sufficiently to betake themselves to their heels. Two or three persons were killed in this ridiculous engagement, the most conspicuous of whom was a Capt. Hinófos, who commanded the regular troops.

A very curious but fully authentic anecdote may not be inappropriately inserted here, in which this individual was concerned. On one occasion, being about to start on a belligerent expedition, he directed his orderly-sergeant to fill a powder-flask from an unbroached keg of twenty-five pounds. The sergeant, having bored a hole with a gimlet, and finding that the powder issued too slowly, began to look about for something to enlarge the aperture, when his eyes haply fell upon an iron poker which lay in a corner of the fire-place. To heat the poker and apply it to the hole in the keg was the work of but a few moments; when an explosion took place which blew the upper part of the building into the street, tearing and shattering everything else to atoms. Miraculous as their escape may appear, the sergeant, as well as the captain who witnessed the whole operation, remained more frightened than hurt, although they were both very severely scorched and bruised. This ingenious sergeant was afterwards Secretary of State to Gov. Gonzalez, of revolutionary memory, and has nearly ever since held a clerkship in some of the offices of state, but is now captain in the regular army.

I come now to speak of the *Apaches*, the most extensive and powerful, yet the most vagrant of all the savage nations that inhabit the interior of Northern Mexico. They are supposed to number some fifteen thousand souls, although they are subdivided into various petty bands, and scattered over an immense tract of country. Those that are found east of the Rio del Norte are generally known as *Mezcaleros*, on account of an article of food much in use among them, called *mezcal;** but by far the greatest portion of the nation is located in the west, and is mostly known by the sobriquet of *Coyoteros*, in consequence, it is said, of their eating the *coyote* or prairie-wolf. The Apaches are perhaps more given to itinerant habits than any other tribe in Mexico. They never construct houses, but live in the ordinary wigwam, or tent of skins and blankets. They manufacture nothing—cultivate nothing: they seldom resort to the chase, as their country is destitute of game—but depend almost entirely upon pillage for the support of their immense population, some two or three thousand of which are warriors.

For their food, the Apaches rely chiefly upon the flesh of the cattle and sheep they can steal from the Mexican ranchos and haciendas. They are said, however, to be more fond of

---

* *Mezcal* is the baked root of the *maguey* (*agave Americana*) and of another somewhat similar plant.

the meat of the mule than that of any other animal. I have seen about encampments which they had recently left, the remains of mules that had been slaughtered for their consumption. Yet on one occasion I saw their whole trail, for many miles, literally strewed with the carcasses of these animals, which, it was evident, had not been killed for this purpose. It is the practice of the Apache chiefs, as I have understood, whenever a dispute arises betwixt their warriors relative to the ownership of any particular animal, to kill the brute at once, though it be the most valuable of the drove; and so check all further cavil. It was to be inferred from the number of dead mules they left behind them, that the most harmonious relations could not have existed between the members of the tribe, at least during this period of their journeyings. Like most of the savage tribes of North America, the Apaches are passionately fond of spirituous liquors, and may frequently be seen, in times of peace, lounging about the Mexican villages, in a state of helpless inebriety.

The range of this marauding tribe extends over some portions of California, most of Sonora, the frontiers of Durango, and at certain seasons it even reaches Coahuila: Chihuahua, however, has been the mournful theatre of their most constant depredations. Every nook and corner of this once flourishing state has been subjected to their inroads. Such is the imbecility of the local governments, that the savages, in order to dispose of their stolen property without even a shadow of molestation, frequently enter into partial treaties of peace with one department, while they continue to wage a war of extermination against the neighboring states. This arrangement supplies them with an ever-ready market, for the disposal of their booty and the purchase of munitions wherewith to prosecute their work of destruction. In 1840, I witnessed the departure from Santa Fé of a large trading party freighted with engines of war and a great quantity of whiskey, intended for the Apaches in exchange for mules and other articles of plunder which they had stolen from the people of the south. This traffic was not only tolerated but openly encouraged by the civil authorities, as the highest public functionaries were interested in its success— the governor himself not excepted.

The Apaches, now and then, propose a truce to the government of Chihuahua, which is generally accepted very nearly upon their own terms. It has on some occasions been included that the marauders should have a *bonâ fide* right to all their stolen property. A *venta* or quit-claim brand, has actually been marked by the government upon large numbers of mules and horses which the Indians had robbed from the citizens. It is hardly necessary to add that these truces have rarely been observed by the wily savages longer than the time necessary for the disposal of their plunder. As soon as more mules were needed for service or for traffic—more cattle for beef—more scalps for the war-dance—they would invariably return to their deeds of ravage and murder.

The depredations of the Apaches have been of such long duration, that, beyond the immediate purlieus of the towns, the whole country from New Mexico to the borders of Durango is almost entirely depopulated. The haciendas and ranchos have been mostly abandoned, and the people chiefly confined to towns and cities. To such a pitch has the temerity of those savages reached, that small bands of three or four warriors have been known to make their appearance within a mile of the city of Chihuahua in open day, killing the laborers and driving off whole herds of mules and horses without the slightest opposition. Occasionally a detachment of troops is sent in pursuit of the marauders, but for no other purpose, it would seem, than to illustrate the imbecility of the former, as they are always sure to make a precipitate retreat, generally without even obtaining a glimpse of the enemy.* And yet the columns of a little weekly sheet published in Chihuahua always teem with flaming accounts of prodigious feats of valor performed by the 'army of operations' against *los bárbaros:* showing how "the enemy was pursued with all possible vigor"—how the soldiers "displayed the great-

---

* It has been credibly asserted, that, during one of these 'bold pursuits,' a band of Comanches stopped in the suburbs of a village on Rio Conchos, turned their horses into the wheat-fields, and took a comfortable *siesta*—desirous, it seemed, to behold their pursuers face to face; yet, after remaining most of the day, they departed without enjoying that pleasure.

est bravery, and the most unrestrainable desire to overhaul the dastards," and by what extraordinary combinations of adverse circumstances they were "compelled to relinquish the pursuit." Indeed, it would be difficult to find a braver race of people than the *Chihuahueños** contrive to make themselves appear upon paper. When intelligence was received in Chihuahua of the famous skirmish with the French, at Vera Cruz, in which Santa Anna acquired the glory of losing a leg, the event was celebrated with uproarious demonstrations of joy; and the next number of the *Noticioso*† contained a valiant fanfaronade, proclaiming to the world the astounding fact, that one Mexican was worth four French soldiers in battle: winding up with a "*Cancion Patriótica,*" of which the following exquisite verse was the *refrain*:

> "*Chihuahuenses, la Patria gloriosa*
> *Otro timbre á su lustre ha añadido;*
> *Pues la* ınʌıɔʇɐ, ɐl Ɔɐllɐ ınpoɯɐqlǝ
> AL VALOR MEXICANO *ha cedido*."

Literally translated:

> Chihuahuenses! our glorious country
> Another ray has added to her lustre;
> For the *invincible, indomitable Gallia*
> Has succumbed to Mexican valor.

By the inverted letters of "*invicta, la Galia indomable,*" in the third line, the poet gives

* Or *Chihuahuenses*, citizens of Chihuahua.
† *Noticioso de Chihuahua* of December 28, 1838.

the world to understand that the kingdom of the Gauls had at length been whirled topsy-turvy, by the glorious achievements of *el valor Mexicano!*

From what has been said of the ravages of the Apaches, one would be apt to believe them an exceedingly brave people; but the Mexicans themselves call them cowards when compared with the Comanches; and we are wont to look upon the latter as perfect specimens of poltroonery when brought in conflict with the Shawnees, Delawares, and the rest of our border tribes.

There was once a celebrated chief called Juan José at the head of this tribe, whose extreme cunning and audacity caused his name to be dreaded throughout the country. What contributed more than anything else to render him a dangerous enemy, was the fact of his having received a liberal education at Chihuahua, which enabled him, when he afterwards rejoined his tribe, to outwit his pursuers, and, by robbing the mails, to acquire timely information of every expedition that was set on foot against him. The following account of the massacre in which he fell may not be altogether uninteresting to the reader.

The government of Sonora, desirous to make some efforts to check the depredations of the Apaches, issued a proclamation, giving a sort of *carte blanche* patent of 'marque and reprisal,' and declaring all the booty that might be taken from the savages to be the rightful property of the captors. Accordingly, in the spring of 1837, a party of some 20 men composed chiefly of foreigners, spurred on by the love of gain, and never doubting but the Indians, after so many years of successful robberies, must be possessed of a vast amount of property, set out with an American as their commander, who had long resided in the country. In a few days they reached a *ranchería* of about fifty warriors with their families, among whom was the famous Juan José himself, and three other principal chiefs. On seeing the Americans advance, the former at once gave them to understand, that, if they had come to fight, they were ready to accommodate them; but on being assured by the leader, that they were merely bent on a trading expedition, a friendly interview was immediately established between the parties. The American captain having determined to put these obnoxious chiefs to death under any circumstances, soon caused a little field-piece which had been concealed from the Indians to be loaded with chain and canister shot, and to be held in readiness for use. The warriors were then invited to the camp to receive a present of flour, which was placed within range of the cannon. While they were occupied in dividing the contents of the bag, they were fired upon and a considerable number of their party killed on the spot! The remainder were then attacked with small arms, and about twenty slain, including Juan José and the other chiefs. Those who escaped became afterwards their own avengers in a manner which proved terribly disastrous to another party of Americans, who happened at the time to be trapping on Rio Gila not far distant. The enraged savages resolved to take summary vengeance upon these unfortunate trappers; and falling upon them, massacred them every one! They were in all, including several Mexicans, about fifteen in number.*

The projector of this scheme had probably been under the impression that treachery was justifiable against a treacherous enemy. He also believed, no doubt, that the act would be highly commended by the Mexicans who had suffered so much from the depredations of these notorious chiefs. But in this he was sadly mistaken; for the affair was received with general reprehension, although the Mexicans had been guilty of similar deeds themselves, as the following brief episode will sufficiently show.

In the summer of 1839, a few Apache prisoners, among whom was the wife of a distin-

* The Apaches, previous to this date, had committed but few depredations upon foreigners—restrained either by fear or respect. Small parties of the latter were permitted to pass the highways of the wilderness unmolested, while large caravans of Mexicans suffered frequent attacks. This apparent partiality produced unfounded jealousies, and the Americans were openly accused of holding secret treaties with the enemy, and even of supplying them with arms and ammunition. Although an occasional foreigner engaged in this clandestine and culpable traffic, yet the natives themselves embarked in it beyond comparison more extensively, as has been noted in another place. This unjust impression against Americans was partially effaced as well by the catastrophes mentioned in the text, as by the defeat and robbery (in which, however, no American lives were lost), of a small party of our people, about the same period, in *La Jornada del Muerto*, on their way from Chihuahua to Santa Fé.

guished chief, were confined in the calabozo of Paso del Norte. The bereaved chief, hearing of their captivity, collected a band of about sixty warriors, and, boldly entering the town, demanded the release of his consort and friends. The commandant of the place wishing to gain time, desired them to return the next morning, when their request would be granted. During the night the forces of the country were concentrated; notwithstanding, when the Apaches reappeared, the troops did not show their faces, but remained concealed, while the Mexican commandant strove to beguile the Indians into the prison, under pretence of delivering to them their friends. The unsuspecting chief and twenty others were entrapped in this manner, and treacherously dispatched in cold blood: not, however, without some loss to the Mexicans, who had four or five of their men killed in the fracas. Among these was the commandant himself, who had no sooner given the word, "¡ *Maten á los carajos!*" (kill the scoundrels!) than the chief retorted, "¡ *Entónces morirás tu primero, carajo!*" (then you shall die first, carajo!) and immediately stabbed him to the heart!

But as New Mexico is more remote from the usual haunts of the Apaches, and, in fact, as her scanty ranchos present a much less fruitful field for their operations than the abundant haciendas of the South, the depredations of this tribe have extended but little upon that province. The only serious incursion that has come within my knowledge, was some ten years ago. A band of Apache warriors boldly approached the town of Socorro on the southern border, when a battle ensued between them and the Mexican force, composed of a company of regular troops and all the militia of the place. The Mexicans were soon completely routed and chased into the very streets, suffering a loss of thirty-three killed and several wounded. The savages bore away their slain, yet their loss was supposed to be but six or seven. I happened to be in the vicinity of the catastrophe the following day, when the utmost consternation prevailed among the inhabitants, who were in hourly expectation of another descent from the savages.

Many schemes have been devised from time to time, particularly by the people of Chihuahua, to check the ravages of the Indians, but generally without success. Among these the notorious *Proyecto de Guerra*, adopted in 1837, stands most conspicuous. By this famous 'war-project' a scale of rewards was established, to be paid out of a fund raised for that purpose. A hundred dollars reward were offered for the scalp of a full grown man, fifty for that of a squaw, and twenty-five for that of every papoose! To the credit of the republic, however, this barbarous *proyecto* was in operation but a few weeks, and never received the sanction of the general government; although it was strongly advocated by some of the most intelligent citizens of Chihuahua. Yet, pending its existence, it was rigidly complied with. I saw myself, on one occasion, a detachment of horsemen approach the Palacio in Chihuahua, preceded by their commanding officer, who bore a fresh scalp upon the tip of his lance, which he waved high in the air in exultation of his exploit! The next number of our little newspaper contained the official report of the affair. The soldiers were pursuing a band of Apaches, when they discovered a squaw who had lagged far behind in her endeavors to bear away her infant babe. They dispatched the mother without commiseration and took her scalp, which was the one so 'gallantly' displayed as already mentioned! The officer concluded his report by adding, that the child had *died* not long after it was made prisoner.

The *Yutas* (or *Eutaws*, as they are generally styled by Americans) are one of the most extensive nations of the West, being scattered from the north of New Mexico to the borders of Snake river and Rio Colorado, and numbering at least ten thousand souls. The habits of the tribe are altogether itinerant. A band of about a thousand spend their winters mostly in the mountain valleys northward of Taos, and the summer season generally in the prairie plains to the east, hunting buffalo. The vernacular language of the Yutas is said to be distantly allied to that of the Navajoes, but it has appeared to me much more guttural, having a deep sepulchral sound resembling ventriloquism. Although these Indians are nominally at peace with the New Mexican government, they do not hesitate to lay the hunters and traders who happen to fall in with their scouring parties under severe contributions; and on some occasions they have been known to proceed even to personal violence. A prominent Mexican officer* was scourged not long ago by a party of Yutas, and yet the government has never dared to resent the outrage. Their hostilities, however, have not been confined to Mexican traders, as will be perceived by the sequel.

In the summer of 1837, a small party of but five or six Shawnees fell in with a large band of Yutas near the eastern borders of the Rocky Mountains, south of Arkansas river. At first they were received with every demonstration of friendship; but the Yutas, emboldened no doubt by the small number of their visitors, very soon concluded to relieve them of whatever surplus property they might be possessed of. The Shawnees, however, much to the astonishment of the marauders, instead of quietly surrendering their goods and chattels, offered to defend them; upon which a skirmish ensued that actually cost the Yutas several of their men, including a favorite chief; while the Shawnees made their escape unhurt toward their eastern homes.

A few days after this event, and while the Yutas were still bewailing the loss of their people, I happened to pass near their *rancherías* (temporary village) with a small caravan which mustered about thirty-five men. We

* Don Juan Andrés Archuleta, who commanded at the capture of Gen. McLeod's division of the Texans.

had hardly pitched our camp, when they began to flock about us—men, squaws, and papooses—in great numbers; but the warriors were sullen and reserved, only now and then muttering a curse upon the Americans on account of the treatment they had just received from the Shawnees, whom they considered as half-castes, and our allies. All of a sudden, a young warrior seized a splendid steed which belonged to our party, and, leaping upon his back, galloped off at full speed. Being fully convinced that, by acquiescing in this outrage, we should only encourage them to commit others, we resolved at once to make a peremptory demand for the stolen horse of their principal chief. Our request being treated with contumely, we sent in a warlike declaration, and forthwith commenced making preparations for descending upon the *rancherías*. The war-whoop resounded immediately in every direction; and as the Yutas bear a very high character for bravery and skill, the readiness with which they seemed to accept our challenge began to alarm our party considerably. We had defied them to mortal combat merely by way of bravado, without the least expectation that they would put themselves to so much inconvenience on our account. It was too late, however, to back out of the scrape.

No sooner had the alarm been given than the *rancherías* of the Indians were converted into a martial encampment; and while the mounted warriors were exhibiting their preliminary feats of horsemanship, the squaws and papooses flew like scattered partridges to the rocks and clefts of a contiguous precipice. One-third of our party being Mexicans, the first step of the Indians was to proclaim a general *indulto* to them, in hopes of reducing our force, scanty as it was already. "My Mexican friends," exclaimed in good Spanish, a young warrior who daringly rode up within a few rods of us, "we don't wish to hurt *you;* so leave those Americans, for we intend to kill every one of *them.*" The Mexicans of our party to whom this language was addressed, being rancheros of some mettle, only answered, "*Al diablo!* we have not forgotten how you treat us when you catch us alone: now that we are with Americans who will defend their rights, expect ample retaliation for past insults." In truth, these rancheros seemed the most anxious to begin the fight,—a remarkable instance of the effects of confidence in companions.

A crisis seemed now fast approaching: two swivels we had with us were levelled and primed, and the matches lighted. Every man was at his post, with his rifle ready for execution, each anxious to do his best, whatever might be the result; when the Indians, seeing us determined to embrace the chances of war, began to open negotiations. An aged squaw, said to be the mother of the principal chief, rode up and exclaimed, "My sons! the Americans and Yutas have been friends, and our old men wish to continue so: it is only a few impetuous and strong-headed youths who want to fight." The stolen horse having been restored soon after this harangue, peace was joyfully proclaimed throughout both encampments, and the *capitanes* exchanged ratifications by a social smoke.

The little tribe of Jicarillas also harbored an enmity for the Americans, which, in 1834, broke out into a hostile *rencontre*. They had stolen some animals of a gallant young backwoodsman from Missouri, who, with a few comrades, pursued the marauders into the mountains and regained his property; and a fracas ensuing, an Indian or two were killed. A few days afterward all their warriors visited Santa Fé in a body, and demanded of the authorities there, the delivery of the American offenders to their vengeance. Though the former showed quite a disposition to gratify the savages as far as practicable, they had not helpless creatures to deal with, as in the case of the Indian prisoners already related. The foreigners, seeing their protection devolved upon themselves, prepared for defence, when the savages were fain to depart in peace.

CHAPTER XVI.

Incidents of a Return Trip from Santa Fé—Calibre of our Party—Return Caravans—Remittances—Death of Mr. Langham—Burial in the Desert—A sudden Attack—Confusion in the Camp—A Wolfish Escort—Scarcity of Buffalo—Unprofitable Delusion—Arrival—Table of Camping Sites and Distances—Condition of the Town of Independence—The Mormons—Their Dishonesty and Immorality—Their high-handed Measures, and a Rising of the People—A fatal Skirmish—A chivalrous Parade of the Citizens—Expulsion of the Mormons—The Meteoric Shower, and Superstition, etc.—Wanderings and Improprieties of the 'Latter-day Saints'—Gov. Boggs' Recipe—The City of Nauvoo—Contemplated Retribution of the Mormons.

I do not propose to detain the reader with an account of my journeyings between Mexico and the United States, during the seven years subsequent to my first arrival at Santa Fé. I will here merely remark, that I crossed the plains to the United States in the falls of 1833 and 1836, and returned to Santa Fé with goods each succeeding spring. It was only in 1838, however, that I eventually closed up my affairs in Northern Mexico, and prepared to take my leave of the country, as I then supposed, forever. But in this I was mistaken, as will appear in the sequel.

The most usual season for the return of the

caravans to the United States is the autumn, and not one has elapsed since the commencement of the trade which has not witnessed some departure from Santa Fé with that destination. They have also crossed occasionally in the spring, but without any regularity or frequency, and generally in very small parties. Even the 'fall companies,' in fact, are small when compared with the outward-bound caravans; for besides the numbers who remain permanently in the country, many of those who trade southward return to the United States *via* Matamoros or some other Southern port. The return parties of autumn are therefore comparatively small, varying in number from fifty to a hundred men. They leave Santa Fé some four or five weeks after their arrival—generally about the first of September. In these companies there are rarely over thirty or forty wagons; for a large portion of those taken out by the annual caravans are disposed of in the country.

Some of the traders who go out in the spring, return the ensuing fall, because they have the good fortune to sell off their stock promptly and to advantage: others are compelled to return in the fall to save their credit; nay, to preserve their homes, which, especially in the earlier periods, have sometimes been mortgaged to secure the payment of the merchandise they carried out with them. In such cases, their goods were not unfrequently sold at great sacrifice, to avoid the penalties which the breaking of their engagements at home would involve. New adventurers, too, are apt to become discouraged with an unanticipated dullness of times, and not unfrequently sell off at wholesale for the best price they can get, though often at a serious loss. But those who are regularly engaged in this trade usually calculate upon employing a season—perhaps a year, in closing an enterprise—in selling off their goods and making their returns.

The wagons of the return caravans are generally but lightly laden: one to two thousand pounds constitute the regular return cargo for a single wagon; for not only are the teams unable to haul heavy loads, on account of the decay of pasturage at this season, but the approaching winter compels the traders to travel in greater haste; so that this trip is usually made in about forty days. The amount of freight, too, from that direction is comparatively small. The remittances, as has already been mentioned, are chiefly in specie, or gold and silver bullion. The gold is mostly *dust*, from the Placer or gold mine near Santa Fé: the silver bullion is all from the mines of the South—chiefly from those of Chihuahua. To these returns may be added a considerable number of mules and asses—some buffalo rugs, furs, and wool,—which last barely pays a return freight for the wagons that would otherwise be empty. Coarse Mexican blankets, which may be obtained in exchange for merchandise, have been sold in small quantities to advantage on our border.

On the 4th of April, 1838, we departed from Santa Fé. Our little party was found to consist of twenty-three Americans, with twelve Mexican servants. We had seven wagons, one dearborn, and two small field-pieces, besides a large assortment of small-arms. The principal proprietors carried between them about $150,000 in specie and bullion, being for the most part the proceeds of the previous year's adventure.

We moved on at a brisk and joyous pace until we reached Ocaté creek, a tributary of the Colorado, a distance of a hundred and thirty miles from Santa Fé, where we encountered a very sudden bereavement in the death of Mr. Langham, one of our most respected proprietors. This gentleman was known to be in weak health, but no fears were entertained for his safety. We were all actively engaged in assisting the more heavily laden wagons over the miry stream, when he was seized with a fit of apoplexy and expired instantly. As we had not the means of giving the deceased a decent burial, we were compelled to consign him to the earth in a shroud of blankets. A grave was accordingly dug on an elevated spot near the north bank of the creek, and on the morning of the 13th, ere the sun had risen in the east, the mortal remains of this most worthy man and valued friend were deposited in their last abode,—without a tomb-stone to consecrate the spot, or an epitaph to commemorate his virtues. The deceased was from St. Louis, though he had passed the last eleven years of his life in Santa Fé, during the whole of which period he had seen neither his home nor his relatives.

The melancholy rites being concluded, we resumed our line of march. We now continued for several days without the occurrence of any important accident or adventure. On the 19th we encamped in the Cimarron valley, about twelve miles below the Willow Bar. The very sight of this desolate region, frequented as it is by the most savage tribes of Indians, was sufficient to strike dismay into the hearts of our party; but as we had not as yet encountered any of them, we felt comparatively at ease. Our mules and horses were 'staked' as usual around the wagons, and every man, except the watch, betook himself to his blanket, in anticipation of a good night's rest. The hour of midnight had passed away, and nothing had been heard except the tramping of the men on guard, and the peculiar grating of the mules' teeth, nibbling the short grass of the valley. Ere long, however, one of our sentinels got a glimpse of some object moving stealthily along, and as he was straining his eyes to ascertain what sort of apparition it could be, a loud Indian yell suddenly revealed the mystery. This was quickly followed by a discharge of fire-arms, and the shrill note of the 'Pawnee whistle,' which at once made known the character of our visitors. As usual, the utmost confusion prevailed in our camp: some, who had been snatched from the land of dreams, ran their heads against the wagons—others called out for their guns while they had them in their hands. During the height of the bustle and uproar, a Mexican servant was observed leaning with his back against a wagon, and his fusil elevated at an angle of forty-five degrees, cocking and pulling the trigger without ceasing, and exclaiming at every snap, "*Carajo, no sirve!*"—Curse it, it's good for nothing.

The firing still continued—the yells grew fiercer and more frequent; and everything betokened the approach of a terrible conflict. Meanwhile a number of persons were engaged in securing the mules and horses which were staked around the encampment; and in a few minutes they were all shut up in the *corral*—a hundred head or more in a pen formed by seven wagons. The enemy failing in their principal object—to frighten off our stock, they soon began to retreat; and in a few minutes nothing more was to be heard of them. All that we could discover the next morning was, that none of our party had sustained any injury, and that we had not lost a single animal.

The Pawnees have been among the most formidable and treacherous enemies of the Santa Fé traders. But the former have also suffered a little in turn from the caravans. In 1832, a company of traders were approached by a single Pawnee chief, who commenced a parley with them, when he was shot down by a Pueblo Indian of New Mexico who hap pened to be with the caravan. Though this cruel act met with the decided reprobation of the traders generally, yet they were of course held responsible for it by the Indians.

On our passage this time across the 'prairie ocean' which lay before us, we ran no risk of getting bewildered or lost, for there was now a plain wagon trail across the entire stretch of our route, from the Cimarron to Arkansas river.

This track, which has since remained permanent, was made in the year 1834. Owing to continuous rains during the passage of the caravan of that year, a plain trail was then cut in the softened turf, on the most direct route across this arid desert, leaving the Arkansas about twenty miles above the 'Caches.' This has ever since been the regular route of the caravans; and thus a recurrence of those distressing sufferings from thirst, so frequently experienced by early travellers in that inhospitable region, has been prevented.

We forded the Arkansas without difficulty, and pursued our journey to the Missouri border with comparative ease; being only now and then disturbed at night by the hideous howlings of wolves, a pack of which had constituted themselves into a kind of 'guard of honor,' and followed in our wake for several hundred miles—in fact to the very border of the settlements. They were at first attracted no doubt by the remains of buffalo which were killed by us upon the high plains, and afterwards enticed on by an occasional fagged animal, which we were compelled to leave behind, as well as by the bones and scraps of food, which they picked up about our camps. Not a few of them paid the penalty of their lives for their temerity.

Had we not fortunately been supplied with a sufficiency of meat and other provisions, we might have suffered of hunger before reaching the settlements; for we saw no buffalo after crossing the Arkansas river. It is true that, owing to their disrelish for the long dry grass of the eastern prairies, the buffalo are rarely found so far east in autumn as during the spring; yet I never saw them so scarce in this region before. In fact, at all seasons, they are usually very abundant as far east as our point of leaving the Arkansas river.

Upon reaching the settlements, I had an opportunity of experiencing a delusion which had been the frequent subject of remark by travellers on the Prairies before. Accustomed as we had been for some months to our little mules, and the equally small-sized Mexican ponies, our sight became so adjusted to their proportions, that when we came to look upon the commonest hackney of our frontier horses, it appeared to be almost a monster. I have frequently heard exclamations of this kind from the new arrivals:—"How the Missourians have improved their breed of horses!"—"What a huge gelding!"—"Did you ever see such an animal!" This delusion is frequently availed of by the frontiersmen to put off their meanest horses to these deluded travellers for the most enormous prices.

On the 11th of May we arrived at Independence, after a propitious journey of only thirty-eight days.* We found the town in a thriving condition, although it had come very near being laid waste a few years before by the Mormons, who had originally selected this section of the country for the site of their New Jerusalem. In this they certainly displayed far more taste and good sense than they are generally supposed to be endowed

* Having crossed the Prairies between Independence and Santa Fé six times, I can now present a table of the most notable camping sites, and their respective intermediate distances, with approximate accuracy—which may prove acceptable to some future travellers. The whole distance has been variously estimated at from 750 to 800 miles, yet I feel confident that the aggregate here presented is very nearly the true distance.

From INDEPENDENCE to	M.	Agg.		M.	Agg.
Round Grove,	35		Sand Cr. (leav. Ark. r.)	50	437
Narrows,	30	65	Cimarron r.(Lower sp.)	8	445
110-mile Creek,	30	95	Middle spr. (up Cim. r.)	36	481
Bridge Cr.,	8	103	Willow Bar,	26	507
Big John Spring,			Upper Spring,	18	525
(crossing sev'l Crs.)	40	143	Cold spr. (leav.Cim. r.)	5	530
Council Grove,	2	145	M'Nees's Cr.,	25	555
Diamond Spring,	15	160	Rabbit-ear Cr.,	20	575
Lost Spring,	15	175	Round Mound,	8	583
Cottonwood Cr.,	12	187	Rock Creek,	8	591
Turkey Cr.,	25	212	Point of Rocks,	19	610
Little Arkansas,	17	229	Rio Colorado,	20	630
Cow Creek,	20	249	Ocatè,	6	636
Arkansas River,	16	265	Santa Clara Spr.,	21	657
Walnut Cr.(up Ark. r.)	8	273	Rio Mora,	22	679
Ash Creek,	19	292	Rio Gallinas (Vegas),	20	699
Pawnee Fork,	6	298	Ojo de Bernal (spr.),	17	716
Coon Creek,	33	331	San Miguel,	6	722
Caches,	36	367	Pecos village,	23	755
Ford of Arkansas,	20	387	SANTA FÉ,	25	780

with: for the rich and beautiful uplands in the vicinity of Independence might well be denominated the 'garden spot' of the Far West. Their principal motive for preferring the border country, however, was no doubt a desire to be in the immediate vicinity of the Indians, as the reclamation of the 'Lost tribes of Israel' was a part of their pretended mission.

Prior to 1833, the Mormons, who were then flocking in great swarms to this favored region, had made considerable purchases of lots and tracts of land both in the town of Independence and in the adjacent country. A general depot, profanely styled the 'Lord's Store,' was established, from which the faithful were supplied with merchandise at moderate prices; while those who possessed any surplus of property were expected to deposit it in the same, for the benefit of the mass. The Mormons were at first kindly received by the good people of the country, who looked upon them as a set of harmless fanatics, very susceptible of being moulded into good and honest citizens. This confidence, however, was not destined to remain long in the ascendant, for they soon began to find that the corn in their cribs was sinking like snow before the sun-rays, and that their hogs and their cattle were by some mysterious agency rapidly disappearing. The new-comers also drew upon themselves much animadversion in consequence of the immorality of their lives, and in particular their disregard for the sacred rites of marriage.

Still they continued to spread and multiply, not by conversion but by immigration, to an alarming extent; and in proportion as they grew strong in numbers, they also became more exacting and bold in their pretensions. In a little paper printed at Independence under their immediate auspices, everything was said that could provoke hostility between the 'saints' and their 'worldly' neighbors, until at last they became so emboldened by impunity, as openly to boast of their determination to be the sole proprietors of the 'Land of Zion;' a revelation to that effect having been made to their prophet.

The people now began to perceive, that, at the rate the intruders were increasing, they would soon be able to command a majority of the county, and consequently the entire control of affairs would fall into their hands. It was evident, then, that one of the two parties would in the course of time have to abandon the country; for the old settlers could not think of bringing up their families in the midst of such a corrupt state of society as the Mormons were establishing. Still the nuisance was endured very patiently, and without any attempt at retaliation, until the 'saints' actually threatened to eject their opponents by main force. This last stroke of impudence at once roused the latent spirit of the honest backwoodsmen, some of whom were of the pioneer settlers of Missouri, and had become familiar with danger in their terrific wars with the savages. They were therefore by no means appropriate subjects for yielding what they believed to be their rights. Meetings were held for the purpose of devising means of redress, which only tended to increase the insolence of the Mormons. Finally a mob was collected, which proceeded at once to raze the obnoxious printing establishment to the ground, and to destroy all the materials they could lay hands upon. One or two of the Mormon leaders who fell into the hands of the people, were treated to a clean suit of 'tar and feathers,' and otherwise severely punished. The 'Prophet Joseph,' however, was not then in the neighborhood. Having observed the storm-clouds gathering apace in the frontier horizon, he very wisely remained in Ohio, whence he issued his flaming mandates.

These occurrences took place in the month of October, 1833, and I reached Independence from Santa Fé while the excitement was raging at its highest. The Mormons had rallied some ten miles west of the town, where their strongest settlements were located. A hostile encounter was hourly expected: nay, a skirmish actually took place shortly after, in which a respectable lawyer of Independence, who had been an active agent against the Mormons, was killed. In short, the whole country was in a state of dreadful fermentation.

Early on the morning after the skirmish just referred to, a report reached Independence that the Mormons were marching in a body towards the town, with the intention of sacking and burning it. I had often heard the cry of "Indians!" announcing the approach of hostile savages, but I do not remember ever to have witnessed so much consternation as prevailed at Independence on this memorable occasion. The note of alarm was sounded far and near, and armed men, eager for the fray, were rushing in from every quarter. Officers were summarily selected without deference to rank or station: the 'spirit-stirring drum' and the 'ear-piercing fife' made the air resound with music; and a little army of as brave and resolute a set of fellows as ever trod a field of battle, was, in a very short time, paraded through the streets. After a few preliminary exercises, they started for a certain point on the road where they intended to await the approach of the Mormons. The latter very soon made their appearance, but, surprised at meeting with so formidable a reception, they never even attempted to pull a trigger, but at once surrendered at discretion. They were immediately disarmed, and subsequently released upon condition of their leaving the country without delay.

It was very soon after this affair that the much talked of phenomenon of the meteoric shower (on the night of November 12th) occurred. This extraordinary visitation did not fail to produce its effects upon the superstitious minds of a few ignorant people, who began to wonder whether, after all, the Mor mons might not be in the right; and whether this was not a sign sent from heaven as a remonstrance for the injustice they had been guilty of towards that chosen sect.* Sometime afterward, a terrible misfortune occurred which was in no way calculated to allay the superstitious fears of the ignorant. As some eight or ten citizens were returning with the ferry-boat which had crossed the last Mormons over the Missouri river, into Clay county, the district selected for their new home, the craft filled with water and sunk in the middle of the current; by which accident three or four men were drowned! It was owing perhaps to the craziness of the boat, yet some persons suspected the Mormons of having scuttled it by secretly boring auger-holes in the bottom just before they had left it.

After sojourning a few months in Clay county, to the serious annoyance of the inhabitants (though, in fact, they had been kindly received at first), the *persecuted* 'Latter day Saints' were again compelled to shift their quarters further off. They now sought to establish themselves in the new county of Caldwell, and founded their town of Far West, where they lingered in comparative peace for a few years. As the county began to fill up with settlers, however, quarrels re-

---

* In Northern Mexico, as I learned afterwards, the credulity of the superstitious was still more severely tried by this celestial phenomenon. Their Church had been deprived of some important privileges by the Congress but a short time before, and the people could not be persuaded but that the meteoric shower was intended as a curse upon the nation in consequence of that sacrilegious act.

peatedly broke out, until at last, in 1838, they found themselves again at open war with their neighbors. They appear to have set the laws of the state at defiance, and to have acted so turbulently throughout, that Governor Boggs deemed it necessary to order out a large force of state militia to subject them: which was easily accomplished without bloodshed. From that time the Mormons have harbored a mortal enmity towards the Governor: and the attempt which was afterwards made to assassinate him at Independence, is generally believed to have been instigated, if not absolutely perpetrated, by that deluded sect.

Being once more forced to emigrate, they passed into Illinois, where they founded the famous 'City of Nauvoo.' It would seem that their reception from the people of this state was even more strongly marked with kindness and indulgence than it had been elsewhere, being generally looked upon as the victims of persecution on account of their religious belief; yet it appears that the good people of Illinois have since become about as tired of them as were any of their former neighbors. It seems very clear then, that fanatical delusion is not the only sin which stamps the conduct of these people with so much obliquity, or they would certainly have found permanent friends somewhere; whereas it is well known that a general aversion has prevailed against them wherever they have sojourned.

Before concluding this chapter, it may be

proper to remark, that the Mormons have invariably refused to sell any of the property they had acquired in Missouri, but have on the contrary expressed a firm determination to reconquer their lost purchases. Of these, a large lot, situated on an elevated point at Independence, known as the 'Temple Lot,' upon which the 'Temple of Zion' was to have been raised,—has lately been 'profaned,' by cultivation, having been converted into a cornfield!

END OF VOL. 1.

GLOSSARY,

Containing such Spanish or Hispano-Mexican words as occur undefined in this work, or recur without definition after having been once translated.

A, al, to, to the.
Abajo, down, under, below.
Acequia, ditch, canal.
Adelantado, governor of a province.
A dios, adieu, farewell.
Administrador de Rentas, a custom-house officer.
Adobe, a sort of unburnt brick.
Afuera, without, abroad.
Aguador, water-carrier.
Aguardiente, brandy.
Alacran, scorpion.
Alameda, public walk, with rows of trees, usually the *álamo.*
Alamo (in Mexico), cotton-wood.
Alcalde, justice of the peace.
Alegria, mirth; a plant.
Allí, there.
Amigo, friend.
Ancheta, adventure of goods.
Angelito, little angel.
Angostura, narrowness.
Aparejo, sort of pack-saddle.
Aqui, here.
Arancel, tariff.
Armas, arms.
Arriba, up, above.
Arriero, muleteer.
Asambléa, assembly.
Astucia, cunning, artifice.
Atajo, drove of pack mules, &c.
Atole, sort of thick gruel.
Auto, act, edict.
Azotéa, flat roof, terrace.

Baile, ball, dance.
Bandolin, species of small guitar.
Bárbaro, barbarous; a savage.
Barra, ingot, bar of silver, &c.
Baston, staff, cane.
Blanco, white.
Bolsa, pocket, purse.
Bonanza, prosperity.
Bonito, pretty.
Bota, boot, leggin.
Bravo, brave, bold.

Bueno, good.
Burro, ass.

Caballada, drove of horses, &c.
Caballero, gentleman, knight.
Caballo, horse.
Cacique, Indian chief or prince.
Café, coffee; coffee-house.
Calabozo, dungeon, jail.
Caliente, warm, hot.
Camino, road.
Campo, field, camp.
Campo santo, cemetery without a church.
Cancion, song, poem.
Cañada, valley.
Cañon, deep gorge or ravine; cannon.
Capilla, chapel.
Capitan, captain.
Carajo, an oath; scoundrel.
Caravana, caravan.
Cárcel, prison, jail.
Carga, load.
Cargador, carrier.
Cargamento, cargo.
Carnero, male sheep.
Carreta, cart.
Carro, wagon, &c.
Casa, house.
Cautivo, captive.
Ceja, brow.
Centralismo, central government.
Cerro, mound.
Chacal, jackal.
Chico, small; small person.
Chile, red pepper.
Cibolero, buffalo-hunter.
Cibolo, the American buffalo.
Cigarrito, little cigar.
Cigarro, cigar.
Cimarron, wild.
Claco, small copper coin.
Coche, coach.
Cocina, kitchen.
Cocinera, female cook.
Cola, tail; glue.
Colorado, red.

322   GLOSSARY.

Comanchero, Comanche trader.
Comiso, confiscation.
Consumo, consumption.
Contra-revolucion, counter-revolution.
Cordillera, chain of mountains.
Corral, yard, pen.
Correr, to run.
Coyote, prairie-wolf.
Crepúsculo, dawn, twilight.
Cristo, Christ.
Cruz, cross.
Cuñado, brother-in-law

De, del, of, of the, &c.
Decreto, decree.
Derecho, tax; right.
Descubrimiento, discovery.
Dia, day.
Diablo, devil.
Dictador, dictator.
Diligencia, diligence; stage-coach.
Dios, God.
Doblon, doubloon.
Domingo, Sunday; Dominic.
Don, Sir, Mr.; gift.
Doña, Madam, Mrs., Miss.
Dorado, gilt.
Dos, two.
Dulce, sweet.

Eclesiástico, ecclesiastical.
El, the; he, him.
Enáguas, sort of petticoat.
En junta, in council.
Enmendadura, enmendation.
Entrada, entrance.
Entrerenglonadura, interlineation.
Escritor, writer.
Escuadron, squadron.
Español, Spanish; Spaniard.
Está, is, he is, it is, &c.
Estacado, staked.
Estrangero, stranger, foreigner.
Estufa, cell; stove.

Factura, invoice.
Fandango, dance; ball.
Fiera, wild beast.
Fe, faith.
Feria, fair.
Fierro, iron; branding-iron, &c.
Fiesta, feast.
Fonda, eating-house, inn.
Fraile, Fray, friar.
Frijol, bean.
Fueros, chartered privileges.

Gachupin, Spaniard in America.
Gallina, hen.
Gallo, cock.
Ganado, cattle.
Gefe, chief.
Gobernador, governor.
Gobernadorcillo, petty governor, or chief.
Gobierno, government.
Grama, species of grass.
Gran, grande, great, large.
Grandeza, greatness, grandeur.
Grano, grain.

Guage, gourd, flask.
Guardia, guard, watch; watch-house
Guerra, war.
Guia, sort of passport for goods
Guisado, cooked, stewed.
Guitarra, guitar.

Hacienda, estate; lands; treasure.
Haciendero, proprietor of an hacienda.
Herradura, horse-shoe.
Herrero, blacksmith.
Hidalgo, nobleman.
Hoja, leaf, husk, &c.
Hombre, man.
Hombre bueno, arbitrator.

Ilustrisimo, most illustrious.
Imprenta, printing-office.
Inocente, innocent.

Jacal, hut, wigwam.
Jola, copper coin, penny.
Jornada, day's travel; journey.
Juez, judge.
Junta, council; union.

La, las, the; her, it, them.
Labor, labor; field; mining-pit.
Labrador, laborer, farmer.
Ladron, thief, robber.
Laguna, lake.
Lanzada, thrust with a lance.
Lazador, nooser.
Lazito, little lazo.
Lazo, noosing rope.
Legua, league.
Lépero, vagabond, *sans-culotte*.
Ley, law.
Limosnero, beggar.
Llano, plain; prairie; smooth.
Lo, los, the; it, them, &c.
Lobo, wolf.

Madre, mother.
Manifiesto, manifest; bill of goods presented to the custom-house.
Manta, covering; cotton-cloth.
Marco, weight of eight ounces; mark.
Mayor, greater, superior.
Mayordomo, overseer.
Médano, sand-hill.
Medio, half; picayune.
Menor, less, inferior.
Mesa, table; table-plain.
Meson, inn, hotel.
Mestizo, mongrel.
Mezquite, a tree, acacia.
Mi, mis, my.
Militar, military.
Monte, a game; grove; mount
Mora, mulberry.
Muerto, dead; dead man.
Mula, mule; unsalable item.

Negro, black; a black person.
Noria, machine for drawing water; well.
Norte, north.
Noticioso, giving information.
Número, number.

GLOSSARY.

Oficial, official; officer.
Ojo, eye; spring of water.
Oro, gold.

Padre, father; priest.
Padrino, godfather, sponsor.
Paisano, countryman.
Palacio, palace.
Panza, paunch.
Papa, pope; potato.
Parage, place; camping-site.
Pariente, relative, kin.
Parroquia, parish; parish church.
Pasa, raisin.
Paséo, pleasure walk or ride.
Paso, pass, passage; step.
Pastor, pastor; shepherd.
Patio, court, enclosed yard.
Pato, duck.
Patriótico, patriotic.
Pauta, rule, model.
Pelo, hair.
Penitencia, penance, penitence.
Perro, dog.
Peso, dollar; weight.
Piedra, stone.
Pinole, food of parched Indian meal stirred in water.
Placer, pleasure; gold region.
Plata, silver.
Plaza, square; place; village.
Poquito, very little.
Portal, porch, corridor.
Prefecto, prefect.
Presidio, garrison, fort.
Presto, quick, soon.
Profano, profane.
Pronunciamento, act of making a public declaration.
Proyecto, project, plan.
Público, public.
Pueblo, people; Catholic Indians, &c.
Puerta, door.
Puro, pure; pure tobacco cigar.

Ranchera, country woman.
Ranchería, village of wild Indians.
Ranchero, inhabitant of a rancho.
Rancho, stock-farm.
Raspadura, erasure; rasping.
Real, a coin; royal, real, grand.
Rebozo, muffler, species of scarf.
Remedio, remedy, medicine.
Rey, king.
Rico, rich; rich man.
Rio, river.

Sala, hall, parlor.
Salina, salt pond or pit.
San, santo, santa, saint, holy
Sandia, watermelon.
Sangre, blood.
Santísimo, most holy.
Saquéo, sack, pillage.
Sarape, sort of blanket.
Semana, week.
Señor, sir, Mr.; lord.
Señora, madam, Mrs.; lady.
Señoria, lordship.
Señoria ilustrísima, title of a bishop, &c
Señorita, madam, miss, Mrs., &c.
Sierra, ridge of mountains; saw.
Siesta, afternoon's sleep.
Silla, chair; saddle.
Sistema, system.
Sol, sun.
Soldado, soldier.
Sombrero, hat.
Sonoreño, citizen of Sonora.
Su, sus, his, her, its, their.

Tarde, evening.
Tierra, country, land,
Tierra Afuera (in Mexico), the exterior, or country near the coast, &c.
Tilma, Indian mantle.
T'io, uncle.
Todo, all, every, whole.
Tornillo, screw.
Tortilla, thin cake, diminutive of *torta* cake, loaf.

Vado, ford.
Valiente, valiant, brave.
Valle, valley, dale.
Vaquero, cowherd.
Vaquita, diminutive of *vaca*, cow.
Vara, Spanish yard of 33 inches.
Venta, sale; sale-brand; inn
Verdadero, true.
Verde, green.
Vicio, vice.
Viernes, Friday.
Un, uno, a, one.

Y, é, and.
Yeso, gypsum.

Zambo, offspring of the Indian and negro.
Zaguan, entry, porch.
Zarco, light blue.
Zorra, fox

CPSIA information can be obtained at www.ICGtesting.com
Printed in the USA
266774BV00003B/60/P